CW00723201

CON^T

Editor
Julia Lee

Art Editor
Alexandra Bourdelon

Consultant Editor
Mark Rasmussen

Advertisement Manager
Brian Case

Senior Sales Executive
Sophie North

Sales Consultant
Jay Jones

Production
George Kesta

Illustrations supplied by
Mark Rasmussen

Publisher
MyHobbyStore Ltd,
Hadlow House, 9 High
Street, Green Street
Green, Kent BR6 6BG.

SPECIAL FEATURES

ABOVE: A Henry VII type V sovereign which sold for £160,000 (see p11)

LATEST MARKET PRICES

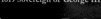

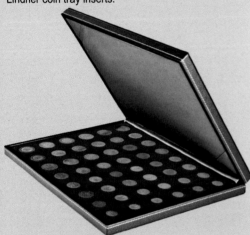

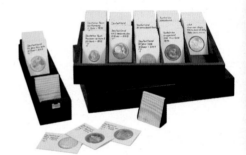

THE YEAR IN COINS

Find out what were the biggest sellers at auction in the last 12 months and the latest state of the British market

This year has been another successful one for British coins. A broad range of good material has again been offered and the market continues to mature in a steady and controlled manner.

The great rarities have enjoyed a meteoric rise this year as a result of fierce competition between a few extremely wealthy individuals at home and abroad who have taken a shine to the British series.

Collectors should not be too alarmed or frustrated by the rising prices, as whilst it may squeeze their budgets a little, coins are now regarded as good value compared with other collectables. Bear in mind that the British coin market was dormant for two decades and has only witnessed real increases in the last five years. It is also not surprising in the current economic climate, as savings are offering little return.

Collectors have always been encouraged, and rightly so, to acquire coins in extremely fine grade or better. However, aesthetically-pleasing examples in lesser condition are readily available at very modest prices when compared to their high grade counterparts. It is not surprising, therefore, that the prices are rising noticeably for very fine in particular.

Despite the current economic gloom, collectors remain confident and are buying intelligently when material is offered. As long as the opportunities to obtain a good representative, or even specialist, collection continue, collecting British coins will be an attractive and serious endeavour.

CELTIC

The Celtic series has recently suffered from a lack of supply and sadly little new material has come on to the market over the last year. It would appear that there are presently fewer

ABOVE: A Cunobelin gold stater realised £5,500 at Spink

ABOVE: This 'Biga' type stater realised £3,400 at Spink

ABOVE: An Anarevitos gold stater, auctioned by Chris Rudd for £21,000.

collectors for this series, and it seems underrated at present.

The only significant offering was the collection belonging to Major Clem Lister, which was sold by Spink through their Auction 204 in September. This small, useful group, covering a broad range of types and denominations attracted much attention and sold well. Pretty type coins, such as staters, in high grades and the rarer types were most sought-after. A Cunobelin gold stater in good VF realised a hammer price of £5,500 and a 'Biga' type stater realised £3,400. Each of these pieces had an estimate of £1,200-£1,500.

It is always exciting to report a new coin for the series which should be entered in the catalogue as a new type. It was a gold stater of fine style of Anarevitos of Cantiaci, auctioned by Chris Rudd in his List 117 in May. In good VF it sold for £21,000 against an estimate of £12,500.

HAMMERED GOLD

The enduring popularity of the hammered gold series is not surprising, for nowhere else can you acquire an intricate gold item of Richard II, or an official portrait of Henry VIII for a relatively modest financial outlay. The strength of this market is particularly impressive and is demonstrated by the large price increases each year, confirming the popularity of this series amongst those who can afford to collect it.

Unusually, there were a considerable number

ABOVE: This Henry VII type V sovereign sold at DNW for £160,000

ABOVE: A Henry VII type IV sovereign, which was auctioned for £150,000 at Spink

ABOVE: A 1643 triple unite which was bid up to £100,000 at Spink

prices would have dipped and there would have been plenty of unsolds. But there is the largest-ever collector base for British series at present and it seems that even in these pressured times, people are spending disposable income on coins, so prices are not dropping.

There were a number of important highlights. In September, a beautifully struck type V Henry VII sovereign was offered in DNW's Auction 89. This extremely rare coin was chased up by a number of determined bidders before being knocked down for £160,000 – a high price, but a magnificent example.

Spink in Auction 206 in December offered an unusually full good VF type IV sovereign of Henry VII. This type is difficult to find in such a high grade and had been purchased from the celebrated Ryan sale in 1950 for £220, so an estimate of £50,000-£60,000 was conservative. Fierce competition ensured it easily breached six figures and it was finally secured for a staggering £150,000.

Rarity is not always the issue. The triple unites of Charles I are not rare but continue to exceed market expectations because they are attractive. In 1980 *British Coins Market Values* priced triple unites in fine condition at £3,000 and in VF at £6,500. A dip followed because of the crash in the 1980s, but by 2005, the beginning of the current boom, they reached £4,500 and £10,000. Last year, they were valued

of high denomination pieces offered for sale which suggests some speculative collectors are taking advantage of the high prices. If this had occurred at a time when the market was more stagnant, as was witnessed in the early 1980s,

ABOVE: This 1644 triple unite fetched £140,000 at Spink

from £12,000 and £27,500 respectively, and this year from £18,500 and £38,500. However, in EF they can realise up to three times the price of a VF example, depending on the style and the quality of strike. For example, in Spink Auction 206 in December, an EF example, dated 1643, realised a hammer price of £100,000 against an estimate of £40,000-£50,000. This was followed by another, dated 1644, which was a very rare variety in good VF, which also exceeded its estimate of £60,000 and reached a hammer price of £140,000.

HAMMERED SILVER

This fascinating and varied coinage, commencing in the 7th century and running to the 17th century, covers a thousand years of British history from which one can acquire either a tiny early Saxon sceat from approximately £100 or a large and majestic Charles I Oxford 'Rawlins' Pound for over £100,000.

A feature has been the continued strength of the market for Saxon and Norman coins and, although they are rising in price, few look

overvalued. The Saxon and Norman series were once fairly uncommercial and only collected by a handful of specialist collectors. From the mid 1980s to the late 1990s there was a much greater availability of good material. But today demand is so considerable, coins are hard to find.

Key rarities and high-grade attractive pennies, even of the more common types, have been particularly in demand, with choice portrait coins attracting the highest premiums.

Bruun Rasmussen Auction 816, in December, obtained DKK 80,000 (£9,000) for a holed and VF example of the exceedingly rare Agnus Dei type penny of Aethelred II. CNG's Mailbid Sale 87, in May, realised $1,400 (estimate $700) for an almost EF common two-line type penny of Eadgar.

A pleasing, almost EF, Edward the Martyr portrait penny of Ipswich was successfully secured by a collector for £10,000 in Spink's September Auction 204, against a £3,000-£4,000 estimate.

CNG's Triton XIV sale, in January, featured

ABOVE: The hammer price was £22,900 for this superb 'standing figures' type penny of Stephen and Queen Matilda from York, also at CNG

ABOVE: This Alfred the Great portrait/cross and lozenge type penny sold for £25,810 at CNG

ABOVE: A two-star type penny of William I, which reached £5,200 at Spink

ABOVE: A John class 5ai penny, but with the sceptre to right, of which only a few are known, realised an extraordinary £4,800, at Spink

ABOVE: A very pretty sixth bust of James I sixpence with a beautifully struck portrait realised £800 at DNW

a superb Alfred the Great portrait/cross and lozenge type penny, in excellent metal and extremely fine condition. Despite a minor die flaw on the hair, it sold for a substantial $40,000 (£25,810), which was double its estimate. The same sale realised $35,500 (£22,900) for a superb 'standing figures' type penny of Stephen and Queen Matilda from York.

A very photogenic mint state example of a common two-star type penny of William I realised a world-record price of £5,200 (high estimate £900) in Spink Auction 206 in December.

Bargains can be still be obtained by the astute collector. Mark Rasmussen had one of only three known examples of the facing bust type of Edward the Confessor of Nottingham at £800 in his summer 2010 list. Although once mounted, it was a well-struck example.

Metal detectorists continue to unearth fresh material which stimulates the market. An example was a very fine Wulfred penny found in Oxborough, Norfolk, which sold for £4,700 in Timeline's September sale, against an estimate of £2,000-£2,500.

The short- and long- cross coinage remains popular. A John class 5ai penny, but with the

sceptre to right, of which only a few are known, realised an extraordinary £4,800, against an estimate of £600-800 in Spink Auction 204 in September.

The standardised type coins of the medieval period are less visually rewarding than the realistic portrait issues of the later Tudor and Stuart periods. Therefore, apart from specialist collectors who focus on a particular denomination or monarch, many collectors are content with an overall representation of coinage of the period in high grade. Consequently, the common types in top condition can attain surprisingly high prices and are hard to source.

As reported last year, high-grade Tudor and Stuart portrait coins are difficult to find. The best offering came in the form of the late Alfred Bole collection of sixpences dispersed in several parts by DNW. This is the largest and most comprehensive collection of the denomination ever to be offered at public auction.

Part I, sold in September in Auction 89, included a good run of 'fine issue' sixpences of Edward VI. They were generally in good-VF condition or better and each sold for between £700 and £800. A very pretty sixth bust of

ABOVE: An exceptionally rare Philip and Mary sixpence, with 1554 below the bust, netted £5,800 at DNW

ABOVE: This extremely rare Scarborough sixpence of Charles I sold for £42,000, also at DNW

James I with a beautifully struck portrait realised £800. A group C 'fine-work' plume over shield sixpence of Charles I, from the famous Lingford collection, fetched £7,200, against an estimate £4,000-£5,000.

The collection also contained a number of important rarities. A clear F example of an exceptionally rare Philip and Mary sixpence, with 1554 below the bust, deserved its £5,800 hammer price. An extremely rare Scarborough sixpence of Charles I from the Lockett collection, which was estimated at £25,000-£30,000, sold for £42,000.

MILLED GOLD

Milled gold is extremely popular here and, especially, in the USA. Generally, values have stabilised. However exceptional examples, especially from the early milled period, will still fetch significant prices in some instances.

A very pleasing Cromwell broad fetched £24,000 in DNW Auction 89, in September, against quite a low estimate of £8,000-£10,000.

The guinea series is more abundant between F and VF condition. EF pieces are getting increasingly hard to find. Baldwin's Auction no 68 in September featured a good VF Anne 'Vigo' five guineas piece of 1703. This sold to a phone bidder for £76,000.

A less than perfect but almost EF Anne pre-union five guineas of 1706 fetched £36,000, a high price bearing in mind its condition. In September, a lustrous Charles II 1678 two

ABOVE: A George II 1729 EIC half-guinea sold for £5,000 at DNW

guineas with great eye appeal fetched a modest £9,200 in DNW Auction 89. In February, Goldberg Auction 62 sold a similar piece dated 1676. Arguably slightly better, it sold for a whopping $55,000 (approximately £35,000). Would the DNW piece have fetched a similar price in the USA?

A practically mint state Charles II 1676 elephant and castle guinea deserved its hammer price of £13,000 in St James's Auction 17 in May. Finally, DNW Auction 89 featured a George II 1739 EIC guinea and a George II 1729 EIC half-guinea, both remarkable coins in mint state which fetched £10,000 and £5,500 respectively. Coins of this superb calibre are rarely seen these days.

There have always been a lot of collectors for the 'new coinage' from 1816. The sovereign market continues to grow and demand is high, especially for the rare dates and for coins in uncirculated state.

St James's Auctions consistently seem to offer a fine selection of material. In December, a practically mint George V 1917 London sovereign realised almost top estimate of £7,400 in St James's Auction 16. An example of a high price for a relatively common date was an 1822 sovereign of George IV in brilliant mint state which fetched a staggering £5,500 in St James's Auction 17 in May, more than double the high estimate. This must be a record for this coin.

The smaller half-sovereign is still not as popular, but it does seem interest is growing as these little coins are extremely rare in high grade, often rarer than their larger counterpart. In July, Sincona Auction 1 offered a pair of Victorian pattern sovereigns – an 1837 sovereign

ABOVE: This Cromwell broad realised £24,000 at DNW

ABOVE: This Charles II 1678 two guineas with great eye appeal fetched a modest £9,200, also at DNW

ABOVE: A 1790 'nude Britannia' restrike halfpenny by Taylor in gold, which achieved £24,000 at St James's

fetched 29,000 Swiss Francs (£21,500) and an 1866 sovereign reached 35,000 Swiss Francs (£26,000).

The larger denominations and proof sets have shot up in price over the last year. As these are popular with the speculative collector, the fleur de coin prices in some instances are now double what they were a couple of years ago. In Spink Auction 204 in September, a Victoria 1839 proof set fetched £60,000.

A feature of the season was the Mitchell David collection of pattern and proofs sold by St James's Auction 15 in September. It contained a number of Soho pieces struck in gold, which had previously been sold at an auction in Plymouth in 2008, and had originally been purchased from the famous Murdoch sale in 1904. Its attractive and professional catalogue helped it attract considerable attention.

One of the Plymouth coins was a medallic size crown piece, probably struck by Weyl on a thin flan, which is unpublished and unofficial. It sold for approximately £18,000 in 2008 at the Plymouth sale. In September, it now realised £114,000! A number of George III gold pieces also from the same source sold strongly. A 1790 restrike halfpenny by Taylor in gold, which bears a nude Britannia on the reverse, fetched a staggering £24,000.

MILLED SILVER

The scarcity of high-grade pre-1816 milled coins and their current substantial prices has brought an increased interest in the middle grades, and so values have risen.

Prices have also been driven up by an influx

of new buyers over the last few years who do not have the same expectations as collectors in the past. In the 1960s and 1970s, it was always drummed into collectors that they should only collect EF or better. In hindsight, this was probably unrealistic as the middle grades can be just as rewarding and there is more choice and availability.

The post-1816 milled has always been a buoyant market and condition in this area is more important. Uncirculated pieces command premiums over EF examples and are always scarce. Naturally, rare dates are increasingly sought-after, for example, an Edward VII 1905 halfcrown in uncirculated condition could fetch as much as £10,000 in a public auction, whereas a fine example could probably be picked up fairly readily for £300-400.

Part 1 of the late Alfred Bole collection of sixpences, featured in September in DNW Auction 89, had a number of good-quality

ABOVE: A William III 1696 second bust sixpence fetched the princely sum of £5,200 at DNW

ABOVE: An Anne 1707 E (Edinburgh) proof sixpence and from the legendary Manville collection sold for £3,400, also at DNW

ABOVE: An exceedingly rare Edward VIII pattern sixpence was chased up to £34,000 at DNW

Coincraft

An open letter to Dealers

When a dealer sold us some coins a while ago I asked him why we were not doing more business together, his answer was, that he didn't want to bother us. Hell, we want to be bothered, especially when it comes to business. You will find that Claire, Ian, Barry and myself (Richard) are easy to talk to and we are always interested in buying material. On large lots or collections we are even willing to put up the money for you.

We now have 18 full time and 3 part time staff and we need material to offer our collectors. As the busiest coin firm in the United Kingdom, we now send out 30 different catalogues a year, we need material. Single pieces, hoards, accumulations and of course collections. We buy British and world coins, British and world banknotes, ancient coins and antiquities, medallions, bulk coins and banknotes, in fact almost anything.

Please give us a call and join the many satisfied dealers who do business with Coincraft everyday. We will say yes or no, without messing you around. When we agree a price, we will write you a cheque on the spot. We need you and will treat you right, if you haven't tried us, please do. You will find dealing with Coincraft easy, pleasurable and I hope, profitable.

Richard Lobel
Founder of Coincraft

ABOVE: An exceedingly rare pattern George VI double florin of 1950 sold for £10,000 at St James's Auctions

currency, proof and pattern pieces. A William III 1696 second bust sixpence in about EF condition, fetched the princely sum of £5,200. An Anne 1707 E (Edinburgh) proof example in delightful condition and from the legendary Manville collection sold for £3,400. The extremely rare George IV pattern 1820 realized £2,500, against an estimate of £1,200-£1,500. A George V 1924 trial in gold realised £6,800 against an estimate of £8,000-£10,000. An exceedingly rare Edward VIII pattern example was chased up to £34,000, which was more than double the low estimate.

Mark Rasmussen's winter list offered an exceptional Charles II 1673 crown at £6,500 and an almost FDC Victoria 1853 'gothic' crown at £9,500. Roddy Richardson's Summer 2011 List featured the very rare Edward VII 1910 pattern crown at £12,000 and the ever popular George III 1817 'Three Graces' crown at £17,500.

In the Mitchell David collection of patterns and proofs at St James's Auction 15 in

September, a very important piece came up – an exceedingly rare pattern George VI double florin of 1950 sold for £10,000, against an estimate of £6,000-£8,000.

COPPER & BRONZE

The early copper coinage has steady support amongst the collectors. It has been less reactive to the boom, so there has been no marked increase in prices from last year.

However, choice examples will fetch extremely strong prices. There is not as much interest in varieties and errors as there used to be, as these tend to be available in low grade. The interest now seems to be for basic types in high grade, but collecting by date is still extremely popular.

Later bronze coinage, in particular the penny, has always been a great favourite with collectors. The 'bun' penny, as it is affectionately known, continues to be one of the most popular coins in the British series, with uncirculated examples with full lustre commanding high prices.

The highlight of the year was the George V pattern model penny, undated (1933), by Lavrillier, offered in Baldwin's Auction No 68 in September. This piece is believed to be unique and fetched £5,000.

SCOTTISH

Although small, the Scottish market is heavily supported by a group of enthusiastic collectors. The coins are much scarcer than their comparable English counterparts.

For the sterling collector, Mark Rasmussen's

ABOVE: An undated 1933 pattern model penny, believed to be unique, fetched £5,000 at Baldwin's

ABOVE: A magnificent portrait testoon of Queen Mary went for £26,000 at Spink

ABOVE & RIGHT: A 1576 gold twenty pound piece of James VI, which realised £85,000 at Spink

IRISH

Considering the plight of the Irish economy, prices continue to be firm for the series. Collectors are having difficulty in obtaining fresh material and when offered it sells well.

ABOVE: This Edward IV Dublin 'crown' groat realised £3,000 at Spink

The only two pieces of any significance are an Edward IV Dublin 'crown' groat which realised £3,000 in Spink Auction 207 in March and an Irish Free State 1943 halfcrown in St James's Auction 17 in May. This is seldom seen and it realised £2,750.

ANGLO-GALLIC

The Anglo-Gallic market has again been extremely quiet due to the lack of supply. The high quality strike and design found on the gold coins makes them a very attractive and complimentary series to collect. Very few examples have been offered and have realised predictably strong prices.

Baldwin's auction No69, May 2010, contained an Edward III third issue leopard d'or, GVF but with a fine striking perforation, at £11,000. Meanwhile, prices for the silver and billon issues appear to be stable.

recent lists have featured a nice run of early sterling from several interesting mints. List 20 featured an Alexander III transitional coinage type 1c Sterling in GF which was listed at £675. The list also included a gold lion of Robert III in VF at £3,250.

The handsome portrait testoons of Queen Mary are one of the most iconic type coins of the Scottish series. In December, a magnificent example dated 1562 was sold in Spink Auction 206. This piece carried an estimate of £5,000-£6,000 but this was almost certainly a little conservative as it eventually fetched a whopping £26,000. This clearly demonstrates that collectors are prepared to pay exaggerated, but not hysterical, prices for the very best coins.

There was also an example of a 1576 gold twenty pound piece of James VI which realised £85,000, three times the price of the testoon.

Rare high-grade silver coins are now fetching disproportionately high prices to their gold counterparts. For example, when these same two coins were offered in 1996, the twenty pound fetched six times the price of the testoon.

ABOVE: This Edward III third issue leopard d'or achieved £11,000 at Baldwin's

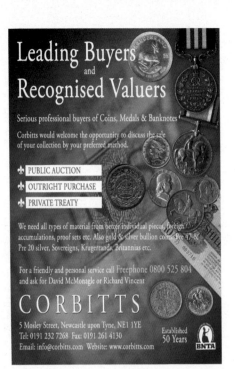

St James's Auctions

We are now taking consignments for our
2012 Auctions

0% Commission*

*There are no hidden costs,
you get the entire hammer price!
For more information please contact us
at the address below.*

For enquiries and to consign contact:
St James's Auctions, (Knightsbridge Coins-Stephen Fenton)
43 Duke Street, St James's
London ,SW1Y 6DD

Tel: 020 7930 7597 / 7888 / 8215 Fax: 020 7930 8214
E-mail: info@stjauctions.com

* This applies to individual lots over £1,000

TIPS FOR COLLECTING

If you are new to the hobby, here is some advice to get you started and put you in touch with the experts

HOW MUCH IS IT WORTH?

There was a time when newcomers to coin collecting would ask the question 'What is it?'

Nowadays, the most common question dealers hear is 'What is it worth?'

The aim of *British Coins Market Values* is to try to place a value on all the coins in the British Isles, in other words England, Wales, Scotland and Ireland, the Channel Islands as well as the Anglo-Gallic series and British banknotes.

This is a difficult task because many items do not turn up in auctions or lists every year, even though they are not really rare.

However, we can estimate a figure so that you can have an idea of what you will have to pay.

HOW TO SELL AT AUCTION

Potential sellers have considerable choice when it comes to auction houses.

In London alone there are several: Spink & Son Ltd, A H Baldwin & Sons Ltd, St. James's Auctions, Dix Noonan Webb, Morton & Eden and Bonhams.

There are also smaller companies up and down the country, such as Croydon Coin Auctions and London Coins.

The best approach for the seller is to compare the auction houses' catalogues and if possible attend the auctions so that you can see how well they are conducted.

Talk over your collection with the specialist, for you may have specific cataloguing requirements and you may find that one of the firms will look after your needs better than the others.

A well-known coin requires little expertise and will probably sell at a certain price in most auctions.

However, if you require cataloguing of a specialist collection of a more academic nature, for example early medieval coinages, then you need to know what a company is capable of before you discuss a job rate.

You should remember that, while it is not complicated to sell by auction, and a good auction house will guide you through the process, you may have to wait three or four months from the time you consign the coins to the auctioneers before you receive any money.

There are times when items at auction manage to achieve very high prices, and other times when, for some reason, they fail to reach even a modest reserve.

Finally, auctioneers will usually charge you at least 10% of the knock-down price, and will charge the buyer a premium of up to 22.5% plus VAT.

HOW TO TRADE WITH DEALERS

The British coin market is very much dependent upon and benefits from the support of a strong network of dealers, with their professional numismatic expertise and long experience of the business. Fortunately, the needs of the collector, at any level, are eminently well served by them.

Most offer a large and varied stock of coins for sale at marked prices. All dealers will provide advice and guidance on any aspect of collecting or disposal free of charge. When selling to a dealer, it is true that they generally prefer to obtain fresh material.

A proportion of the dealers also offer to sell on a commission basis. The retail prices are discussed in advance, allowing the collector a degree of control and a far more active role in the dispersal of their collection. Hence, the dealer offers a valuable and unique personal service and it is this relationship which has been responsible for helping to form some of our greatest numismatic collections.

BULLION COINS

Bullion coins can be priced by looking at the price of gold, which is fixed twice daily by a group of leading banks. Most newspapers carry

this information in their financial pages.

Anyone can buy bullion coins, such as sovereigns or Krugerrands, and they are not subject to VAT.

Normally, when you sell a bullion coin you expect the coin dealer to make a few pounds profit on each coin.

For mounted or damaged coins do not expect more than their intrinsic value.

HOW TO COLLECT COINS

You should obviously purchase your coins from a reputable dealer or auction house.

You can be sure of some protection if you choose a member of the British Numismatic Trade Association or the International Association of Professional Numismatists.

Membership lists, detailing their main interests, can be obtained from the respective secretaries:

☐ Mrs Rosemary Cooke, PO Box 2, Rye, East Sussex TN31 7WE.
Tel/Fax: 01797 229988. E-mail: bnta@lineone.net
☐ Jean-Luc Van Der Schueren, 14 Rue de la Bourse, B 1000 Brussels, Belgium.
Tel: +32 2 513 3400. Fax: +32 2 513 2528.

However, many are not members of either organisation, and it does not mean that they are not honest and professional. The best approach is simply to find one who will unconditionally guarantee that the coins you buy from him are genuine and accurately graded.

As a general rule, you should only buy coins in the best condition available, normally considered to be Extremely Fine or better. This applies particularly to the milled (post-1600) series, which is more commercial and therefore there is more emphasis on condition.

Hammered coins should be clear, legible and struck in good metal, with Very Fine being perfectly acceptable. One can obtain specimens in higher grade but they are much more difficult to get than their milled counterparts.

Collectors should be prepared that in some series and in the case of great rarities, they might have to make do with a coin that is only Fine or even Poor.

It very much depends on factors such as type, reign and rarity and of course affordability, so be realistic.

It is worth taking out subscriptions with auction houses so that you regularly receive their catalogues, because this is an excellent way to keep up with current market prices and trends, as well as the collections that are being offered. Arguably just as important are dealers'

fixed price lists, where coins can be chosen and purchased at leisure by mail order or alternatively from the Internet.

The most famous list is Spink's *Numismatic Circular*, first published in 1892 and still going strong with 6 issues a year.

It is more than a price list, being an important forum for numismatic debate, the reporting of new finds and other useful information (annual subscription £20 in the UK).

A good cross-section of other dealers, who produce excellent retail lists, either for mail order or online, in alphabetical order, follows.

☐ A H Baldwin & Sons, 11 Adelphi Terrace, London WC2N 6BJ. Hammered and milled.
☐ Lloyd Bennett, PO Box 2, Monmouth, Gwent NP25 3YR. Hammered, milled, tokens.
☐ Dorset Coin Company, 193 Ashley Road, Parkstone, Poole, Dorset BH14 9DL.
All coins and banknotes.
☐ Format, Unit K, Burlington Court 2nd Floor, 18 Lower Temple Street, Birmingham B2 4JD.
All British.
☐ K B Coins, 50 Lingfield Road, Martins Wood, Stevenage, Hertfordshire SG1 5SL. Hammered, milled.
☐ Knightsbridge Coins, 43 Duke Street, St James, London SW1Y 6DD. Hammered, milled.
☐ Timothy Millet, PO Box 20851, London SE22 0YN. Medallions.
☐ Simon Monks, Suite 313, St Loyes House, 20 St Loyes Street, Bedford MK40 1ZL. Medallions, tokens, hammered, milled.
☐ Peter Morris, PO Box 223, Bromley, Kent BR1 4EQ. Hammered, milled, tokens.
☐ Spink & Son, 69 Southampton Row,

Bloomsbury London WC1B 4ET. Hammered, milled, tokens, medallions.

☐ S R Porter, 18 Trinity Road, Headington Quarry, Oxford OX3 8QL. Hammered and milled.

☐ Studio Coins, 16 Kilham Lane, Winchester, Hampshire S022 5PT. Hammered.

☐ Mark Rasmussen, PO Box 42, Betchworth, Surrey RH3 7YR. Hammered, milled, medallions, tokens.

☐ Roderick Richardson, The Old Granary Antiques Centre, King's Staithe Lane, King's Lynn, Norfolk PE30 1LZ. Hammered and milled.

☐ Chris Rudd, PO Box 222, Aylsham, Norfolk NR11 6TY. Celtic.

☐ Mike Vosper, PO Box 32, Hockwold, Brandon IP26 4HX. Ancient, Celtic, hammered.

☐ Classical Numismatics Group (Seaby Coins), 14 Old Bond Street, London W1X 4JL. Hammered, some milled.

☐ Simmons Gallery, PO Box 104, Leytonstone, London E11 1ND. Medallions, tokens.

SOCIETIES

Consider joining your local numismatic society, of which there are over 50 across the UK. To find if there is one near you, get in touch with the present Secretary of British Association of Numismatic Societies, Phyllis Stoddart. Tel: 0208 980 5672. www.coinclubs.freeserve.co.uk

BANS organises annual congresses and seminars, and it is a good idea for the serious collector to consider attending these. Details are published in the numismatic press or available via their website.

Collectors who wish to go further can apply for membership of the British Numismatic Society. The Society holds ten meetings each year at the Warburg Institute, Woburn Square, London, WC1H 0AB, in addition to out-of-town lecture days. As a member, you receive a copy of the *British Numismatic Journal*, which has details of current research, articles and book reviews.

The current Secretary of the BNS is Peter Preston-Morely, c/o The Warburg Institute. E-mail: secretary@britnumsoc.org

COIN FAIRS

Whilst it is important to visit museums to see coins, it is worth remembering that there is often a fine array on show at coin fairs around the country, and most dealers do not mind showing coins to would-be collectors, even if they cannot afford to buy them on the spot.

The UK's premier international numismatic show, the BNTA Coinex show, is held in late September every year. For more information call the BNTA Secretary, Rosemary Cooke. Tel: 01797 229988. E-mail: bnta@lineone.net

Mike and Lu Veissid run the London Coin Fairs at the Holiday Inn, Bloomsbury, London. They take place in February, June and November. For all enquiries contact Mike Veissid. Tel: 01964 731781.

The Croydon team of Davidson and Monk organise regular shows at the Bloomsbury, 16-22 Gt. Russell Street, London. Tel: 0208 656 4583.www.lindamonkfairs.co.uk

The monthly Midland Coin and Stamp Fairs are on the second Sunday of every month at the National Motorcycle Museum in Birmingham. For further details, contact Mike Veissid. Tel: 01694 731781. www.midlandcoinfair.co.uk

The Harrogate Coin Show has recently been revived. The venue for this popular spring event is the Old Swan Hotel, Harrogate. Contact Simon Monks. Tel: 01234 270260.

There are also biannual coin and stamp fairs at York racecourse in January and July coordinated by Kate Puleston and Chris Rainey. Tel: 01793 513431 or 0208 946 4489. www.stampshows.co.uk

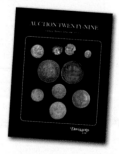

STORING YOUR COINS

Here are some helpful hints, along with some of the best accessories on the market, to help you keep your collection in good condition

ABOVE: One of Peter Nichols' handmade wooden cabinets

Store coins carefully, as a collection which is carelessly or inadequately housed can suffer irreparable damage.

Water vapour causes corrosion and therefore coins should not be stored in damp attics or spare bedrooms but, where possible, in evenly heated warm rooms.

One must be careful only to pick up coins by the edges, as sweaty fingerprints contain corrosive salt.

WOODEN CABINETS

A collection carefully laid out in a wooden cabinet looks very impressive.

Unfortunately, custom-built wooden cabinets are not cheap.

Their main advantages are the choice of tray and hole sizes but also, more importantly, they are manufactured from untreated well-matured wood, ideally mahogany, which has proven to be the perfect material for the long-term storage of coins.

Makers of wooden cabinets include Peter Nichols of St Leonards-on-Sea, East Sussex. Tel: 01424 436682 www.coincabinets.com Another is Rob Davis in Woodville, Derbyshire. Tel: 01332 740828 (evenings).

If you cannot afford a new cabinet, then a second-hand one may be the answer.

These can sometimes be purchased at coin auctions or from dealers but it can be hard to find one with tray hole sizes to suit your coins.

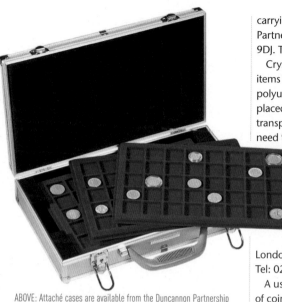

ABOVE: Attaché cases are available from the Duncannon Partnership

Do-it-yourself cabinet-makers should be careful not to use new wood, which will contain corrosive moisture.

ALBUMS, PLASTIC CASES AND CARRYING CASES

There are many of these on the market, some both handsome and inexpensive.

There are also attractive Italian and German-made carrying cases for collectors. These can be obtained from a number of dealers such as Lodge Hill Collectors Accessories. Tel: 01694 731439. www.lodge-hill.co.uk

Coin albums, where the coins are contained in cards with crystal-clear film windows, claim to prevent oxidisation. The cards slide into pages in the album, which is a convenient method of storage, especially for new collectors.

Lindner Publications, Unit 3A, Hayle Industrial Park, Hayle, Cornwall TR27 5JR, supplies useful coin and collecting boxes, as well as albums. Tel: 01736 751910. Fax: 01736 751911. www.prinz.co.uk

An extended range of Lighthouse coin accessories, including presentation and carrying cases, is available from the Duncannon Partnership, 4 Beaufort Road, Reigate, Surrey RH2 9DJ. Tel: 01737 244222. www.duncannon.co.uk

Crystalair Compression packs immobilise items between two layers of clear, inert, polyurethane film that moulds to the object placed between it. They are perfect for storing and transporting valuable and delicate items that also need to be viewed.

For details contact Lane Packaging, Headley Park 8, Headley Road East, Woodley, Reading, Berkshire RG5 4SA. Tel: 0118 944 2425. www.lanepackaging.com

In central London, the best place to visit is Vera Trinder, 38 Bedford Street, London WC2E 9EU, which keeps a good stock. Tel: 0207 257 9940. www.veratrinder.co.uk

A useful new place to obtain a wide range of coin products, including cases, albums and capsules, from different suppliers, is MyHobbyStore. Tel: 0844 848 8222. www.myhobbystore.co.uk

ENVELOPES

Plastic envelopes are useful for exhibitions, but not recommended for long-term storage purposes.

ABOVE: Another type of attaché case

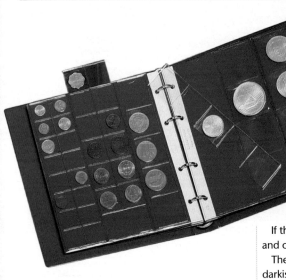

ABOVE: MyHobbyStore supply coin albums

such as a long spell in the sea.

A bath in methylated spirits will usually improve a dirty gold coin. But it is vital that gold coins are not rubbed in any way.

SILVER COINS

Silver coins will discolour easily, and are susceptible to damp or chemicals in the atmosphere. Gentle brushing with a soft, non-nylon, bristle brush will clear loose dirt.

If the dirt is deep and greasy, a dip in ammonia and careful drying on cotton wool should work.

There is no need to clean a coin that has a darkish tone.

COPPER AND BRONZE COINS

There is no safe method of cleaning copper or bronze coins without harming them. Use only a non-nylon, pure bristle brush to deal with dirt.

There is no way of curing verdigris (green spots) or bronze disease (blackish spots) permanently, so do not buy pieces with these problems, unless they are very inexpensive.

Remember that looking after your coins could make you money in the future!

They tend to make the coins 'sweat' which, can lead to corrosion.

Manila envelopes are much more suitable since the paper is dry. Most collectors use them with a cardboard box, a simple, unobtrusive and inexpensive method of coin storage.

The best article on coin and medal storage is by L R Green, Higher Conservation Officer at the Department of Coins and Medals at the British Museum. It appeared in the May 1991 issue of *Spink's Numismatic Circular*.

CLEANING COINS

Every week, coin dealers examine coins that someone has unwittingly ruined by cleaning.

Never clean coins unless they are very dirty or corroded. 'Dirt' does not mean oxide, which on silver coins can give a pleasing bluish tone favoured by collectors.

Do not clean corroded coins found in the ground, because if they are important, they will be handed over to a conservationist.

GOLD COINS

Gold should cause collectors few problems, since it is subject to corrosion only in extreme conditions

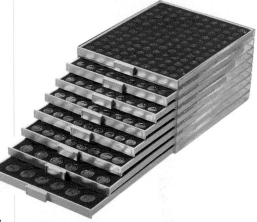

ABOVE: Coin cases are also available from MyHobbyStore

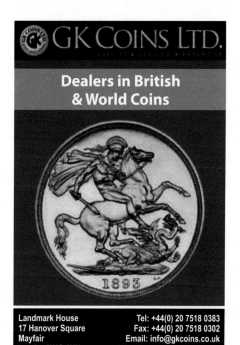

COUNTERFEIT COINS

Forgeries have always been a problem. Here is some advice on the most commonly counterfeited coins

ABOVE: 'Fantasy' Celtic stater

There have been forgeries since the earliest days of coin production, so, of course, new forgeries appear on the scene every year. There is always someone willing to try to deceive the collector and the dealer.

However, nowadays few forgers end up making much money.

As a result of the diligence and ongoing monitoring of the situation by the British Numismatic Trade Association and the International Association of Professional Numismatists, the trade is now more informed about the latest forgeries before they have had a chance to be a serious menace.

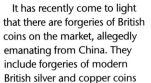

ABOVE: Dennington Edward III noble

It has recently come to light that there are forgeries of British coins on the market, allegedly emanating from China. They include forgeries of modern British silver and copper coins in lower grades, including common coins. Two or more identical coins show the same defects, or purported 'damage', revealing them as fakes. It seems that the counterfeiters sell on the internet, picking up clients in various countries who are then set up as distributors.

At the moment

ABOVE: Ceolwulf penny forgery

there is not a comprehensive list available. Examples reported are: George III Halfcrowns, 1763 'Northumberland' Shilling, the rare 1816 Bank Token Three Shillings, George V 'wreath' Crowns and Victoria 'old head' Halfcrowns. There is also a convincing 1826 penny, with a die-axis deviation to 7mm off-centre and a weight of 18.04g instead of 18.8g; a 1854 penny with a die-axis deviation to 3mm off-centre, weighing 19.02g instead of 18.8g, and an Isle of Man 1813 penny with a die-axis deviation to 3mm off-centre, weight 19.11g instead of 20.3g-20.6g.

They can easily deceive as they appear to have signs of circulation and are toned, and are therefore not easily detectable.

Two hammered gold coins, apparently from the same source, have also been deemed forgeries. They are a Edward VI third period half-sovereign and an Elizabeth I angel.

ABOVE: A new forgery, of the 1826 penny

As always, collectors should buy with caution and from reputable dealers.

Forgeries were last a matter of major concern in the late 1960s and early 1970s. A considerable number of forged 1887 £5 and £2 pieces, early sovereigns and some silver pieces, in particular the 'Gothic' crown, thought to be manufactured in Beirut, came on on to the market.

Also in the early 1970s, the Dennington forgeries could have made a serious impact on the English hammered gold market, but luckily they were detected early on. Fortunately, only a few of these are still in circulation.

In the late 1970s a crop of forgeries of Ancient British coins came to light, causing a panic in academic and trade circles.

This caused a lack of confidence in the trade and it took a number of years for the confidence to return.

A spate of copies of Anglo-Saxon coins from the West Country were being sold as replicas in the early 1990s, but they are still deceptive in the wrong hands.

Bob Forrest compiled a list of them and it was published in the IAPN *Bulletin of Forgeries* in 1995-96, volume 20, number 2.

ABOVE: A copy of an Apollo Ambiani stater

THE DIFFERENT TYPES OF FORGERY

Forgeries can be divided into two main groups: contemporary forgeries which are intended to be used as face-value money and forgeries which are intended to deceive collectors.

The following five methods of reproduction have been used for coins which attempt to deceive collectors:

☐ Electrotyping. These could deceive an expert.

☐ Casting. Old casts are easily recognisable, as they have marks made by air bubbles on the surface, and showing a generally 'fuzzy' effect. Modern cast copies are much more of a problem. They are produced by sophisticated 'pressure-casting', which can be extremely difficult to distinguish from the originals.

☐ The fabrication of false dies. With hammered coins, counterfeits are not difficult for an expert to detect. However, the sophisticated die-production techniques used in Beirut have resulted in good forgeries of modern gold and silver coins.

☐ The use of genuine dies put to illegal use, such as re-striking.

☐ Alteration of a genuine coin, most commonly a George V penny. The 1933 is extremely rare, so other years are often altered to provide the rarer date.

COUNTERFEIT COIN CLUB

There is a Counterfeit Coin Club that produces a small quarterly journal. For membership details write to its President: Ken Peters, 8 Kings Road, Biggin Hill, Kent TN16 3XU.
E-mail: kenvoy@hotmail.co.uk

DENNINGTON FORGERIES

A man called Anthony Dennington was tried at the Central Criminal Court and found guilty of six charges of 'causing persons to pay money by falsely pretending that they were buying genuine antique coins'.

A small number of these pieces are still in the trade, and since they have deceived some collectors and dealers, we have recorded them here, as they appeared in the *International Bureau for the Suppression of Counterfeit Coins Bulletin* in August 1976.

These copies are generally very good and you must beware of them. The following points may be useful guidelines:

☐ The coins are usually slightly 'shiny' in appearance, and the edges are not good, because they have been filed down and polished.

☐ They are usually very 'hard' to touch, whereas there is a certain amount of 'spring' in the genuine articles.

☐ They usually, but not always, feel slightly thick. They do not quite feel like an electrotype but are certainly thicker than normal.

☐ Although the Mary Fine sovereign reproduction is heavier, at 16.1986g, these pieces are usually lighter in weight than the originals.

ABOVE: A Dennington Mary Fine sovereign of 1553

MODERN COINS

As far as forgeries of modern coins are concerned, the most worrying aspect has been the enormous increase in well-produced forgeries in the last 25 years.

They are so well produced that it is often impossible for the naked eye to detect the difference, and it has therefore become the job of the scientist and metallurgist.

Many of these pieces have deceived dealers and collectors, but they do not seem to have caused a crisis of confidence.

This increase in the number of modern counterfeits has been due to the massive rise in

ABOVE: A forged 1832 sovereign

coin values since the 1960s.

The vast majority of these forgeries emanate from the Middle East, where it is not illegal to produce counterfeits of other countries' coins. But the coin trade is alert and reports are circulated quickly whenever a new forgery is spotted.

But with the profits available to the forger, no one should be complacent. At the time of writing, it only takes about £950 worth of gold to make an 1887-dated five pound piece of correct composition, valued approximately at £1650.

Detecting forgeries requires specialist knowledge, so we can only point out to you which coins are commonly counterfeited. In the catalogue section of British Coins Market Values, we have placed F beside a number of coins which have been counterfeited and which frequently turn up.

However, you should watch out for sovereigns, in particular, of which there are forgeries of every

ABOVE: A copy of an Una and Lion 1839 five pounds

ABOVE: A forged 1820 £5

ABOVE: A copy of a 1847 Gothic Crown, edge UNDECIMO

DENNINGTON FORGERIES STILL IN THE TRADE

- ☐ Henry III gold penny
- ☐ Edward III Treaty period noble
- ☐ Edward III Treaty period noble with saltire before King's name
- ☐ Henry IV heavy coinage noble
- ☐ Henry V noble, Class C, mullet at King's sword arm
- ☐ Henry VI mule noble
- ☐ Henry VI noble, annulet issue, London
- ☐ Edward IV ryal, Norwich
- ☐ Edward IV ryal, York
- ☐ Elizabeth I angel
- ☐ Mary Fine sovereign 1553
- ☐ James I unite, mintmark mullet
- ☐ James I rose ryal, third coinage, mint mark lis
- ☐ James I third coinage laurel
- ☐ Commonwealth unite 1651
- ☐ Commonwealth half-unite 1651
- ☐ Charles II touch piece

date from 1900 to 1932 and even recent dates such as 1957 and 1976.

Pieces you should be particularly careful about, especially if they are being offered below the normal catalogue value, are listed in the box.

Most modern forgeries of, for example, Gothic crowns, are offered at prices that are 10% or 20% below the current market price.

The moral is: if something looks too good to be true, it probably is!

ABOVE: A forged 1913 sovereign

OTHER SAFEGUARDS

The best protection against purchasing forgeries is to buy your coins from a reputable dealer or auctioneer who is a member of the BNTA or the IAPN, or one who will unconditionally guarantee that all his coins are genuine.

Legal tender coins, which include £5 and £2 pieces, sovereigns, half sovereigns and crowns, are protected by the Forgery and Counterfeiting

ABOVE: A counterfeit 1822 sovereign

COMMONLY FORGED COINS

- ☐ 1738, 1739 two guineas
- ☐ 1793, 1798 guineas, there could also be other dates
- ☐ 1820 pattern five pounds
- ☐ 1820 pattern two pounds
- ☐ 1839 five pounds, plain edge variety
- ☐ 1887 five pounds
- ☐ 1887 two pounds, many forgeries in circulation
- ☐ 1893 five pounds, two pounds
- ☐ 1902 five pounds, two pounds
- ☐ 1911 five pounds, two pounds
- ☐ 1817, 1819 (altered date), 1822, 1825, 1827, 1832, 1887, 1889, 1892, 1892M, 1908C, 1913C sovereigns; 1900-1932 inclusive, plus 1957
- ☐ 1959, 1963, 1966, 1967, 1974, 1976
- ☐ 1847 Gothic crowns
- ☐ 1905 halfcrowns

Act. Contact the police if you believe this Act may have been contravened.

If your dealer is unhelpful over a non-legal tender item which you have purchased, and which you think has been falsely described, you can take legal action under the Trades Description Act 1968. This is a long and difficult process. Contact your local Trading Standards Office or Consumer Protection department.

ABOVE: A forged 1827 sovereign

LITERATURE ON FORGERY

The back issues of *Spink's Numismatic Circular* and *Seaby's Coin & Medal Bulletin* are useful sources of information on the forgeries that have been recorded over the years.

The ISBCC also produced a series of forgery bulletins, mainly on modern coins, which can now only be found secondhand.

The most useful work on hammered coins is by L A Lawrence in the *British Numismatic Journal* back in 1905!

ABOVE: A copy of a Mary ryal

RECENT FORGERIES

- ☐ George III halfcrowns
- ☐ George III 1763 'Northumberland' shilling
- ☐ George III 1816 Bank Token three shillings
- ☐ George V 'wreath' crowns
- ☐ Victoria 'old head' halfcrowns
- ☐ Edward VI third period half-sovereign
- ☐ Elizabeth I angel

COIN, MEDAL & BANKNOTE FAIRS

THE LONDON COIN FAIR

HOLIDAY INN

London, Bloomsbury, Coram Street, WC1N 1HT

2011 dates: 19th November

2012 dates: 11th February, 26th May, 3rd November

THE MIDLAND COIN FAIR

NATIONAL MOTORCYCLE MUSEUM

Bickenhill, Birmingham, B92 0EJ

(Opposite the NEC on the M42/A45 junction)

2011 dates: 13th November, 11th December

2012 dates: 8th January, 12th February, 11th March, 8th April, 13th May, 10th June, 12th August, 9th September, 14th October, 11th November, 9th December

BLOOMSBURY COIN FAIR

BLOOMSBURY HOTEL

16-22 Great Russell Street
London WC1 3NN

2011 dates: 3rd September, 3rd December

2012 dates: 7th January, 3rd March, 5th May, 7th July, 1st September, 1st December

For more information please contact:
Lu Veissid, Hobsley House, Frodesley, Shrewsbury SY5 7HD
Tel: 01694 731781   Email: l.veissid@btinternet.com

www.coinfairs.co.uk

COIN GRADING

The basics of grading and details of the different conditions

It is important that newcomers to collecting should get to know the different grades of condition before buying or selling coins.

The system of grading most commonly used in Britain recognises the following main classes in descending order of quality: Brilliant Uncirculated (B Unc, BU), Uncirculated (Unc), Extremely Fine (EF), Very Fine (VF), Fine (F), Fair, Poor.

Beginners often get confused when they first encounter these grades.

The word 'fine' implies a coin of high quality, yet this grade is near the bottom of the scale. Fine is, in fact, about the lowest grade acceptable to most collectors of modern coinage in Britain.

But, to some extent, the grade 'is in the eye of the beholder', and there are always likely to be differences of opinion as to the exact grade of a coin.

Some collectors and dealers have tried to make the existing scale of definitions more exact by adding letters such as N (Nearly), G (Good, meaning slightly better than the grade), A (About or Almost) and so on. In cases where a coin wears more on one side than the other, two grades are shown, the first for the obverse, the second for the reverse such as: GVF/EF.

Any major faults not apparent from the use of a particular grade are often described separately. These include dents and noticeable scratches, discoloration, areas of corrosion, edge knocks and holes.

SPECIAL TERMS

Full mint lustre

There are two schools of thought on the use of the terms Brilliant Uncirculated and Uncirculated. The former is often considered to be the most useful and descriptive term for coins of copper, bronze, nickel-brass or other base metals, which display what is known as 'full mint lustre'.

When this term is being used it is often necessary to employ the grade Uncirculated to describe coins which have never been circulated but have lost the original lustre of a newly minted coin.

However, some dealers and collectors tend to classify as Uncirculated all coins which have not circulated, whether they are brilliant or toned, and do not use the term Brilliant Uncirculated.

Fleur de coin

Sometimes FDC (fleur de coin) is used to define top-grade coins, but it really only applies to pieces in perfect mint state with no flaws or surface scratches.

With modern methods of minting, slight damage to the surface is inevitable, except in the case of proofs, and therefore Brilliant Uncirculated or Uncirculated best describe the highest grade of modern coins.

The word 'proof' should not be used to denote a coin's condition. Proofs are pieces struck on specially prepared blanks from highly polished dies and usually have a mirror-like finish.

Fair and Poor

Fair is applied to very worn coins which still have the main parts of the design distinguished and Poor denotes a grade in which the design and rim are worn almost flat and few details are discernible.

AMERICAN GRADING

The American grading system is quite different to the British one. It purports to be a lot more accurate, but is actually much more prone, in our opinion, to be abused, and we prefer the British dealers' more conservative methods of grading.

American dealers use many more terms, ranging from Mint State to About Good. The latter could be described as 'very heavily worn, with portions of lettering, date and legend worn smooth. The date may be partially legible'. In Britain we would simply say 'Poor'.

There is also a numerical method of describing coins, often used in the United States. For example, an MS-65 coin would be Mint State and a 65 would mean 'an above average Uncirculated coin which may be brilliant or lightly toned but has some surface marks'.

The MS system seemed to be acceptable at first but there are two schools of thought in the United States and you will quite frequently see coins graded in the more traditional manner in sale catalogues.

GRADING EXAMPLES

It would be impossible to show every coin in different grades. We show instead representative examples from three different periods in the British series, to illustrate the middle range of coin conditions.

Each coin is shown in Extremely Fine, Very Fine and Fine conditions.

Extremely Fine
This describes coins which have been put into circulation, but have received only the minimum amount of damage since. There may be a few slight marks or minute scratches in the field, which is the flat area around the main design, but otherwise the coin should show very little sign of having been in circulation.

Very Fine
Coins in very fine condition show some amount of wear on the raised surfaces, but all other detail is still very clear. Here, all three coins have had a little wear which can be seen in the details of the hair and face. However, they are still in attractive condition from the collector's viewpoint.

Fine
In this grade coins show noticeable wear on the raised parts of the design; most other details should still be clear.

GRADES OF COIN

EXTREMELY FINE (EF)

VERY FINE (VF)

FINE (F)

ABBREVIATIONS & TERMS

These are the abbreviations and terms used in the price guide section

* Asterisks against some dates indicate that no firm prices were available at the time of going to press

2mm The P of PENNY is 2mm from the trident on some 1895 pennies. Otherwise, the gap is 1mm

AE numismatic symbol for copper or copper alloys

Arabic 1 or Roman I varieties of the 1 in 1887

arcs decorative border of arcs which vary in number

B on William III coins, minted at Bristol

BB beaded border

BBITANNIAR lettering error

Bank of England issued overstruck Spanish dollars for currency use in Britain 1804-1811

black farthings 1897-1918, artificially darkened to avoid confusion with half sovereigns

brilit lettering error

B Unc, BU Brilliant Uncirculated condition

BV bullion value

C on milled gold coins, minted at Ottawa, Canada

C on William III coins, minted at Chester

close colon colon close to DEF

crosslet 4 having upper and lower serifs on the horizontal bar of the 4 (compare plain 4)

cu-ni cupro-nickel

debased in 1920 the silver fineness in British coins was debased from .925 to .500

'Dorrien and Magens' issue of shillings by a group of bankers, which were suppressed on the day of issue

ABOVE: E.I.C. initials

DRITANNIAR lettering error

E minted at Exeter on William III coins

E, E* on Queen Anne coins, minted at Edinburgh

Edin Edinburgh

EEC European Economic Community

EF over price column Extremely Fine condition

ABOVE: English shilling, 1937-46

E.I.C. East India Co, supplier of metal

Eleph, eleph & castle elephant or elephant and castle provenance mark, below the bust. Taken from the badge of the African ('Guinea') Company, which imported the metal for the coins

Eng English shilling. In 1937, English and Scottish versions of the shilling were introduced. English designs have lion standing on a crown between 1937-1951 and three leopards on a shield between 1953-66

exergue segment below main design, usually containing the date

Ext extremely

F face value only

F over price column Fine condition

F forgeries exist of these pieces. In some cases the forgeries are complete fakes. In others where a particular date is rare, the date of a common coin has been altered. Be very cautious when buying any of these coins

ABOVE: Victoria Gothic florin

Fair rather worn condition

fantasies non-currency items, often just produced for the benefit of collectors

far colon colon further from DEF than in close colon variety

FDC fleur de coin. A term used to describe coins in perfect mint condition, with no flaws, scratches or other marks

fillet hair band

flan blank for a coin or medal

GEOE lettering error

Gothic Victorian coins featuring Gothic-style portrait and lettering

guinea-head die used for obverse of guinea

ABOVE: The Jubilee Head was introduced in 1887 to mark Victoria's Golden Jubilee

ABOVE: KN mintmark

H mintmark of The Mint, Birmingham

hd head

hp, harp for example early, ordinary varieties of the Irish harp on reverse

hearts motif in top right-hand corner of Hanoverian shield on reverse

im initial mark

inc incised, sunk in

inv inverted

JH Jubilee Head

KN mintmark of the Kings Norton Metal Company

ABOVE: 'Military' guinea, reverse

L.C.W. Initials of Leonard Charles Wyon, engraver

LIMA coins bearing this word were struck from bullion captured from vessels carrying South American treasure, which may have come from Lima, Peru

low horizon on normal coins the horizon meets the point where Britannia's left leg crosses behind the right. On this variety the horizon is lower

LVIII etc regnal year in Roman numerals on the edge

matt type of proof without a mirror-like finish

M on gold coins minted at Melbourne, Australia

'military' popular name for the 1813 guinea struck for the payment of troops fighting in the Napoleonic Wars

mm mintmark

mod eff modified effigy of George V

mule coin struck from wrongly paired dies

N on William III coins, minted at Norwich

obv obverse, usually the 'head' side of a coin

OH Old Head

OT ornamental trident

P on gold coins, minted at Perth, Australia

pattern trial piece not issued for currency

piedfort a coin which has been specially struck on a thicker than normal blank. In France, where the term originates, the kings seem to have issued them as presentation pieces from the 12th century onwards. In Britain, medieval and Tudor examples are known, and their issue has been reintroduced by the Royal Mint, starting with the twenty pence piedfort of 1982

plain on silver coins, no provenance marks in angles between shields on reverse

plain 4 with upper serif only to horizontal bar of 4

plumes symbol denoting

ABOVE: Plumes provenance mark

Welsh mines as the source of the metal

proof coin specially struck from highly polished dies. Usually has a mirror-like surface

prov a provenance mark on a coin, such as a rose, plume or elephant, which indicates the supplier of the bullion from which the coin was struck

PT plain trident

raised in relief, not incuse

RB round beads in border

rev reverse, 'tail' side of coin

r & p roses and plumes

rose symbol denoting west of England mines as the source of the metal

PRITANNIAR lettering error

QVARTO fourth regnal year, on edge

QVINTO fifth regnal year, on edge

rsd raised

S on gold coins minted at Sydney, Australia

SA on gold coins mined at Pretoria, South Africa

Scot Scottish shilling. In 1937, English and Scottish versions of the shilling were introduced. Scottish designs has a lion seated on crown, holding a sword and sceptre between 1937-51 and a lion rampant on a shield between 1953-66

SS C South Sea Company, the source of the metal

SECUNDO second regnal year, on edge

SEPTIMO seventh regnal year, on edge

'spade' the spade-like shape of the shield on George III gold coins

TB toothed beads in border

TERTIO third regnal year, on edge

trnctn base of head or bust where the neck or shoulders terminate

Unc Uncirculated condition

var variety

VF above price column Very Fine condition

VIGO struck from bullion captured in Vigo Bay, Spain

VIP 'very important person'.   ABOVE: 1723 halfcrown with
The so-called VIP crowns were   W.C.C. initials
the true proofs for the years of issue. Probably most of the limited number struck would have been presented to high-ranking officials

W.C.C. Welsh Copper Company, indicating the supplier of the metal

wire type figure of value in thin wire-like script

W.W., ww initials of William Wyon, engraver

xxri lettering error

y, Y on William III coins minted in York

YH Young Head

Lighthouse®

VOLTERRA coin etuis for QUADRUM coin capsules

[NEW]

Our high-quality **VOLTERRA** coin etuis are now also available for storing **QUADRUM** coin capsules. Choose between 7 different designs for precise fitting and representative presentation of 1 to 6 **QUADRUM** coin capsules.

	Overall size	Ref. No.	Price
1 x *QUADRUM*	80 x 80 mm (3 1/4 x 3 1/4")	339 043	£ 11.50
1 x *QUADRUM*	95 x 95 mm (3 3/4 x 3 3/4")	339 047	£ 15.95
2 x *QUADRUM*	148 x 93 mm (5 5/6 x 3 2/3")	339 048	£ 17.15
3 x *QUADRUM*	193 x 93 mm (7 3/5 x 3 2/3")	339 049	£ 18.25
4 x *QUADRUM*	260 x 93 mm (10 1/5 x 3 2/3")	339 050	£ 20.55
5 x *QUADRUM*	310 x 93 mm (12 1/5 x 3 2/3")	339 051	£ 22.95
6 x *QUADRUM*	193 x 150 mm (7 3/5 x 6")	339 052	£ 22.95

Digital coin scales

The practical pocket size makes our digital coin scale ideal for use on the move as well.
• LCD display. • Foldaway.
• Battery operated 2 x 3 V AAA.
• Overall size: 80 x 120 mm
(3 1/4 x 4 3/4")

0.01 - 50 g
Measuring tolerance +/- 0.02 g
Ref. No. 303 863 **£48.50**

0.1 - 500 g
Measuring tolerance +/- 0.2 g
Ref. No. 326 729 **£43.50**

VARIO currency album

The **VARIO** currency albums consists of:
• **VARIO** binder with sturdy 4-ring mechanism.
• 10 clear **VARIO** pages for bank notes up to 190 x 80 mm (7 1/2 x 3 1/4").
• 11 sort interleaves **VARIO**.
• Banknotes can be viewed from both sides.

Hunter green	Ref. No. 304 979	**£25.50**
Burgundy	Ref. No. 315 579	

THE DUNCANNON PARTNERSHIP · 4 Beaufort Road · REIGATE · SURREY · RH2 9DJ

Telephone 0 17 37/24 42 22 · FAX 0 17 37/22 47 43 · **www.duncannon.co.uk**

MARKET PRICES

CELTIC COINAGE

The early British series is the hardest to price, as the market has developed considerably since the publication of R D Van Arsdell's *Celtic Coinage of Britain* in 1989, an essential book for collectors.

A number of forgeries of this series exist, some of relatively recent production, and numerous items from undeclared hoards are also on the market. It is therefore essential to buy from a reputable dealer.

We are very grateful for the help of Robert Van Arsdell who produced the synopsis of the material we have used.

We have kept this very basic, and linked it for easy reference with *The Coinage of Ancient Britain* by R P Mack, third edition (now out of print), and with the *British Museum Catalogue of British Iron Age Coins* by R Hobbs, where possible.

In the listings, Mack types are indicated by 'M' and BMC types by 'B'. The V numbers relate to the Van Arsdell catalogue. The existence of forgeries is indicated by F.

The map on the right shows the distribution of the tribes in Britain based on the map in *The Coinage of Ancient Britain*, by R P Mack, published by Spink and B A Seaby Ltd.

KEY TO TOWNS:
1. Calleva Atrebatum (Silchester)
2. Verulamium (St Albans)
3. Camulodunum (Colchester)

■ GOLD STATERS WITHOUT LEGENDS

AMBIANI

	F	VF
Large flan type M1, 3, V10, 12	£1650	£5500
Defaced die type M5, 7, V30, 33	£500	£1600
Abstract type M26, 30, V44, 46	£395	£975
Gallic War type M27, a, V50, 52 F	£195	£400

Gallo-Belgic Stater

SUESSIONES

	F	VF
Abstract type M34a, V85	£485	£1375

VE MONOGRAM

	F	VF
M82, a, b, V87 F	£395	£1100

WESTERHAM

	F	VF
M28, 29, V200, 202, B1-24	£285	£650

Chute Gold Stater

CHUTE

	F	VF
M32, V1205, B35-76 F	£175	£375

CLACTON

	F	VF
Type I M47, V1458, B137-144	£400	£1275
Type II M46, a, V30, 1455, B145-179	£350	£1200

CORIELTAUVI

	F	VF
Scyphate type M-, V-, B3187-93	£275	£650

CORIELTAUVI (N E COAST TYPE)

	F	VF
Type I M50-M51a, V800, B182-191	£225	£525
Type II M52-57, S27, V804	£210	£500

NORFOLK	F	VF
Wolf type M49, a, b, V610, B212-278	£285	£750

CORIELTAUVI		
South Ferriby Kite & Domino type, M449-450a, V811, B3146-3186	£285	£750

Corieltauvi (South Ferriby) Stater

WHADDON CHASE	F	VF
M133-138, V1470-1478, B279-350 F	£250	£625
Middle, Late Whaddon Chase V1485-1509	£300	£775

WONERSH		
M147, 148, V1522, B351-56	£450	£1200

WEALD		
M84, 229, V144, 150, B2466-68	£900	£2750

ICENI		
Freckenham Type I M397-399, 403b, V620, B3384-95	£350	£925
Freckenham Type II M401, 2, 3a, 3c, V626, B3396-3419	£350	£875
Snettisham Type M-, V-, B3353-83	£600	£1575

ATREBATIC		
M58-61, V210-216, B445-76	£275	£625

SAVERNAKE FOREST		
M62, V1526, B359-64	£275	£625

DOBUNNIC		
M374, V1005, B2937-40	£675	£1750

Iceni Stater

■ GOLD QUARTER STATERS WITHOUT LEGENDS

AMBIANI		
Large flan type M2, 4, V15, 20 F	£350	£925

	F	VF
Defaced die type M6, 8, V35, 37	£275	£675

GEOMETRIC		
M37, 39, 41, 41A, 42, V65, 146, 69, 67	£90	£200

SUSSEX		
M40, 43-45, V143, 1225-1229	£85	£185

VE MONOGRAM		
M83, V87 F	£135	£350

ATREBATIC		
M63-6, 69-75, V220-256, B478-546	£130	£350

KENTISH		
Caesar's Trophy type V145	£135	£325

■ GOLD STATERS WITH LEGENDS

COMMIUS		
M92, V350, B724-730	£400	£1250

TINCOMARUS		
M93, 93, V362, 363, B761-74	£625	£1775

VERICA		
Equestrian type M121, V500, B1143-58	£350	£900
Vine leaf type M125, V520, B1159-76	£385	£950

EPATICCUS		
M262, V575, B2021-23	£1250	£3500

DUBNOVELLANUS		
In Kent M283, V176, B2492-98	£425	£1200
In Essex M275, V1650, B2425-40	£385	£1050

EPPILLUS		
In Kent M300-1, V430, B1125-28	£1850	£5500

ADDEDOMAROS		
M226, 7, V1605, B2390-94 F Three types	£300	£875

TASCIOVANUS		
Bucranium M149, V1680, B1591-1607 F	£400	£1150
Equestrian M154-7, V1730-1736, B1608-13	£375	£925

TASCIO/RICON		
M184, V1780, B1625-36	£825	£2000

SEGO		
M194, V1845, B1625-27	£2000	£5750

ANDOCO		
M197, V1860, B2011-14	£750	£1950

Tasciovanus 'Celtic Warrior' Stater

Cunobeline Stater

CUNOBELINE	F	VF
Two horses M201, V1910, B1769-71	£900	£2000
Corn ear M203 etc V2010, V1772-1835 F	£275	£650

ANTED of the Dobunni		
M385-6, V1062-1066, B3023-27 F	£600	£1650

EISU		
M388, V1105, B3039-42 F	£700	£1950

INAM		
M390, V1140, B3056 F	£1250	£4000

CATTI		
M391, V1130, B3057-60 F	£575	£1600

COMUX		
M392, V1092, B3061-63 F	£1250	£3750

CORIO		
M393, V1035, B3064-3133	£600	£1650

BODVOC		
M395, V1052, B3135-42 F	£950	£2650

Volisios Dumnocoveros Stater

VEP CORF		
M549-460, V940, 930, B3296-3304 F	£425	£975

DUMNOC TIGIR SENO		
M461, V972, B3325-27	£725	£2275

VOLISIOS DUMNOCOVEROS	F	VF
M463, V978, B3330-36	£450	£1300

Cunobeline Quarter Stater

■ GOLD QUARTER STATERS WITH LEGENDS

TINCOMARUS		
Abstract type M95, V365	£175	£425
Medusa head type M97, V387, B811-24	£225	£575
Tablet type M101-4, V387-390, B825-79	£135	£300

EPPILLUS		
Calleva M107, V407, B986-1015	£145	£325

VERICA		
Horse type M111-114, V465-468, B1143-46	£135	£375

TASCIOVANUS		
Horse type M152-3, V1690, 1692, B1641-1650	£125	£295

CUNOBELINE			
Various types, B1836-55	from	£175	£425

■ SILVER COINS WITHOUT LEGENDS

DUROTRIGES		
Silver Stater M317, V1235, B2525-2731 F	£45	£125
Geometric type M319, V1242, B2734-79	£30	£90
Starfish type M320, V1270, B2780-81	£65	£200

DOBUNNIC		
Face M374a, b, 5, 6, 8, V1020, B2950-3000	£35	£110
Abstract M378a-384d, V1042, B3012-22	£30	£85

CORIELTAUVI		
Boar type M405a, V855, B3194-3250	£60	£200
South Ferriby M410 etc, V875	£45	£125

ICENI		
Boar type M407-9, V655-659, B3440-3511	£30	£100
Wreath type M414, 5, 440, V679, 675, B3763-74	£35	£110
Face type M412-413e, V665, B3536-55	£75	£375

QUEEN BOUDICA	F	VF
Face type M413, 413D, V790, 792, B3556-3759	£50	£175
COMMIUS		
Head left M446b, V355, 357, B731-58	£45	£160

■ SILVER COINS WITH LEGENDS

EPPILLUS	F	VF
Calleva type M108, V415, B1016-1115	£50	£165
EPATICCUS		
Eagle type M263, V580, B2024-2289	£40	£125
Victory type M263a, V581, B2294-2328	£35	£120
VERICA		
Lim type M123, V505, B1332-59	£50	£165
CARATACUS		
Eagle Type M265, V593, B2376-2384 F	£135	£395
TASCIOVANUS		
Equestrian M158, V1745, B1667-68	£80	£295
VER type M161, V1699, B1670-73	£80	£295
CUNOBELINE		
Equestrian M216-8, 6, V1951 1983, 2047, B1862	£80	£275
Bust right M236, VA2055, B1871-73	£75	£250

Anted, silver Unit

ANTED of the Dobunni	F	VF
M387, V1082, B3032-38	£40	£125
EISU		
M389, V1110, B3043-55	£40	£120
BODVOC		
M396, V1057, B3143-45 F	£125	£450
ANTED of the Dobunni		
M419-421, V710, 711, 715 B3791-4009	£30	£75
ECEN		
M424, V730, B4033-4215	£25	£65
EDNAM		
M423, 425b, V740, 734, B4219-4281	£30	£65

ECE	F	VF
M425a, 426, 7, 8, V761, 764, 762, 766, B4348-4538	£25	£60
AESU		
M432, V775, B4558-72	£50	£125
PRASUTAGUS		
King of the Iceni (husband of Boudica) B4577-4580	£675	£1950
ESUP ASU		
M4566, VA924, B3272	£70	£225
VEP CORF		
M460b, 464, V394, 950, B3277-3382, B3305-3314	£50	£110
DUMNOC TIGIR SENO		
M462, V974, 980, B3339	£165	£550
VOLISIOS DUMNOCOVEROS	£185	£575
ALE SCA		
M469, V996	£125	£450

■ BRONZE, BASE METAL COINS WITHOUT LEGENDS

POTIN	F	VF
Experimental type M22a, V104	£30	£80
Class I M9-22, V122-131	£25	£70
Class II M23-25, V136-139	£25	£70
Thurrock Types V1402-1442	£35	£90
ARMORICAN		
Billon stater	£40	£145
Billon quarter stater	£50	£175
DUROTRIGES		
Bronze stater M318, V1290	£20	£50
Cast type M332-370, V1322-1370	£35	£110
NORTH THAMES		
M273, 274, 281, V1646, 1615, 1669	£35	£110
NORTH KENT		
M295, 296, V154	£65	£235

■ BRONZE COINS WITH LEGENDS

DUBNOVELLANUS in Essex	F	VF
M277, 8, V1665, 1667	£50	£190
TASCIOVANUS		
Head, beard M168, 9, V1707	£40	£140

VERLAMIO	F	VF
M172, V1808	£40	£135
Head, VER M177, V1816	£45	£165
Boar, VER M179, V1713	£45	£165
Equestrian M190, V1892	£65	£250
Centaur M192, V1882	£75	£300

ANDOCOV	F	VF
M200, V1871	£50	£195

CUNOBELINE	F	VF
Victory, TASC M221, V1971	£35	£135
Victory, CUN M22, a, V1973	£40	£150
Winged animal, M225, V2081	£40	£150
Head, beard, M226, 9, V2131, 2085	£35	£150

	F	VF
Panel, sphinx, M230, V1977	£40	£150
Winged beast, M231, V1979	£40	£150
Centaur, M242, V2089	£30	£130
Sow, M243, V2091	£30	£130
Warrior, M244, V2093	£30	£125
Boar, TASC, M245, V1983	£40	£160
Bull, TASC M246, V2095	£30	£140
Metal worker, M248, V2097	£40	£160
Pegasus, M249, V2099	£30	£130
Horse, CAMV, M250, V2101	£40	£150
Jupiter, horse, M251, V2103	£45	£160
Janus head, M252, V2105	£45	£160
Jupiter, lion, M253, V1207	£35	£145
Sphinx, fig, M260, a, V2109	£35	£160

HAMMERED GOLD 1344-1662

Prices in this section are approximately what collectors can expect to pay for the commonest types of the coins listed. For most other types prices will range upwards from these amounts.

Precise valuations cannot be given since they vary from dealer to dealer and have to be determined by a number of factors such as a coin's condition, which is of prime importance in deciding its value.

For more detailed information, look at *English Hammered Coins, Volumes 1 and 2*, by J J North (Spink, 1994, 1992).

Serious collectors should also obtain *The Herbert Schneider Collection, Volume 1: English Gold Coins 1257-1603* (Spink, 1996) and *Volume 2: English Coins 1603-20th Century* (Spink, 2002).

■ THE PLANTAGENET KINGS

HENRY III 1216-1272
Gold penny
One sold for £159,500 (including buyer's premium) at a Spink auction in 1996

Edward III Treaty Quarter-noble

EDWARD III 1327-77
Third coinage

		F	VF
Double-florins or Double Leopards		**ext. rare**	
Florins or leopards		**ext. rare**	
Half-florins or helms		**ext. rare**	
Nobles	from	**£1750**	**£6250**
Half-nobles	from	**£2500**	**£6750**
Quarter-nobles	from	**£500**	**£1275**

Fourth coinage
Pre-treaty period with France (before 1315)
With French title

	F	VF
Nobles	£875	£1950
Half-nobles	£625	£1500
Quarter-nobles	£275	£650

Transitional treaty period, 1361
Aquitaine title added

	F	VF
Nobles	£900	£2750
Half-nobles	£500	£1375
Quarter-nobles	£275	£600

Edward III Transitional Treaty Half-noble

Treaty period 1361-9
Omits FRANC

	F	VF
Nobles, London	£850	£1950
Nobles, Calais (C in centre of reverse)	£925	£2150
Half-nobles, London	£575	£1400
Half-nobles, Calais	£825	£1925
Quarter-nobles, London	£265	£550
Quarter-nobles, Calais	£295	£625

Post-treaty period 1369-77
French title resumed

	F	VF
Nobles, London	£925	£2150
Nobles, Calais (flag at stern or C in centre)	£950	£2375
Half-nobles, London	£1675	£4250
Half-nobles, Calais	£1250	£3250

There are many other issues and varieties in this reign. These prices relate to the commoner pieces.

Richard II Calais Noble

RICHARD II 1377-99

Nobles, London	£1100	£2750
Nobles, Calais (flag at stern)	£1250	£2950
Half-nobles, London	£1425	£3750
Half-nobles, Calais (flag at stern)	£1500	£4750
Quarter-nobles, London	£525	£1000

There are many different varieties and different styles of lettering.

Henry VI annulet London Noble

Henry IV heavy coinage London Noble

HENRY IV 1399-1413	F	VF
Heavy coinage		
Nobles (120g) London	£7250	£20000
Nobles, Calais (flag at stern)	£7750	£22500
Half-nobles, London	£5500	*
Half-nobles, Calais	£6250	*
Quarter-nobles, London	£1250	£3250
Quarter-nobles, Calais	£1475	£4250
Light coinage		
Nobles (108g)	£1675	£5250
Half-nobles	£2500	£6750
Quarter-nobles	£700	£1750

HENRY VI 1422-61	F	VF
Annulet issue, 1422-27		
Nobles, London	£850	£2150
Nobles, Calais (flag at stern)	£925	£2500
Nobles, York	£1500	£3750
Half-nobles, London	£725	£1650
Half-nobles, Calais	£1000	£3250
Half-nobles, York	£1750	£4000
Quarter-nobles, London	£275	£600
Quarter-nobles, Calais	£300	£700
Quarter-nobles, York	£395	£900
Rosette-mascle issue 1427-30		
Nobles, London	£1625	£4500
Nobles, Calais	£1950	£5750
Half-nobles, London	£2250	£5950
Half-nobles, Calais	£2650	£7000
Quarter-nobles, London	£825	£2650
Quarter-nobles, Calais	£975	£2750

Henry V Noble

HENRY V 1413-22		F	VF
Nobles, many varieties	from	£950	£2250
Half-nobles		£875	£2600
Quarter-nobles		£400	£800

This reign sees an increase in the use of privy marks to differentiate issues.

Henry VI rosette-mascle Calais Noble

Pinecone-mascle issue 1430-4		
Nobles, London	£1625	£4500
Half-nobles, London	£2875	£8000
Quarter-nobles	£925	£2850
Leaf-mascle issue 1434-5		
Nobles, London	£3000	£8500
Half-nobles, London	£2750	£7500
Quarter-nobles	£975	£3250

Leaf-trefoil issue 1435-8	F	VF
Nobles	£3000	£8500
Half-nobles	£2950	£9250
Quarter-noble	£975	£3000

Trefoil issue 1438-43		
Nobles	£2750	£8000

Henry VI Pinecone-mascle Noble

Leaf-pellet issue 1445-54		
Nobles	£3000	£8750

Cross pellet issue 1454-60		
Nobles	£3500	£10000

EDWARD IV 1st reign 1461-70		
Heavy coinage 1461-65		
Nobles (108g)	£4500	£13250
Quarter-noble		ext. rare

Light coinage 1464-70		
Ryals or rose-nobles (120g) London	£850	£1925
Flemish copy	£600	£1425

Edward IV Light coinage Norwich Ryal

	F	VF
Ryals, Bristol (B in waves)	£1250	£3000
Ryals, Coventry (C in waves)	£2150	£4950
Ryals, Norwich (N in waves)	£2250	£5850
Ryals, York (E in waves)	£1100	£2750
Half-ryals, London	£700	£1925
Half-ryals, Bristol (B in waves)	£1450	£3950
Half-ryals, Coventry (C in waves)	£4850	£12000
Half-ryals, Norwich (N in waves)	£3750	£10250
Half-ryals, York (E in waves)	£825	£2150
Quarter-ryals	£450	£950
Angels	£8500	*

HENRY VI restored 1470-71		
Angels, London	£1450	£3850
Angels, Bristol (B in waves)	£2500	£7250
Half-angels, London	£4250	*
Half-angels, Bristol (B in waves)	£5500	*

EDWARD IV 2nd reign 1471-83		
Angels, London	£725	£1950
Angels, Bristol (B in waves)	£2500	£6250
Half-angels, some varieties	£650	£1750

EDWARD IV or V 1483		
im halved sun and rose		
Angels	£4500	£12500
Half-angels	£4500	*

RICHARD III 1483-85		
Angels, reading EDWARD, im		
boar's head on obverse, halved sun		
and rose on reverse	£7250	£19500
Angels, reading RICHARD or RICAD	£4750	£11000
Half-angels	£6500	*

Edward IV second reign Angel

■ THE TUDOR MONARCHS

HENRY VII 1485-1509
Sovereigns of 20 shillings			
(all extremely rare)	from	£30000	£65000
Ryals		£35000	*
Angels, varieties, different ims	from	£825	£1950
Half-angels		£750	£1850

Henry VIII first coinage Angel, Im portcullis

	F	VF
Angels	£825	£1950
Half-angels	£775	£1825
Quarter-angels	£675	£1825
Crowns, HENRIC 8, London	£750	£1925
Crowns, Southwark	£750	£1925
Crowns, Bristol	£800	£1950
Halfcrowns, London	£600	£1350
Halfcrowns, Southwark	£600	£1350
Halfcrowns, Bristol	£825	£2000

Henry VIII Third coinage type I Sovereign

HENRY VIII 1509-47
First coinage 1509-26

		F	VF
Sovereigns of 20 shillings im crowned portcullis only		£9500	£27500
Angels (6s 8d)	from	£825	£1950
Half-angels		£675	£1525

Second coinage 1526-44

		F	VF
Sovereigns of 22s 6d, various ims		£9000	£24500
Angels (7s 6d)	from	£1250	£3000
Half-angels im lis		£1150	£3250
George-nobles im rose		£9500	£26500
Half-George-noble		£9000	*
Crowns of the rose im rose		£7000	*
Crowns of the double rose			
HK (Henry and Katherine of Aragon)		£875	£2000
HA (Henry and Anne Boleyn)		£2500	£5500
HI (Henry and Jane Seymour)		£950	£2350
HR (HENRICUS REX)		£850	£2000
Halfcrowns of the double-rose			
HK		£725	£1850
HI		£950	£2500
HR		£1100	£2650

Third coinage 1544-47

		F	VF
Sovereigns of 20s, London	from	£6750	£15250
Sovereigns of 20s, Southwark		£6000	£14500
Sovereigns of 20s, Bristol	from	£8500	£22500
Half-sovereigns, London		£1200	£3250
Half-sovereigns, Southwark		£1200	£3250
Half-sovereigns, Bristol		£2750	£6250

EDWARD VI 1547-53
Posthumous coinage in the name of Henry VIII, 1547-51

	F	VF
Sovereigns, London	£7750	£21500
Sovereigns, Bristol	£9250	£26500
Half-sovereigns, London	£1100	£2650
Half-sovereigns, Southwark	£1100	£2650
Crowns, London	£725	£1875
Crowns, Southwark	£800	£2000
Halfcrowns, London	£650	£1450
Halfcrowns, Southwark	£650	£1450

Coinage in Edward's own name
First period 1547-49

	F	VF
Half-sovereigns, Tower, reads EDWARD 6	£2750	£7750

Edward VI second period Sovereign im arrow

	F	VF
Half-sovereigns, Southwark	£2250	£6750
Crown	£3500	*
Halfcrowns	£2750	*

Second period 1549-50

	F	VF
Sovereigns	£7250	£18500
Half-sovereign, uncrowned bust, London	£3850	£10000
Half-sovereigns, SCUTUM on obverse	£1750	£5500
Half-sovereigns, Durham House MDXLVII	£6500	*
Half-sovereigns, crowned bust, London	£1850	£5250
Half-sovereigns, half-length bust, Durham House	£6500	*
Crowns, uncrowned bust	£1850	£5750
Crowns, crowned bust	£1850	£5750
Halfcrowns, uncrowned bust	£1850	£5750
Halfcrowns, crowned bust	£1475	£4250

Mary 1553 Sovereign

PHILIP AND MARY 1554-8	F	VF
Angels, im lis	£6000	£15000
Half-angels	£9500	*

Edward VI third period Sovereign im tun

Third period 1550-53

'Fine' sovereigns of 30s,		
king enthroned	£31500	£75000
Sovereigns of 20s, half length figure	£4500	£13500
Half-sovereigns, similar to last	£1800	£4850
Crowns, similar but SCUTUM on reverse	£1850	£5250
Halfcrowns, similar	£1950	£5500
Angels	£9500	*
Half-angels		ext. rare

MARY 1553-4

Sovereigns, different dates, some undated,		
im pomegranate or half rose	£7000	£16500
Ryals, dated MDLIII (1553)	£25000	*
Angels, im pomegranate	£2750	£7000
Half-angels	£5250	£10500

Elizabeth I sixth issue Ryal

ELIZABETH I 1558-1603
Hammered issues

'Fine' Sovereigns of 30s,		
different issues from	£6250	£15500
Ryals	£14750	£35000
Angels, different issues	£1150	£3000
Half-angels	£950	£2650
Quarter-angels	£900	£2400

Elizabeth I second issue Quarter-angel

	F	VF
Pounds of 20s, different ims	from £3250	£8000
Half-pounds, different issues	£2000	£5250
Crowns	£1475	£3500
Halfcrowns	£1100	£2850

	F	VF
Britain crowns	£385	£750
Halfcrowns	£285	£600
Thistle crowns, varieties	£325	£700

Elizabeth I sixth issue Crown

Milled issues

	F	VF
Half-pounds, one issue but different marks	£4000	£10500
Crowns	£2950	£7500
Halfcrowns	£3850	£9250

■ THE STUART KINGS

James I third coinage Rose-ryal

James I, third coinage Spur-ryal

James I third coinage Laurel

JAMES I 1603-25
First coinage 1603-4

Sovereigns of 20s, two busts	£3250	£9000
Half-sovereigns	£4250	£14000
Crowns	£2850	£7500
Halfcrowns	£925	£3250

Second coinage 1604-19

Rose-ryals of 30s	£3000	£8750
Spur-ryals of 15s	£8500	£18750
Angels	£1500	£4750
Half-angels	£3250	£8500
Unites, different busts	£850	£2000
Double crowns	£500	£1250

Third coinage 1619-25

Rose-ryals, varieties	£3850	£9750
Spur-ryals	£7000	£18750
Angels	£2750	£6000
Laurels, different busts	£850	£1750
Half-laurels	£575	£1100
Quarter-laurels	£300	£675

CHARLES I 1625-49
Tower mint 1625-42
Initial marks: lis, cross-calvary, negro's head, castle, anchor, heart, plume, rose, harp, portcullis, bell, crown, tun, triangle, star, triangle-in-circle.

Charles I Tower mint Unite, im heart

	F	VF
Angels, varieties	£4000	£8500
Angels, pierced as touchpieces	£1250	£2950
Unites	£825	£1850
Double-crowns	£525	£1150
Crowns	£300	£625

Charles I Tower mint Double-crown, im heart

Tower mint under Parliament 1642-9
Ims: (P), (R), eye, sun, sceptre
Unites, varieties	£1500	£3250
Double-crowns	£875	£2000
Crowns	£395	£875

Briot's milled issues 1631-2
Ims: anemone and B, daisy and B, B
Angels		ext. rare
Unites	£4500	£11000
Double-crowns	£3500	£8250
Crowns	£4500	£11000

Coins of provincial mints
Bristol 1645
Unites	ext. rare
Half-unites	ext. rare

Chester 1644
Unites	ext. rare

Exeter 1643-44
Unites	ext. rare

Oxford 1642-46
Triple unites,	from	£18500	£38500
Unites	from	£2750	£7500
Half-unites	from	£2450	£5750

Truro 1642-43	F	VF
Half-unites		ext. rare
Shrewsbury 1644		
Triple unites and unites		ext. rare
Worcester 1643-44		
Unites		ext. rare

Charles I 1643 Oxford Triple unite

Siege pieces 1645-49
Pontefract 1648-49
Unites F		ext. rare

Commonwealth 1651 Unite

COMMONWEALTH 1649-60
Unites im sun	£3000	£6250
im anchor	£8500	£19250
Double-crowns im sun	£1875	£4000
im anchor	£6000	£12500
Crowns, im sun	£1275	£3000
im anchor	£4000	£9500

Commonwealth 1650 Crown

CHARLES II 1660-85
Hammered Coinage 1660-62

Charles II hammered coinage Unite

		F	VF
Unites, two issues	from	£2750	£6000
Double-crowns		£1500	£4250
Crowns		£1650	£4500

HAMMERED SILVER

In this section, coins are mainly valued in Fine or Very Fine condition. Prices are based on coins of good metal and that are not chipped or cracked.

However, pennies of the early Plantagenets, where higher-grade coins are seldom available, are valued in Fair or Fine condition.

Again it should be noted that prices are for the commonest types only, and are the amounts collectors can expect to pay, rather than dealers' buying prices.

Prices for the Saxon and Norman series are based on common mint towns. Rarer mints command higher premiums.

Descriptions such as 'cross/moneyer's name' indicate that a cross appears on the obverse and the moneyer's name on the reverse. For more details see *Standard Catalogue of British Coins* (Spink, annual), and *English Hammered Coins, volumes 1 and 2* by J J North, Spink (1991, 1994).

■ ANGLO-SAXON SCEATS AND STYCAS

Examples of Sceats

EARLY PERIOD c600-750		F	VF
Silver Sceats	from	£80	£195
Large numbers of types and varieties.			

NORTHUMBRIAN KINGS c737-867			
Silver Sceats c737-796	from	£100	£295
Copper Stycas c 810-867	from	£20	£55

Struck for many kings. Numerous moneyers and different varieties. The copper Styca is the commonest coin in the Anglo-Saxon series.

ARCHBISHOPS OF YORK c732-900			
Silver Sceats	from	£65	£185
Copper Stycas	from	£20	£55

■ KINGS OF KENT

HEABERHT c764	F	VF
Pennies monogram/cross		ext. rare
One moneyer (Eoba).		

ECGBERHT c765-780		
Pennies monogram/cross	£1100	£4250
Two moneyers (Babba and Udd).		

EADBERHT PRAEN 797-798		
Pennies EADBERHT REX/moneyer	£1300	£4400
Three moneyers.		

CUTHRED 789-807		
Pennies non-portrait, various designs from	£750	£2400
Bust right	£900	£2500
Different moneyers and varieties.		

BALDRED c825		
Pennies bust right	£1300	£3850
Cross/cross	£785	£2250
Different types and moneyers.		

ANONYMOUS		
Pennies bust right	£875	£2750
Different types and moneyers.		

■ ARCHBISHOPS OF CANTERBURY

JAENBERHT 766-792			
Pennies various types			
non-portrait	from	£1100	£3750

AETHELHEARD 793-805			
Pennies various types			
non-portrait	from	£925	£3250

WULFRED 805-832			
Pennies various groups			
portrait types	from	£775	£2850

CEOLNOTH 833-870			
Pennies various groups, portrait types	from	£685	£2000

AETHELRED		
Pennies various types,		
portrait, non portrait	£2300	£7600

PLEGMUND 890-914			
Pennies various types non-portrait	from	£725	£2000

Offa portrait Penny

■ KINGS OF MERCIA

OFFA 757-796

		F	VF
Pennies non-portrait	from	£650	£1500
Portrait	from	£1250	£4250

CYNETHRYTH (wife of Offa)

	F	VF
Pennies portrait	£2850	£9250
Non-portrait	£1500	£4850

COENWULF 796-821

		F	VF
Pennies various types, portrait,		£875	£2750
non-portrait	from	£625	£1750

Coenwulf portrait Penny

CEOLWULF 821-823

	F	VF
Pennies various types, portrait	£950	£3750

BEORNWULF 823-825

	F	VF
Pennies various types, portrait	£925	£3500

LUCIDA 825-827

	F	VF
Pennies two types, portrait F	£3000	£9750

WIGLAF 827-829, 830-840

	F	VF
Pennies two groups, portrait, non-portrait	£2300	£6850

BERHTWULF 840-852

	F	VF
Pennies two groups, portrait, non-portrait	£1000	£3600

BURGRED 852-874

	F	VF
Pennies one type portrait, five variants	£275	£575

CEOLWULF II 874-c 877

	F	VF
Pennies two types portrait	£1400	£4250

■ KINGS OF EAST ANGLIA

BEONNA c758

	F	VF
Silver Sceat	£800	£2500

AETHELBERHT died 794

Pennies, portrait type F	ext. rare

EADWALD c796

	F	VF
Pennies, non-portrait types	£950	£3450

AETHELSTAN I c850

	F	VF
Pennies various types, portrait, non-portrait	£475	£1400

AETHELWEARD c 850

	F	VF
Pennies, non-portrait types	£625	£1750

EADMUND 855-870

	F	VF
Pennies, non-portrait types	£400	£950

■ VIKING INVADERS 878-954

ALFRED

		F	VF
Imitations of Alfred Pennies and Halfpennies			
Many different types, portrait	from	£2500	£6250
non-portrait.	from	£650	£1750

Danish East Anglia, c885-954

AETHELSTAN II 878-890/1

	F	VF
Pennies cross/moneyer	£1350	£3650

OSWALD

	F	VF
Pennies A/cross	£1450	£4500

ST EADMUND

	F	VF
Pennies memorial coinage, various legends	£185	£400
Many moneyers.		
Halfpennies	£475	£1450
Many moneyers.		

St Eadmund memorial Penny

ST MARTIN OF LINCOLN c917

	F	VF
Pennies sword/cross	£2350	£7750

AETHELRED I c870

	F	VF
Pennies temple/cross	£1750	£5400

York
SIEVERT-SIEFRED-CNUT c897

	F	VF
Crosslet/small cross	£185	£425
Many different groups and varieties.		
Halfpennies	£525	£1350
Many different groups and varieties.		

EARL SIHTRIC unknown

	F	VF
Pennies non-portrait	£2400	£7000

REGNALD c 910

	F	VF
Pennies various types, some blundered	£1800	£6000

SIHTRIC I 921-926/7

	F	VF
Pennies sword/cross	£2000	£7250

ANLAF GUTHFRITHSSON 939-941

	F	VF
Pennies raven/cross	£2000	£6250
Cross/cross	£1850	£5750
Flower/cross	£2250	£7250

OLAF SIHTRICSSON 941-944, 948-952

	F	VF
Pennies various types	£1850	£5750

SIHTRIC II c941-943

	F	VF
Pennies shield/standard	£1900	£6250

REGNALD II c941-943

	F	VF
Pennies cross/cross	£1900	£6250
Shield/standard	£2000	£7250

ERIC BLOODAXE 948, 952-954

	F	VF
Pennies cross/moneyer	£3100	£9500
Sword/cross	£3400	£10750

ST PETER OF YORK c905-925

		F	VF
Pennies various types	from	£325	£800
Halfpennies, various types	from	£675	£1750

■ KINGS OF WESSEX

BEORHTRIC 786-802

Two types, non-portrait	ext. rare

ECGBERHT 802-839

	F	VF
Pennies four groups, portrait, non-portrait	£1250	£4000

Mints of Canterbury, London, Rochester, Winchester

AETHELWULF 839-858

	F	VF
Pennies four phases, portrait, non-portrait	£525	£1650

from mints of Canterbury, Rochester

AETHELBERHT 858-866

	F	VF
Pennies two types portrait from	£525	£1650

Many moneyers.

AETHELRED I 865-871

	F	VF
Pennies portrait types from	£600	£1750

Many moneyers.

ALFRED THE GREAT 871-899

	F	VF
Pennies portrait in style of Aethelred I	£725	£2250
Four other portrait types, commonest		
has the London monogram reverse	£1850	£5250
Halfpennies	£625	£1700
Pennies non-portrait types from	£500	£1100
Many different styles of lettering.		
Halfpennies	£500	£1100

Alfred the Great Halfpenny, London monogram on reverse

EDWARD THE ELDER 899-924

	F	VF
Non-portrait types		
Pennies cross/moneyer's name in two lines	£275	£625
Halfpennies cross/moneyer's		
name in two lines	£850	£2400

Edward the Elder, non-portrait Penny

	F	VF
Portrait types		
Pennies bust/moneyer's name	£925	£3250
Many types, varieties and moneyers.		
Pennies design has buildings,		
floral designs and others	£1650	£5750
Many types, varieties and moneyers.		

■ KINGS OF ALL ENGLAND

AETHELSTAN 924-39

	F	VF
Non-portrait types		
Pennies cross/moneyer's name in two lines	£375	£800
Cross/cross	£325	£900

	F	VF
Portrait types		
Pennies bust/moneyer's name in two lines	£875	£3400
Bust/small cross	£775	£3000

Many other issues, some featuring buildings. There are also different mints and moneyer's names.

EADMUND 939-46

	F	VF
Non-portrait types		
Pennies cross or rosette/moneyer's		
name in two lines	£325	£775
Halfpennies, cross or rosette/moneyer's		
name in two lines	£825	£2400

	F	VF
Portrait types		
Pennies crowned bust/small cross	£825	£2850
Helmeted bust/cross crosslet	£975	£3500

Many other issues and varieties; also different mint names and moneyers.

EADRED 946-55

	F	VF
Non-portrait types		
Pennies cross/moneyer's name in two lines	£285	£650
Halfpennies cross/moneyer's		
name in two lines	£675	£1850
Pennies rosette/moneyer's name	£375	£875

	F	VF
Portrait types		
Pennies crowned bust/small cross	£775	£2650

Many variations and mint names and moneyers.

HOWEL DDA King of Wales, died c948

	F	VF
Pennies small cross/moneyer's name in two lines (Gillys)		**ext. rare**

EADWIG 955-59
Non-portrait types

		F	VF
Pennies cross/moneyer's name	from	**£500**	**£1650**

Many variations, some rare.
Halfpennies, non portrait types

		F	VF
cross/moneyer's name		**£1050**	**£3250**

Portrait types

		F	VF
Pennies bust/cross from		**£3400**	**£10500**

EADGAR 959-75
Non-portrait types

		F	VF
Pennies cross/moneyer's name	from	**£265**	**£500**
Cross/cross from		**£265**	**£525**
Rosette/rosette from		**£285**	**£685**
Halfpennies	from	**£900**	**£2750**

Eadgar, non portrait Penny

Portrait types

	F	VF
Pennies pre-reform, bust right	**£950**	**£3250**
Halfpennies, diademed bust/London monogram	**£775**	**£2650**
Pennies reform (c972), bust left	**£950**	**£3000**

Many other varieties.

EDWARD THE MARTYR 975-78
Portrait types

	F	VF
Pennies bust left/small cross	**£1100**	**£3400**

Many different mints and moneyers.

AETHELRED II 978-1016

Aethelred II last small cross type Penny

		F	VF
Pennies first small cross type from	from	**£700**	**£2250**
First hand type from	from	**£190**	**£425**
Second hand type from	from	**£180**	**£400**
Benediction hand type	from	**£925**	**£3250**

		F	VF
CRUX type from	from	**£145**	**£300**

Aethelred II CRUX type Penny

Aethelred II long cross type Penny

	F	VF
Long cross type	**£160**	**£325**
Helmet type	**£155**	**£350**
Agnus Dei type	**£5400**	*

Other issues and varieties, many mints and moneyers.

CNUT 1016-35

		F	VF
Pennies quatrefoil type	from	**£140**	**£285**

Cnut quatrefoil type Penny

		F	VF
Pointed helmet type	from	**£130**	**£265**

Cnut pointed helmet type Penny

		F	VF
Short cross type	from	**£115**	**£250**
Jewel cross type	from	**£500**	**£1450**

Other types, and many different mints and moneyers.

HAROLD I 1035-40

		F	VF
Pennies jewel cross type	from	**£325**	**£775**
Long cross type with trefoils	from	**£315**	**£725**
Long cross type with fleurs-de-lis		**£315**	**£725**

Many different mint names and moneyers.

HARTHACNUT 1035-42	F	VF
Pennies jewel cross type, bust left	£1250	£3650
Bust right	£1100	£3400
Arm and sceptre type	£875	£2850
Different mint names and moneyers.		
Pennies Scandinavian types struck at Lund	£285	£650

EDWARD THE CONFESSOR 1042-66		
Pennies PACX type	£275	£650
Radiate crown/small cross type	£140	£300
Trefoil quadrilateral type	£150	£325
Small flan type	£120	£260
Expanding cross type	£145	£365

Edward the Confessor transitional pyramids type Penny

Pointed helmet type	£145	£375
Sovereign/eagles type	£160	£425
Hammer cross type	£140	£350

Edward the Confessor hammer cross type Penny

Bust facing/small cross type	£140	£315
Pyramids type	£145	£350
Transitional pyramids type	£1400	£3850

Other issues, including a unique gold penny; many different mints and moneyers.

Harold II Pax type Penny, bust left, without sceptre

HAROLD II 1066		
Pennies Pax type, crowned head left,		
with sceptre	£775	£2000
without sceptre	£850	£2250

	F	VF
Pennies Pax type crowned head right,		
with sceptre	£1750	£5650

■ THE NORMAN KINGS

WILLIAM I 1066-87		F	VF
Pennies profile left/cross fleury type	from	£385	£950
Bonnet type	from	£280	£625
Canopy type	from	£425	£1100
Two sceptres type	from	£340	£850
Two stars type	from	£285	£585
Sword type	from	£365	£950

William I profile/cross fleury type Penny

Profile right/cross and			
trefoils type	from	£485	£1350
PAXS type	from	£265	£550

WILLIAM II 1087-1100

William II cross voided type Penny

Pennies profile right type	from	£765	£2000
Cross in quatrefoil type	from	£700	£1750
Cross voided type	from	£700	£1750
Cross pattée over fleury type	from	£750	£1850
Cross fleury and piles type	from	£850	£2250

Henry I large bust/cross and annulets type Penny

HENRY I 1100-1135

		F	VF
Pennies annulets type	from	£550	£1450
Profile/cross fleury type	from	£385	£1050
PAXS type	from	£360	£950
Annulets and piles type	from	£385	£1050
Voided cross and fleurs type	from	£850	£2400
Pointing bust and stars type	from	£1650	£5250
Facing bust/quatrefoil and piles type	from	£375	£975
Large profile/cross and annulets type	from	£1750	£5650
Facing bust/cross in quatrefoil type	from	£800	£2100
Full bust/cross fleury type		£285	£700
Double inscription type		£625	£1650
Small profile/cross and annulets type		£525	£1400
Star in lozenge fleury type		£500	£1300
Pellets in quatrefoil type		£280	£685
Quadrilateral on cross fleury type		£215	£475
Halfpennies		£1850	£5750

STEPHEN I 1135-54

		F	VF
Pennies cross moline (Watford) type	from	£275	£725

Stephen 'Watford' Penny

	F	VF
Similar, reads PERERIC	£725	£1850
Voided cross and mullets type	£325	£765
Cross and piles type	£425	£1100
Cross pommée (Awbridge) type	£315	£765

There are also a number of irregular issues produced during the civil war, all of which are very rare. These include several extremely rare and attractive pieces bearing the names of Empress Matilda and barons, such as Eustace Fitzjohn and Robert de Stuteville.

◼ THE PLANTAGENET KINGS

HENRY II 1154-89

Henry II cross and crosslets (Tealby) Penny

	F	VF
Pennies cross and crosslets ('Tealby' coinage)	£130	£325

The issue is classified by bust variants into six groups, struck at 32 mints.

	F	VF
Pennies short cross	£80	£185

The 'short cross' coinage was introduced in 1180 and continued through successive reigns until Henry III brought about a change in 1247. HENRICVS REX appears on all these coins but they can be classified into reigns by the styles of the busts and lettering. CR Wren's guide *The Short Cross Coinage 1180-1247* is the best book to identify coins of this series.

RICHARD I 1189-99

	F	VF
Pennies short cross	£85	£215

JOHN 1189-1216

	F	VF
Pennies short cross	£80	£185

John short cross Penny

HENRY III 1216-72

	F	VF
Pennies short cross	£35	£90
Long cross no sceptre	£30	£70
Long cross with sceptre	£30	£70

Henry III, long cross Penny with sceptre

The 'long cross' pennies, first introduced in 1247, are divided into two groups: those with sceptre and those without. They also fall into five basic classes, with many varieties. CR Wren's *The Voided Long Cross Coinage, 1247-79* is the best guide to identification.

Edward I, 1st coinage, long cross Penny

CGS UK

Experience, Objectivity, Professionalism

Guarantee of Authenticity

CGS UK pledge to pay the submitter the full market value of any coin encapsulated and reported as genuine by CGS UK, if it can be subsequently proved that the said coin is a fake or forgery, still intact in the original encapsulation with no evidence of tampering.

LEAGUE TABLES

Shows the best known collections by monarch and denomination.

POPULATION REPORT

A complete report of every coin every graded by CGS by coin type and grade.

VALUATION REPORT

Shows the value of any CGS coin by type and grade.

MY PAGE

The CGS my page allows collectors to effectively manage their collections by one simple input of the UIN number.

MY COLLECTION

This is where your collection is initially input (by UIN number) and where sold or disposed of items may be deleted.

VIRTUAL COIN GALLERY

This will show an image of both sides of each coin in your collection.

COLLECTOR'S GALLERY

Compare your collection to those of other collectors.

**Authenticity Guaranteed
Professionally Attributed
Objectively Graded**

Tel: 01474 874895
Email: info@cgs-uk.biz
www.CGS-UK.biz

EDWARD I 1272-1307		F	VF
1st coinage 1272-78			
Long cross pennies	from	£30	£85

Similar in style to those of Henry III but with more realistic beard.

New coinage 1278-1307

Groats		£2650	£6850
Pennies, various classes, mints	from	£20	£55
Halfpennies	from	£35	£90
Farthings	from	£25	£80

Edward I Farthing London

The best guide to this era of coinage is *Edwardian English Silver Coins 1278-1351* (Sylloge of Coins of the British Isles no39).

EDWARD II 1307-27

Pennies, various classes, mints	from	£30	£65
Halfpennies	from	£50	£130
Farthing	from	£35	£95

EDWARD III 1327-77
1st and 2nd coinages 1327-43

Pennies (only 1st coinage) various types and mints	£210	£550
Halfpennies, different types and mints	£25	£70
Farthings	£35	£80

3rd coinage 1344-51, florin coinage

Pennies, various types and mints	£25	£95
Halfpennies	£25	£70
Farthings	£30	£80

Edward III, post-treaty Groat

4th coinage 1351-77

Groats, many types and mints	from	£65	£190
Halfgroats		£40	£130
Pennies		£25	£85
Halfpennies, different types		£30	£110
Farthings, a few types		£110	£325

RICHARD II 1377-99		F	VF
Groats, four types	from	£485	£1600

Richard II Groat

Halfgroats	£325	£900
Pennies, various types, London	£200	£575
York	£75	£225
Durham	£135	£425
Halfpennies, three main types	£35	£95
Farthings, some varieties	£120	£375

HENRY IV 1399-1413

Groats, varieties	from	£2400	£6500
Halfgroats		£725	£2100
Pennies		£385	£1050
Halfpennies		£225	£625
Farthings		£725	£2100

Henry V Groat

HENRY V 1413-22

Groats, varieties	£185	£525
Halfgroats	£140	£385
Pennies	£45	£145
Halfpennies	£30	£120
Farthings	£250	£800

HENRY VI 1422-61
Annulet issue 1422-1427

Groats	£55	£145
Halfgroats	£35	£120
Pennies	£30	£100
Halfpennies	£25	£65
Farthings	£100	£285

Rosette-mascle issue 1427-1430

Groats	£60	£175
Halfgroats	£40	£125

	F	VF
Pennies	£40	£120
Halfpennies	£25	£75
Farthings	£150	£400

Pinecone-mascle issue 1430-1434

Groats	£55	£145
Halfgroats	£45	£135
Pennies	£40	£125
Halfpennies	£25	£70
Farthings	£150	£425

Leaf-mascle issue 1434-1435

Groats	£165	£475
Halfgroats	£120	£350
Pennies	£85	£210
Halfpennies	£35	£90

Leaf-trefoil issue 1435-1438

Groats	£85	£240
Halfgroats	£85	£210
Pennies	£70	£210
Halfpennies	£30	£70
Farthings	£140	£385

Trefoil issue 1438-1443

Groats	£85	£265
Halfgroats	£160	£485
Halfpennies	£30	£85

Trefoil-pellet issue 1443-1445

Groats	£175	£525

Henry VI, leaf-mascle issue Groat

Leaf-pellet issue 1445-1454

Groats	£75	£220
Halfgroats	£80	£225
Pennies	£55	£145
Halfpennies	£25	£70
Farthings	£150	£425

Unmarked issue 1445-1454

Groats	£550	£1650
Halfgroats	£365	£925

Cross-pellet issue 1454-1460

Groats	£150	£350
Halfgroats	£275	£750

	F	VF
Pennies	£50	£145
Halfpennies	£35	£85
Farthings	£250	£600

Lis-pellet issue 1454-1460

Groats	£265	£775

There are many different varieties, initial marks and mints in this reign. These prices are for commonest prices in each issue.

EDWARD IV 1st Reign 1461-1470
Heavy coinage 1461-4

Groats, many classes, all London	£165	£485
Halfgroats, many classes, all London	£250	£650
Pennies, different classes, London, York and Durham	£135	£385
Halfpennies, different classes, all London	£45	£130
Farthings, London	£210	£675

Edward IV light coinage Groat

Light coinage 1464-70

Groats, many different issues, varieties, ims and mints	from	£55	£165
Halfgroats, ditto		£50	£150
Pennies, ditto		£35	£95
Halfpennies, ditto		£30	£85
Farthings, two issues		£285	£825

Henry VI (restored) Groat London

HENRY VI restored 1470-71

Groats, different mints, different ims	from	£185	£525
Halfgroats	from	£265	£700
Pennies	from	£250	£650
Halfpennies	from	£165	£400

EDWARD IV 2nd reign 1471-83

	F	VF
Groats, different varieties, mints	£65	£175
Halfgroats	£45	£140
Pennies	£35	£110
Halfpennies	£30	£90

EDWARD IV or V 1483

im halved sun and rose

	F	VF
Groats	£1100	£3400
Pennies	£1200	£3650
Halfpennies	£285	£750

Richard III Groat London

RICHARD III 1483-85

	F	VF
Groats, reading EDWARD, initial mark boar's head on obverse, halved sun and rose on reverse	£1850	£5250
Groats, reading Ricard, London and York mints, various combinations of ims	£675	£1850
Halfgroats	£875	£2750
Pennies, York and Durham	£300	£800
London mint		unique
Halfpennies	£250	£725
Farthing	£1250	£3650

PERKIN WARBECK, PRETENDER

	F	VF
Groat, 1494	£1350	£3400

■ THE TUDOR MONARCHS

HENRY VII 1485-1509
Facing bust issues

Henry VII open crown type Groat London

	F	VF
Groats, all London		
Open crown without arches	£120	£350
Crown with two arches unjewelled	£95	£250
Crown with two jewelled arches	£70	£180
Similar but only one arch jewelled	£70	£180
Similar but tall thin lettering	£75	£190
Similar but single arch, tall thin lettering	£80	£225
Halfgroats, London		
Open crown without arches, tressure unbroken	£275	£700
Double arched crown	£45	£135
Unarched crown	£40	£100
Some varieties and different ims.		
Halfgroats, Canterbury		
Open crown, without arches	£40	£120
Double arched crown	£35	£120
Some varieties and different ims.		
Halfgroats, York		
Double arched crown	£40	£125
Unarched crown with tressure broken	£40	£120
Double arched crown with keys at side of bust	£35	£110
Many varieties and different ims.		
Pennies, facing bust type		
London	£160	£475
Canterbury, open crown	£250	£525
Canterbury, arched crown	£65	£165
Durham, Bishop Sherwood, S on breast	£65	£165
York	£40	£120
Many varieties and ims.		
Pennies, 'sovereign enthroned' type		
London, many varieties	£40	£120
Durham, many varieties	£35	£100
York, many varieties	£35	£100
Halfpennies, London		
Open crown	£40	£135
Arched crown	£30	£90
Crown with lower arch	£25	£75
Some varieties and ims.		
Halfpennies, Canterbury		
Open crown	£70	£175
Arched crown	£60	£125
Halfpennies, York		
Arched crown and key below bust	£65	£150
Farthings, all London	£350	£900

Profile issues

	F	VF
Testoons im lis, three different legends	£11500	£23000
Groats, all London		
Tentative issue, double band to crown	£250	£700

Henry VII regular issue Groat

	F	VF
Regular issue, triple band to crown	£135	£375
Some varieties and ims.		
Halfgroats		
London	£125	£350
London, no numeral after king's name	£300	£900
Canterbury	£80	£250
York, two keys below shield	£75	£225
York, XB by shield	£250	£700

HENRY VIII 1509-47
First coinage 1509-26 with portrait of Henry VII

	F	VF
Groats, London	£150	£400
Tournai	£750	£2500
Tournai, without portrait	£2250	*
Halfgroats, London	£125	£375
Canterbury, varieties	£70	£200
York, varieties	£70	£200
Tournai	£875	£2350
Pennies, 'sovereign enthroned'		
type, London	£50	£150
Canterbury, varieties	£70	£200
Durham, varieties	£40	£110
Halfpennies, facing bust type,		
London	£30	£70
Canterbury	£60	£175
Farthings, portcullis type, London	£250	£675

Henry VIII second coinage Groat York

Second coinage 1526-44 with young portrait of Henry VIII

	F	VF
Groats, London, varieties, ims	£125	£350
Irish title, HIB REX	£300	£950
York, varieties, ims	£145	£385
Halfgroats, London, varieties, ims	£65	£200
Canterbury, varieties, ims	£60	£165
York, varieties, ims	£60	£165

	F	VF
Pennies 'sovereign enthroned' type		
London, varieties, ims	£35	£120
Canterbury, varieties, ims	£75	£225
Durham	£35	£110
York	£200	£600
Halfpennies, facing bust type		
London, varieties, ims	£25	£80
Canterbury	£35	£100
York, varieties, ims	£75	£225
Farthings, portcullis type	£300	£750

Third coinage 1544-47 and posthumous issues 1547-51 with old bearded portrait

	F	VF
Testoons or shillings		
London, Tower mint, varieties, ims	£900	£3650
Southwark, varieties, ims	£850	£3250
Bristol, varieties, ims	£950	£3750
Groats, six different busts, varieties, ims		
London, Tower mint	£125	£450
Southwark	£125	£475
Bristol	£135	£525
Canterbury	£125	£450
York	£120	£450
London, Durham House	£250	£675

Henry VIII third coinage Groat

Halfgroats, only one style of bust, except York which has two, varieties, ims

	F	VF
London, Tower mint	£85	£250
Southwark	£75	£225
Bristol	£90	£300
Canterbury	£70	£225
York	£80	£240
London, Durham House	£425	£1100

Henry VIII third coinage Halfgroat Bristol

Henry VIII posthumous coinage Halfgroat Canterbury

	F	VF
Pennies, facing bust, varieties, ims		
London, Tower mint	£40	£135
Southwark	£50	£150
London, Durham House	£425	£975
Bristol	£70	£200
Canterbury	£50	£150
York	£50	£150
Halfpennies, facing bust varieties, ims		
London, Tower mint	£45	£125
Bristol	£85	£250
Canterbury	£60	£150
York	£50	£135

EDWARD VI 1547-53
First period 1547-49

	F	VF
Shillings, London, Durham House,		
im bow, patterns?		ext. rare
Groats, London, Tower, im arrow	£950	£3000
London, Southwark, im E, none	£950	£3000
Halfgroats, London, Tower, im arrow	£525	£1450
London, Southwark, im arrow, E	£450	£1250
Canterbury, im none	£425	£1100
Pennies, London, Tower, im	£400	£1100
London, Southwark, im E	£425	£1250
Bristol, im none	£400	£1150
Halfpennies, London, Tower im uncertain	£400	£1250
Bristol, im none	£475	£1375

Edward VI second period Shilling

Second period 1549-50

Shillings, London,		
Tower various ims	£200	£700
Bristol, im TC	£775	£2650
Canterbury, im T or t	£175	£700
London (Durham House),		
im bow, varieties	£175	£750

Third period 1550-53

	F	VF
Base silver (similar to issues of second period)		
Shillings, London, Tower, im lis, lion, rose	£150	£650
Pennies, London, Tower, im escallop	£65	£180
York, im mullet	£60	£175
Halfpennies, London, Tower	£175	£600
Fine silver issue		
Crown 1551 im Y, 1551-53 im tun	£875	£2500

Edward VI 1551 Crown

Halfcrown, walking horse, 1551, im Y	£675	£1850
Galloping horse,		
1551-52, im tun	£725	£1900

Edward VI, fine silver issue Sixpence

Walking horse,		
1553, im tun	£1300	£3750
Shillings, im Y, tun	£125	£450
Sixpences, London (Tower), im y, tun	£125	£525
York, im mullet	£200	£775
Threepences, London (Tower), im tun	£200	£800
York, im mullet	£400	£1450
Pennies, sovereign type	£1250	£4000
Farthings, portcullis type	£1500	*

Mary Groat

MARY 1553-54

	F	VF
Groats, im pomegranate	£125	£425
Halfgroats, similar	£750	£2250
Pennies, reverse VERITAS TEMP FILIA	£700	£2000
Reverse CIVITAS LONDON	£700	£2000

PHILIP AND MARY 1554-58

	F	VF
Shillings, full titles, without date	£425	£1750
Full titles, without date also without XII	£450	£1850
Full titles, dated 1554	£425	£1750
Dated 1554, English titles	£450	£1850
Dated 1555, English titles only	£425	£1800
Dated 1554, English titles only, also without XII	£475	£2000
Dated 1555, English titles only, also without XII	£750	*
Dated 1554 but date below bust	£2500	*
1555 but date below bust	£2750	*
1555 similar to previous but without ANG	£3000	*
Sixpences, full titles, 1554	£400	£1450
Full titles, undated		ext. rare
English titles, 1555	£450	£1650
Similar but date below bust, 1554	£800	*
English titles, 1557	£425	£1750
Similar, but date below bust, 1557	£1000	*
Groats, im lis	£150	£450
Halfgroats, im lis	£500	£1600

Philip and Mary Halfgroat

	F	VF
Pennies, im lis	£475	£1475
Base pennies, without portrait	£75	£225

ELIZABETH I 1558-1603
Hammered coinage, first issue 1558-61
Shillings ELIZABETH

	F	VF
Wire-line circles	£575	£2400
Beaded inner circles	£250	£875
ET for Z	£150	£450

	F	VF
Groats		
Wire-line inner circles	£150	£650
Beaded inner circles	£75	£325
ET for Z	£70	£285
Halfgroats		
Wire-line inner circles	£165	£700
Beaded inner circles	£50	£150
Pennies		
Wire-line inner circles	£200	£850
Beaded inner circles	£35	£95
Countermarked shillings of Edward VI, 1560 61 with portcullis mark		
(current for 4½d) F	£2650	*
with greyhound mark		
(current for 2½d) F	£3250	*

Hammered coinage, second issue 1561-82

	F	VF
Sixpences, dated 1561-82	£65	£200
Threepences, 1561-82	£45	£145
Halfgroats, undated	£50	£170
Threehalfpences, 1561-62, 1564-70, 1572-79, 1581-82	£45	£165
Pennies, undated	£35	£100
Threefarthings, 1561-62, 1568, 1572-78, 1581-82	£75	£225

Elizabeth I 1601 Crown

Hammered coinage, third issue 1583-1603

	F	VF
Crowns, im 1	£1650	£3500

	F	VF
im 2	£2850	£7500
Halfcrowns, im 1	£975	£2500
im 2 F	£3000	£8500
Shillings ELIZAB	£120	£450
Sixpences, 1582-1602	£60	£185
Halfgroats, E D G ROSA etc	£25	£80
Pennies	£25	£80
Halfpennies	£25	£75

There are many different initial marks, such as lis, bell or lion, featured on the hammered coins of Elizabeth I, and these marks enable collectors to date those coins which are not themselves dated. For more details see J J North's *English Hammered Coinage, Volume 2.*

Elizabeth I milled coinage 1561 Sixpence

Milled Coinage

Shillings

	F	VF
Large size	£400	£1250
Intermediate	£325	£875
Small	£275	£750
Sixpences		
1561	£135	£425
1562	£120	£385
1563-64, 1566	£125	£395
1567-68	£125	£350
1570-71	£375	£1250
Groats, undated	£150	£575
Threepences, 1561, 1562-64	£150	£500
Halfgroats	£185	£625
Threefarthings	ext. rare	*

■ THE STUART KINGS

JAMES I 1603-25
First coinage 1603-04

	F	VF
Crowns, reverse begins EXURGAT	£950	£3000
Halfcrowns	£1250	£3500
Shillings, varieties	£90	£400
Sixpences, dated 1603-04, varieties	£70	£225
Halfgroats, undated	£35	£100
Pennies	£25	£70

Second coinage 1604-19

	F	VF
Crowns reverse begins QVAE DEVS	£875	£2850
Halfcrowns	£1350	£3650

James I second coinage Shilling

	F	VF
Shillings, varieties	£80	£325
Sixpences, dated 1604-15, varieties	£50	£175
Halfgroats, varieties	£20	£50
Pennies	£20	£50
Halfpennies	£15	£45

James I third coinage Shilling

Third coinage 1619-25

	F	VF
Crowns	£625	£1750
Plume over reverse shield	£825	£2250
Halfcrowns	£225	£750
Plume over reverse shield	£500	£1475
Shillings	£100	£325
Plume over reverse shield	£225	£750
Sixpences dated 1621-24	£75	£225
Halfgroats	£20	£50
Pennies	£20	£50
Halfpennies	£15	£35

CHARLES I 1625-1649
Tower Mint 1625-1643

	F	VF
Crowns, obverse King on horseback, reverse shield		
1st horseman/square shield im lis, cross-calvary	£750	£2000
Horseman/square shield, plume above shield im lis, cross-calvary, castle	£1000	£3250
2nd horseman/oval shield im plume, rose harp, some varieties from	£650	£1700
3rd horseman/round shield im bell, crown, tun, anchor, triangle, star, portcullis, triangle-in-circle, some varieties, from	£650	£1700
Halfcrowns, obverse King on horseback, reverse shield		

Charles I Tower mint Crown, plume on rev

		F	VF
1st horseman/square shield im lis, cross-calvary, negro's head, castle, anchor, many varieties	from	£225	£725
2nd horseman/oval shield im plume, rose, harp, portcullis, many varieties	from	£125	£385
3rd horseman/round shield im bell, crown, tun, portcullis, anchor, triangle, star, many varieties,	from	£75	£200
4th horseman/round shield im star, triangle in circle		£70	£200

Charles I Tower mint Halfcrown, im triangle

Shillings

		F	VF
1st bust/square shield im lis, cross-calvary, some varieties		£125	£500
2nd bust/square shield im cross-calvary, negro's head, castle, anchor, heart, plume many varieties,	from	£90	£395
3rd bust/oval shield im plume, rose		£70	£250

		F	VF
4th bust/oval or round shield im harp, portcullis, bell, crown, tun, many varieties,	from	£50	£175
5th bust/square shield im tun, anchor, triangle, many varieties		£60	£200
6th bust/square shield im anchor, triangle, star, triangle-in-circle, many varieties		£45	£165
Sixpences			
1st bust/square shield, date above, 1625 im lis, cross-calvary, 1626 im cross calvary		£100	£350
2nd bust/square shield, date above, 1625, 1626 im cross-calvary, 1626, 1627 im negro's head, 1628, 1629 im castle, 1629 im heart, 1630 im heart, plume		£110	£425
3rd bust/oval shield, im plume, rose,		£70	£225
4th bust/oval or round shield, im harp, portcullis, bell, crown, tun		£50	£150

Charles I Tower mint Sixpence im crown

		F	VF
5th bust/square shield im tun, anchor, triangle, many varieties	from	£60	£200
6th bust/square shield im triangle, star		£50	£200
Halfgroats, crowned rose both sides im lis, cross-calvary, negro's head		£25	£80
2nd bust/oval shield im plume, rose		£25	£80
3rd bust/oval shield in rose, plume		£30	£90
4th bust/oval or round shield, im harp, crown, portcullis, bell, tun, anchor, triangle, star, many varieties	from	£20	£50
5th bust/round shield, im anchor		£30	£90
Pennies, uncrowned rose both sides im one or two pellets, lis, negro's head		£20	£60
2nd bust/oval shield im plume		£25	£75
3rd bust/oval shield im plume, rose		£20	£60
4th bust/oval shield im harp, one or two pellets, portcullis, bell, triangle		£15	£50
5th bust/oval shield im one or two pellets, none		£15	£50
Halfpennies, uncrowned rose both sides im none		£15	£40

Tower Mint, under Parliament 1643-48

Crowns, obverse King on horseback, reverse shield

	F	VF
4th horseman/round shield im P, R, eye sun	£700	£1850
5th horseman/round shield im sun, sceptre	£850	£2250

Charles I Parliament Shilling,

Halfcrowns, obverse King on horseback, reverse shield		
3rd horseman/round shield im P, R, eye sun	£50	£200
im P, foreshortened horse	£150	£450
5th tall horseman/round shield im sun, sceptre	£75	£250
Shillings, reverse all square shield		
6th bust, crude, im P, R, eye, sun	£45	£165
7th bust, tall, slim, im sun, sceptre	£60	£245
8th bust, shorter, older, im sceptre	£70	£285
Sixpences, reverse all square shields		
6th bust im P, R, eye sun	£70	£200
7th bust im R, eye, sun, sceptre	£60	£185
8th bust (crude style) im eye, sun	£125	£400
Halfgroats, 4th bust/round shield im P, R, eye sceptre	£20	£70
7th bust, old/round shield im eye, sun, sceptre	£20	£70
Pennies, 7th bust/oval shield im one or two pellets	£20	£70

Charles I Briot's issue Crown

	F	VF
Briot's first milled issue 1631-32, im flower and B		
Crowns	£950	£2500
Halfcrowns	£525	£1500
Shillings	£350	£850
Sixpences	£165	£450
Halfgroats	£65	£140
Pennies	£70	£180

Briot's second milled issue 1638-39, im anchor and B, anchor and mullet		
Halfcrowns	£350	£850
Shillings	£150	£450
Sixpences	£90	£240

Briot's first milled issue Sixpence

Briot's hammered issue 1638-39, im anchor, triangle over anchor		
Halfcrowns	£825	£2000
Shillings	£350	£875

0
Charles I 1645 Exeter Crown

Provincial Mints

York 1642-44, im lion

		F	VF
Halfcrowns, varieties	from	£300	£750
Shillings		£225	£650
Sixpences		£275	£850
Threepences		£70	£175

Aberystwyth 1638-42 im open book

		F	VF
Halfcrowns, varieties	from	£950	£3500
Shillings		£475	£1500
Sixpences		£400	£1100
Groats		£75	£180

Charles I Aberystwyth Groat

	F	VF
Threepences	£50	£145
Halfgroats	£55	£150
Pennies	£70	£225
Halfpennies	£200	£525

Aberystwyth-Furnace 1647-48, im crown

		F	VF
Halfcrowns	from	£2500	£7000
Shillings		£3500	*
Sixpences		£1500	£3750
Groats		£275	£650
Threepences		£250	£575
Halfgroats		£350	£850
Pennies		£750	£2000

Shrewsbury 1642 im plume without band

		F	VF
Pounds, varieties	from	£2850	£7000
Halfpounds		£1450	£3500
Crowns		£950	£2850
Halfcrowns		£725	£2000
Shillings		£1650	£5500

Oxford 1642-46 im plume with band

		F	VF
Pounds, varieties	from	£2500	£6500
Halfpounds		£1100	£2750
Crowns		£1000	£2650
Halfcrowns		£325	£750
Shillings		£375	£1100
Sixpences		£300	£850
Groats		£175	£500
Threepences		£125	£350
Halfgroats		£125	£350
Pennies		£225	£600

Bristol 1643-45 im Bristol monogram, acorn, plumelet

		F	VF
Halfcrowns, varieties	from	£400	£1000

Charles I York Shilling

	F	VF
Shillings	£485	£1200
Sixpences	£325	£925
Groats	£195	£485
Threepences	£200	£500
Halfgroats	£225	£675
Pennies	£425	£950

Charles I 1644 Bristol Halfcrown

Late 'Declaration' issues 1645-6

These bear the marks A, B and plume.

Ashby de la Zouch mint, 1645

		F	VF
Halfcrowns, varieties	from	£2250	*
Shillings, varieties		£1000	*
Sixpences, varieties		£1000	*
Groats, varieties		£700	£1850
Threepences, varieties		£225	£525

Bridgnorth-on-Severn, 1646

		F	VF
Halfcrowns, varieties	from	£2750	£4000
Shillings, varieties		£650	£1950
Sixpences, varieties		£265	£725
Groats, varieties		£225	£550
Threepence, varieties		£225	£525
Halfgroats, varieties		£425	£975

Truro 1642-43 im rose, bugle

		F	VF
Crowns, varieties	from	£475	£1000
Halfcrowns		£1250	£3250
Shillings		£3750	*

Charles I 1646 Bridgnorth-on-Severn Halfcrown

Exeter 1643-46 im Ex, rose, castle		**F**	**VF**
Halfpounds			**ext. rare**
Crowns, varieties	from	**£450**	**£1050**
Halfcrowns		**£450**	**£1000**
Shillings		**£400**	**£1000**
Sixpences		**£375**	**£900**
Groats		**£150**	**£375**
Threepences		**£150**	**£375**
Halfgroats		**£300**	**£750**
Pennies		**£400**	**£1000**

Worcester 1643-4 im castle, helmet, leopard's head, lion, two lions, lis, rose, star

Halfcrowns, many varieties	from	**£950**	**£2750**

Salopia (Shrewsbury) 1644 im helmet, lis, rose in legend

Halfcrowns, many varieties	from	**£1100**	**£3000**

Worcester or Salopia (Shrewsbury) im bird, boar's head, lis, castle, cross and annulets, helmet, lion, lis, pear, rose, scroll

Shillings, varieties	**£2250**	**£5250**
Sixpences	**£1850**	**£5000**
Groats	**£675**	**£2000**
Threepences	**£425**	**£975**
Halfgroats	**£475**	**£1200**

'HC' mint (probably Hartlebury Castle, Worcester, 1646) im pear, three pears

Halfcrowns	**£1650**	**£4000**

Chester 1644 im cinquefoil, plume, prostrate gerb, three gerbs

Halfcrowns, varieties	**£1250**	**£3500**
Shillings	**£2250**	7500
Threepences	**£950**	**£2750**

Welsh Marches mint? 1644

Halfcrowns	**£1000**	**£2950**

Carlisle besieged 1644-45	**F**	**VF**
Three shillings	**£8500**	**£20000**
Shillings F	**£6500**	**£13500**

Newark besieged 1645-6, surrendered May 1646

Halfcrowns, F	**£825**	**£1750**

Charles I 1645 Newark Halfcrown

Shillings, 1645-46, varieties F	**£675**	**£1500**
Ninepences, 1645-46	**£650**	**£1400**
Sixpences	**£750**	**£1750**

Pontefract besieged 1648-49

Two shillings, 1648	**£6250**	**£16500**
Shillings, 1648, varieties	**£2250**	**£5750**

Charles I 1648 Pontefract Shilling

Scarborough besieged 1644-45
Many odd values issued were issued in Scarborough, all of which are extremely rare. The coin's value was decided by the intrinsic value of the piece of metal from which it was made.
Examples: 5s 8d, 2s 4d, 1s 9d, 1s 3d, 7d F
Collectors can expect to pay at least £12000 or more in F and £19500 in VF for any of these.

COMMONWEALTH 1649-60

Crowns, im sun 1649, 51-54, 56	**£800**	**£1900**
Halfcrowns, im sun 1649, 1651-6	**£250**	**£650**
im anchor 1658-60	**£1250**	**£2750**

Commonwealth 1656 Halfcrown

	F	VF
Shillings, im sun 1649, 1661-87	£175	£425
im anchor 1658-60	£850	£1750
Sixpences, im sun 1649, 1651-7	£150	£375
im anchor 1658-6	£675	£1600
Halfgroats undated	£35	£100
Pennies undated	£30	£80
Halfpennies	£30	£80

CHARLES II 1660-85
Hammered coinage 1660-62

		F	VF
Halfcrowns, three issues	from	£250	£850
Shillings, three issues	from	£165	£500

Charles II hammered issue Shilling

		F	VF
Sixpences, three issues		£135	£450
Fourpences, third issue only		£35	£90
Threepences, third issue	from	£30	£70
Twopences, three issues	from	£25	£65
Pennies, three issues	from	£25	£65

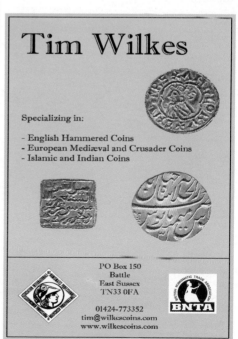

'ROYAL' AND 'ROSE' BASE METAL FARTHINGS

Until 1613 English coins were struck only in gold or silver, because the monarchy thought base metal would diminish the royal prerogative of coining.

However silver coins became far too small and farthings so tiny that they had to be discontinued.

So to meet demands for small change, James I authorised Lord Harington to issue copper farthing tokens.

Subsequently this authority passed in turn to the Duke of Lennox, the Duchess of Richmond and Lord Maltravers.

It ceased by order of Parliament in 1644.

■ ROYAL FARTHING TOKENS

	Fair	F	VF	EF
JAMES I				
Type 1				
Harington, c1613. Larger flan with tin-washed surface, mint-mark between sceptres below crown	£10	£20	£75	£245
Type 2				
Harington, c1613. Larger flan, no tin wash	£15	£15	£40	£150
Type 3				
Lennox, 1614-25. IACO starts at 1 o'clock position	£3	£10	£25	£110
Type 4				
Lennox, 1622-25. Oval flan, IACO starts at 7 o'clock	£8	£26	£65	£225

	Fair	F	VF	EF
CHARLES I				
Type 1				
Richmond, 1625-34 single arched crown	£2	£8	£25	£95
Type 2				
Transitional, c1634 double arched crown	£6	£20	£50	£185
Type 3				
Maltravers, 1634-36 inner circles	£3	£10	£30	£95
Type 4				
Richmond, 1625-34 as Type 1 but oval	£8	£25	£60	£200
Type 5				
Maltravers, 1634-36 double arched crown	£10	£30	£70	£185

■ ROSE FARTHING TOKENS

These have a rose on the reverse.

	Fair	F	VF	EF
Type 1				
Small thick flan	£3	£10	£30	£110
Type 2				
Small thick flan, but single arched crown	£2	£7	£25	£95
Type 3				
Small thick flan, but sceptres below crown	£10	£25	£50	£125

ABOVE: (from left to right) James I Harington farthings, types 1, 2 and 3

ABOVE: (from left to right) Charles I Richmond, Maltravers and rose farthings

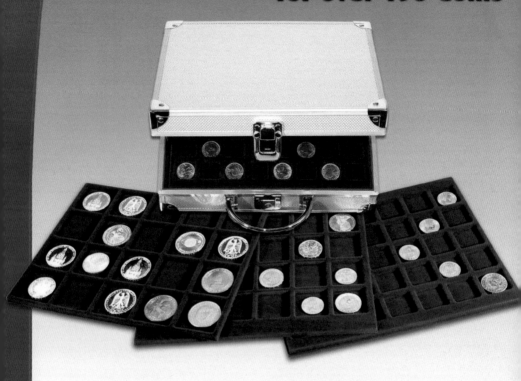

MILLED COINAGE FROM 1656

This listing gives a general indication of value throughout the entire milled series.

As such, only some of the varieties, dates and errors are mentioned.

Again, the prices shown in this guide are the approximate amounts collectors can expect to pay for coins, not dealers' buying prices. Standards of grading also vary.

Information for this guide is drawn from auction results and dealers' lists, with the aim of determining firm valuations, but prices still vary enormously from sale to sale and from one dealer's list to another.

The prices given here aim at a reasonable assessment of the market at the time of compilation.

With some denominations in the silver series, the column headings which indicate condition change at the beginning of the George III coins. The condition, or grade, of a coin is of great importance in determining its value. Refer to the pages on grading (pp52-53) and terms used in this book (pp54-55).

■ CROMWELL GOLD PATTERNS

These were struck by order of Cromwell, with the consent of the Council of State.

Thomas Simon made the dies, and the coins were struck on Peter Blondeau's machine.

The fifty shillings and the broad were struck from the same dies, but the fifty shillings has the edge inscription PROTECTOR LITERIS LITERAE NUMMIS CORONA ER SALUS, while the broad is not as thick and has a grained edge.

No original strikings of the half-broad are known, but some were struck from dies made by John Tanner in 1738.

All three denominations are dated 1656.

	F	VF	EF	Unc
Fifty shillings	*	£45000	£85000	*
Broad	*	£8000	£22500	£30000
Half-broad	*	*	£16500	*

Oliver Cromwell gold Broad 1656

■ FIVE GUINEAS

CHARLES II	F	VF	EF	Unc
1668-78 pointed end of trnctn of bust	£2850	£4950	£17500	*
1668, 69, 75 as above, eleph below bust	£2850	£4950	£17500	*
1675-8 as above, eleph & castle below bust	£2850	£4950	£17500	*
1678-84 rounded end to trnctn	£2850	£4950	£17500	*
1680-4 as above, eleph & castle	£2850	£4950	£17500	*

Charles II 1670 proof Five Guineas

JAMES II	F	VF	EF	Unc
1686 sceptres in wrong order on rev	£2750	£4850	£17000	*
1687-8 sceptres correct	£2700	£4850	£17000	*
1687-8 eleph & castle	£2950	£5500	£17500	*

WILLIAM AND MARY	F	VF	EF	Unc
1691-4 no prov mark	£3000	£6250	£16000	*
1691-4 eleph & castle	£3000	£6250	£16000	*

William and Mary 1692 elephant & castle Five Guineas

WILLIAM III	F	VF	EF	Unc
1699-1700 no				
prov mark	£2500	£5000	£13750	*
1699 eleph & castle	£2500	£5750	£14500	*
1701 new bust				
'fine work'	£2850	£4250	£12500	*

ANNE
Pre-Union with Scotland

	F	VF	EF	Unc
1703 VIGO below bust	*	£75000	£175000	*
1705-6 plain below	£3500	£6000	£25000	*

Post-Union with Scotland

	F	VF	EF	Unc
1706	£2750	£4500	£13500	*
1709 larger lettering				
wider shield and				
crowns	£2850	£5500	£14000	*
1711, 1713-4				
broader bust	£2850	£4750	£14000	*

The pre-Union reverse has separate shields, top and right, for England and Scotland, while post-Union reverses have the English and Scottish arms side by side on the top and bottom shields.

GEORGE I

	F	VF	EF	Unc
1716, 17, 20, 26	£4250	£6750	£25000	*

George I 1716 Five Guineas

GEORGE II

	F	VF	EF	Unc
1729, 31, 35,				
38, 41 YH	£2750	£3750	£11000	*
1729 YH,				
E.I.C. below head	£2750	£4750	£11500	*
1746 OH, LIMA				
below	£2750	£4000	£11000	£20000
1748, 53 OH				
plain below	£3000	£4250	£10000	£18500

GEORGE III

	F	VF	EF	Unc
1770, 73, 77 patterns only	*	*	£95000	£175000

■ TWO GUINEAS

CHARLES II	F	VF	EF	Unc
1664, 65, 69, 71 pointed				
end to trnctn	£1650	£3500	£10000	*
1664 elephant below	£1650	£3500	£10000	*
1675-84 rounded end				
to trnctn	£1500	£3000	£9000	*
1676, 78, 82-84				
eleph & castle				
below bust	£1650	£3500	£9750	*
1678 eleph below				ext. rare

JAMES II	F	VF	EF	Unc
1687	£2000	£4250	£12500	*
1688/7	£2000	£4500	£12500	*

WILLIAM AND MARY

	F	VF	EF	Unc
1691, 93, 94 eleph				
& castle	£2250	£3750	£8500	£12000
1693, 94 no				
prov mark	£2250	£3500	£8000	£11500

WILLIAM III

	F	VF	EF	Unc
1701	£2000	£4500	£10500	*

ANNE

	F	VF	EF	Unc
1709, 11, 13, 14	£1450	£2250	£5750	£9250

GEORGE I

	F	VF	EF	Unc
1717, 20, 26	£1750	£2600	£6500	£9500

GEORGE II

	F	VF	EF	Unc
1734, 35, 38, 39, YH F	£700	£1250	£2500	£4750
1739-40 intermediate				
hd F	£750	£1250	£2500	£4750
1748, 53, OH	£800	£1450	£3500	£5750

GEORGE III

	F	VF	EF	Unc
1768, 73, 77 patterns only	*	*	£26500	£45000

■ BROAD

CHARLES II	F	VF	EF	Unc
1662	£1300	£2650	£5750	*

■ GUINEAS

	F	VF	EF	Unc
1663 pointed trnctn	£1750	£4500	£17500	*
1663 eleph	£1350	£3500	£11000	*
1664 trnctn indented	£1100	£3500	£11000	*
1664 eleph	*	*	£18500	*
1664-73 sloping pointed				
trnctn	£900	£2850	£8500	*
1664, 65, 68 eleph	£1200	£3250	£11000	*
1672-84 rounded trnctn	£800	£2450	£7250	*
1674-84 eleph & castle	£1100	£2750	£8500	*
1677-8 eleph				ext. rare

Charles II 1663 Guinea, elephant below bust

JAMES II	F	VF	EF	Unc
1685-6 1st bust	£725	£1750	£5250	£9500
1685 1st bust eleph & castle	£800	£2250	£6250	*
1686-8 2nd bust	£750	£1750	£5250	£9500
1686-8 2nd bust eleph & castle	£850	£2250	£6750	*

WILLIAM AND MARY				
1689-94 no prov mark	£750	£2000	£5750	£8750
1689-94 eleph & castle	£800	£2500	£6000	*
1692 eleph	£1250	£2950	£8000	*

WILLIAM III				
1695-6 1st bust	£600	£1500	£4750	£7000
1695, 7 eleph & castle	*	*	*	*
1697-1701 2nd bust	£625	£1500	£4750	£6750
1698-1701 eleph & castle	*	*	*ext. rare	
1701 3rd bust 'fine work'	£800	£2250	£6500	*

ANNE				
Pre-Union				
1702, 1705-07 plain below bust	£875	£2000	£5750	£8500
1703 VIGO below	£6500	£20000	£45000	*

Post-Union				
1707-8 1st bust	£750	£1650	£5000	£7000
1707 eleph & castle	£950	£2500	£7000	*
1707-9 2nd bust	£650	£1350	£3500	£5750
1708-9 eleph & castle	£950	£2500	£6500	*
1710-1714 3rd bust	£575	£1000	£3250	£4750

Pre-Union reverse has separate shields, top and right, for England and Scotland. Post-Union reverses have the English and Scottish arms side by side on both the top and bottom shields.

GEORGE I				
1714 1st hd PR. EL. (Prince Elector) in rev legend	£1100	£2750	£5750	£8000
1715 2nd hd, tie with two ends	£550	£1200	£3250	£4850

	F	VF	EF	Unc
1715-16 3rd hd, hair not curling round trnctn	£550	£1100	£3000	£4750
1716-23 4th hd, tie with loop	£550	£1100	£3000	£4750
1721-2 eleph & castle	*			ext. rare
1723-7 5th hd, smaller, older bust	£475	£975	£2850	£4500
1726 eleph & castle	£1650	£4000	*	*

GEORGE II				
1727 1st YH, small lettering	£750	£2000	£5500	£8000
1727-28 1st YH larger lettering	£750	£2150	£5750	£8500
1729-32 2nd YH	£650	£1375	£3650	*
1729, 31-32 E.I.C. below	£800	£2500	£6500	*
1732-38 larger lettering	£600	£1150	£3000	£5000
1732 E.I.C. below	£750	£1875	£5750	*
1739-40, 43 intermediate hd	£500	£950	£2850	£4250
1739 E.I.C. below	£750	£2250	£6750	*
1745-6 larger lettering	£500	£1150	£2850	£4250
1746 LIMA below	£2000	£3950	£8750	*
1746-53, 55-56, 58-59, 60, OH	£475	£850	£2500	£3750

GEORGE III				
1761 1st hd	£900	£2850	£4750	£6250
1763-64 2nd hd	£650	£2000	£4850	*
1765-73 3rd hd	£300	£650	£1500	£3000
1774-79, 81-86 4th hd	£275	£400	£875	£1500
1789-99 5th hd, 'spade' rev F	£265	£375	£600	£900
1813 6th hd, rev shield in Garter ('Military guinea')	£725	£1500	£2950	£4500

George II 1760 Guinea

George III 1813 Guinea

■ HALF-GUINEAS

CHARLES II	F	VF	EF	Unc
1669-72 bust with				
pointed trnctn	£650	£1500	£4250	*
1672-84 rounded				
truncation	£650	£1500	£4250	*
1676-78, 80, 82,				
84 eleph & castle	£750	£1800	£5000	*

JAMES II				
1686-88 no				
prov mark	£675	£1500	£4250	*
1686 eleph & castle	£2000	*	*	*

WILLIAM AND MARY				
1689 1st busts	£650	£1650	£4250	*
1690-4 2nd busts	£600	£1650	£4250	*
1691-2 eleph & castle	£750	£1750	£4850	*
1692 eleph	£1500	*	*	

William and Mary 1689 Half-guinea

WILLIAM III				
1695 no				
prov mark	£475	£950	£2750	*
1695-6 eleph & castle	£650	£1500	£3750	*
1697-1701 larger				
harp on rev	£475	£900	£2750	*
1698 eleph & castle	£600	£1650	£4750	*

ANNE				
Pre-Union				
1702, 05 plain				
below bust	£750	£1950	£5250	*
1703 VIGO below	£3250	£9000	£18500	*

Post-Union

	F	VF	EF	Unc
1707-1714 plain	£375	£700	£2250	£3250

Pre-Union reverse has separate shields, top and right, for England and Scotland. Post-Union reverses have the English and Scottish arms side by side on the top and bottom shields.

GEORGE I				
1715, 17-24 1st hd	£300	£575	£1750	£2850
1721 eleph & castle	*	*	*ext. rare	
1725-27 smaller older				
hd	£275	£425	£1450	£2450

	F	VF	EF	Unc
GEORGE II				
1728-39 YH	£375	£875	£2850	*
1729-32, 39 E.I.C. below	£550	£1350	£3850	*
1740, 43, 45-46				
intermediate hd	£375	£700	£2250	*
1745 LIMA below	£1350	£2850	£6250	*
1747-53, 55-56,				
58-60 OH	£275	£500	£1500	£2650

George II 1756 Half-guinea

GEORGE III				
1762-63 1st hd	£575	£1375	£3000	£4750
1764-66, 68-69,				
72-75 2nd hd	£225	£525	£1350	£2650
1774-75 3rd hd	£850	£1750	£3950	*
1775-79, 81,				
83-86 4th hd	£195	£325	£800	£1500
1787-91, 93-98,				
1800 5th hd	£175	£250	£575	£850
1801-03 6th hd	£130	£185	£400	£675
1804, 06, 08-11,				
13 7th hd	£130	£195	£425	£775

■ THIRD-GUINEAS

GEORGE III				
1797-1800 1st hd	£90	£150	£300	£475
1801-03 date close to				
crown on rev	£90	£150	£300	£475
1804-05, 08-11 2nd hd	£90	£150	£300	£475

■ QUARTER-GUINEAS

GEORGE I				
1718	£110	£185	£385	£525

GEORGE III				
1762	£120	£200	£400	£600

George III 1762 Quarter-guinea

■ FIVE POUNDS

GEORGE III	F	VF	EF	Unc
1820 pattern F	*	*		*£145000

GEORGE IV				
1826 proof	*	*	£11000	£18000

VICTORIA				
1839 proof, 'Una and the Lion' rev F	*	*	£25000	£45000

Victoria 1839 proof Five Pound with 'Una and the Lion'

1887 JH F	BV	£1100	£1500	£1950
1887 proof	*	*	£2250	£4000
1887 proof no B.P.	*	*	£2750	£4850
1893 OH F	BV	£1275	£1850	£2850
1893 proof	*	*	£2750	£4500

EDWARD VII				
1902 F	BV	£1100	£1350	£1950
1902 proof	*	*	£1350	£1700

GEORGE V				
1911 proof F	*	*	*	£2650

GEORGE VI				
1937 proof	*	*	*	£2150

In 1984 the Royal Mint issued the first of an annual issue of Brilliant Uncirculated £5 coins.

These bear the symbol 'U' in a circle to the left of the date on the reverse to indicate the standard of striking.

BV indicates bullion value, at the time of going to press gold is approximately £780 per troy oz.

ELIZABETH II Sovereign Issues	Unc
1953 proof	ext. rare
1980 proof, originally issued in Royal Mint set	BV

	Unc
1981 proof	BV
1982 proof, originally issued in Royal Mint set	BV
1984 proof	BV
1984 BU	BV
1985 proof	BV
1985 BU	BV
1986 BU	BV
1987 new effigy, BU	BV
1988 BU	BV
1989 proof, 500th anniversary of the sovereign, originally issued in Royal Mint set	£1300
1989 BU, 500th anniversary of the sovereign	BV
1990 proof, originally issued in Royal Mint set	BV
1990 BU	BV
1991 proof, originally issued in Royal Mint set	BV
1991 BU	BV
1992 proof, originally issued in Royal Mint set	BV
1992 BU	BV
1993 proof, originally issued in Royal Mint set	BV
1993 BU	BV
1994 proof, originally issued in Royal Mint set	BV
1994 BU	BV
1995 proof, originally issued in Royal Mint set	BV
1995 BU	BV
1996 proof, originally issued in Royal Mint set	BV
1996 BU	BV
1997 proof, originally issued in Royal Mint set	BV
1997 BU	BV
1998 proof, originally issued in Royal Mint set	BV
1998 BU	BV
1999 proof, originally issued in Royal Mint set	BV
1999 BU	BV
2000 proof, originally issued in Royal Mint set	BV
2000 BU	BV
2001 proof, originally issued in Royal Mint set	BV
2001 BU	BV
2002 shield reverse, proof, originally issued in Royal Mint set	BV
2002 BU	BV
2003 proof, originally issued in Royal Mint set	BV
2003 BU	BV
2004 proof, originally issued in Royal Mint set	BV
2004 BU	BV
2005 proof, originally issued in Royal Mint set	BV
2005 BU	BV
2006 proof, originally issued in Royal Mint set	BV
2006 BU	BV
2007 proof, originally issued in Royal Mint set	BV
2008 proof, originally issued in Royal Mint four coin set	BV
2009 proof, Countdown to London 2012	BV
2009 proof, Henry VIII	BV

■ TWO POUNDS

GEORGE III	F	VF	EF	Unc
1820 pattern F	*	*	£13000	£27500

GEORGE IV	F	VF	EF	Unc
1823 St George on rev F	*	£800	£1500	£2950
1826 proof, shield rev	*	*	£3500	£6000

George IV 1823 Two Pounds

WILLIAM IV

	F	VF	EF	Unc
1831 proof	*	*	£4250	£8500

VICTORIA

	F	VF	EF	Unc
1887 JH F	BV	BV	£550	£750
1887 proof	*	*	£900	£1650
1893 OH F	£450	£500	£650	£875
1893 proof	*	*	£975	£1750

EDWARD VII

	F	VF	EF	Unc
1902 F	£450	£500	£700	£900
1902 proof	*	*	£700	£900

GEORGE V

	F	VF	EF	Unc
1911 proof F	*	*	*	£1100

GEORGE VI

	F	VF	EF	Unc
1937 proof	*	*	*	£825

ELIZABETH II

	Unc
1953 proof	ext. rare
1980 proof, originally issued in Royal Mint set	BV
1982 proof, originally issued in Royal Mint set	BV
1983 proof	BV
1985 proof, originally issued in Royal Mint set	BV
1987 proof	BV
1988 proof	BV
1989 500th anniversary of the sovereign, proof	£750
1990 proof	BV
1991 proof	BV
1992 proof	BV
1993 proof	BV
1996 proof	BV
1998 proof, originally issued in Royal Mint set	BV
2000 proof, originally issued in Royal Mint set	BV
2002 shield rev, proof, originially issued in Royal Mint set	BV
2003 proof, originally issued in Royal Mint set	BV
2004 proof, originally issued in Royal Mint set	BV
2005 proof, originally issued in Royal Mint set	BV
2006 proof, originally issued in Royal Mint set	BV
2007 proof, originally issued in Royal Mint set	BV
2008 proof, originally issued in Royal Mint set	BV
2009 proof, issued in Royal Mint set	BV
2009 250th Anniversary Birth Robert Burns	BV

■ SOVEREIGNS

George III 1817 Sovereign

Early sovereigns can attain higher prices in exceptional grade.

GEORGE III	F	VF	EF	Unc
1817 F	£300	£475	£1350	£2400
1818	£700	£1350	£3000	£4500
1819	£28000	£45000	*	*
1820	£300	£475	£1250	£2250

GEORGE IV
Type Laureate head/St George

	F	VF	EF	Unc
1821	£300	£475	£1000	£2250
1821 proof	*	*	£1950	£4000
1822 F	£300	£475	£1000	£2250
1823	£1100	£1850	£4850	*
1824	£375	£475	£1250	£2400
1825	£575	£1200	£3750	£6500

Type bare head/shield

	F	VF	EF	Unc
1825 F	£350	£495	£975	£1950
1826	£350	£495	£950	£2000
1826 proof	*	*	£1750	£3500
1827 F	£350	£495	£975	£1750
1828 F	£3000	£5250	£16000	*
1829	£350	£525	£1200	£2250
1830	£350	£525	£1200	£2250

WILLIAM IV

	F	VF	EF	Unc
1831	£475	£850	£2250	£3850
1831 proof	*	*	£2450	£4500
1832 F	£350	£600	£1450	£2250
1833	£400	£650	£1650	£2850

William IV 1833 Sovereign

	F	VF	EF	Unc
1835	£400	£650	£1650	£2850
1836	£400	£625	£1550	£2750
1837	£425	£675	£1550	£2750

VICTORIA	F	VF	EF	Unc
Type I, YH/shield				
1838	£500	£850	£1875	£3000
1838 wreath leaves different	£1850	*	*	*
1839	£1000	£1750	£3250	*
1839 proof	*	*	£2450	£4750
1841	£3250	£5000	*	*
1842	*	*	£475	£1100
1843	*	*	£375	£950
1843 narrow shield	£3250	£5500	*	*
1844	*	*	£475	£1250
1845	*	*	£475	£1250
1846	*	*	£475	£1250
1847	*	*	£425	£950
1848	*	*	£475	£1250
1849	*	*	£500	£1500
1850	*	*	£475	£1175
1851	*	*	£425	£950
1852	*	*	£425	£950
1853	*	*	£325	£850
1853 proof	*	*	£4750	£9250
1854	*	*	£425	£950
1855	*	*	£300	£750
1856	*	*	£325	£825
1857	*	*	£300	£750
1858	*	*	£300	£700
1859	*	*	£285	£700
1859 'Ansell'	£575	£1600	£5000	*

	F	VF	EF	Unc
1872 M (Melbourne mint) below wreath	*	*	£275	£1000
1872 S	*	*	£375	£1000
1873 die no	*	*	£250	£400
1873 S	*	*	£285	£750
1874 die no	£925	£2750	£5750	£8000
1874 M	*	*	£485	£1500
1875 S	*	*	£395	£900
1877 S	*	*	£395	£900
1878 S	*	*	£395	£900
1879 S	*	*	£395	£900
1880 M	£400	£900	£3000	*
1880 S	*	*	£395	£900
1881 M	*	*	£475	£1650
1881 S	*	*	£485	£1500
1882 M	*	*	£400	£900
1882 S	*	*	£400	£900
1883 M	*	£425	£1250	£2250
1883 S	*	*	£325	£825
1884 M	*	*	£400	£925
1884 S	*	*	£350	£825
1885 M	*	*	£325	£825
1885 S	*	*	£325	£825
1886 M	£700	£1750	£6000	*
1886 S	*	*	£325	£825
1887 M	£800	£1850	£4500	*
1887 S	*	*	£450	£1525

Type II, YH/St George and dragon

	F	VF	EF	Unc
1871	*	*	£250	£495

Victoria 1859 'Ansell' Sovereign

	F	VF	EF	Unc
1860	*	*	£350	£800
1861	*	*	£285	£650
1862	*	*	£285	£650
1863	*	*	£285	£525
1863 die number below wreath on rev	*	*	£285	£525
1863 '827' on trnctn	£4000	£6000	*	*
1864 die no	*	*	£285	£525
1865 die no	*	*	£285	£525
1866 die no	*	*	£285	£525
1868 die no	*	*	£285	£525
1869 die no	*	*	£285	£525
1870 die no	*	*	£285	£525
1871 die no	*	*	£275	£400
1871 S (Sydney mint) below wreath	*	*	£300	*
1872	*	*	£265	£375
1872 die no	*	*	£275	£400

Victoria 1871 St George Sovereign

	F	VF	EF	Unc
1871 S below hd	*	*	£1000	*
1872	*	*	£250	£495
1872 M below hd	*	£350	£900	*
1872 S	*	*	£375	*
1873	*	*	£250	£495
1873 M	*	*	£325	£1200
1873 S	*	*	£375	*
1874	*	*	£225	£475
1874 M	*	*	£325	£1200
1874 S	*	*	£275	£1200
1875 M	*	*	£300	£900
1875 S	*	*	£300	£900
1876	*	*	£250	£575
1876 M	*	*	£300	£900
1876 S	*	*	£300	£900
1877 M	*	*	£300	£900
1878	*	*	£250	£475
1878 M	*	*	£300	£900

	F	VF	EF	Unc
1879	£425	£700	£2750	*
1879 M	*	*	£300	£900
1879 S	*	*	£900	*
1880	*	*	£250	£475
1880 M	*	*	£300	£900
1880 S	*	*	£300	£900
1881 M	*	*	£300	£900
1881 S	*	*	£300	£1000
1882 M	*	*	£325	£975
1882 S	*	*	£300	£725
1883 M	*	*	£300	£725
1883 S	*	*	£400	*
1884	*	*	£250	£450
1884 M	*	*	£265	£650
1884 S	*	*	£300	£725
1885	*	*	£250	£475
1885 M	*	*	£300	£750
1885 S	*	*	£300	£750
1886 M	*	*	£300	£750
1886 S	*	*	£300	£750
1887 M	*	*	£300	£800
1887 S	*	*	£300	£750

Victoria 1887 Jubilee Head Sovereign

Jubilee head coinage

	F	VF	EF	Unc
1887 F	*	*	£235	£300
1887 proof	*	*	£600	£1100
1887 M (Melbourne mint) on ground below dragon	*	*	£235	£395
1887 S (Sydney mint) on ground below dragon	*	*	£275	£650
1888	*	*	£235	£300
1888 M	*	*	£235	£325
1888 S	*	*	£235	£325
1889	*	*	£235	£300
1889 M	*	*	£235	£325
1889 S	*	*	£235	£325
1890	*	*	£235	£300
1890 M	*	*	£235	£325
1890 S	*	*	£235	£300
1891	*	*	£235	£300
1891 M	*	*	£235	£325
1891 S	*	*	£235	£350
1892	*	*	£235	£300
1892 M	*	*	£235	£325
1892 S	*	*	£235	£350
1893 M	*	*	£235	£395
1893 S	*	*	£235	£395

Old head coinage

	F	VF	EF	Unc
1893	*	*	£235	£285
1893 proof	*	*	£700	£1250
1893 M	*	*	£235	£400
1893 S	*	*	£250	£385
1894	*	*	£235	£285
1894 M	*	*	£235	£300
1894 S	*	*	£235	£300
1895	*	*	£235	£285
1895 M	*	*	£235	£300
1895 S	*	*	£250	£385
1896	*	*	£235	£285
1896 M	*	*	£235	£300
1896 S	*	*	£250	£385
1897 M	*	*	£235	£300
1897 S	*	*	£235	£300
1898	*	*	£235	£285
1898 M	*	*	£235	£300
1898 S	*	*	£250	£385
1899	*	*	£235	£285
1899 M	*	*	£235	£300
1899 P (Perth mint) on ground below dragon	*	*	£400	£800
1899 S	*	*	£235	£295
1900	*	*	£235	£285
1900 M	*	*	£235	£295
1900 P	*	*	£235	£295
1900 S	*	*	£235	£295
1901	*	*	£235	£285
1901 M	*	*	£235	£285
1901 P	*	*	£250	£350
1901 S	*	*	£235	£295

EDWARD VII

	F	VF	EF	Unc
1902	*	*	*	£275
1902 proof	*	*	*	£400
1902 M	*	*	*	£265
1902 P	*	*	*	£265
1902 S	*	*	*	£265
1903	*	*	*	£275
1903 M	*	*	*	£265
1903 P	*	*	*	£265
1903 S	*	*	*	£265
1904	*	*	*	£275
1904 M	*	*	*	£265
1904 P	*	*	*	£265
1904 S	*	*	*	£265
1905	*	*	*	£275
1905 M	*	*	*	£265
1905 P	*	*	*	£265
1905 S	*	*	*	£265
1906	*	*	*	£275
1906 M	*	*	*	£265
1906 P	*	*	*	£265
1906 S	*	*	*	£265
1907	*	*	*	£275
1907 M	*	*	*	£265
1907 P	*	*	*	£265
1907 S	*	*	*	£265

	F	VF	EF	Unc
1908	*	*	*	£275
1908 C on ground below dragon F	*	*	£3250	£5000
1908 M	*	*	*	£265
1908 P	*	*	*	£265
1908 S	*	*	*	£265
1909	*	*	*	£275
1909 C	*	*	£375	£900
1909 M	*	*	*	£265
1909 P	*	*	*	£265
1909 S	*	*	*	£265
1910	*	*	*	£275
1910 C	*	*	£350	£875
1910 M	*	*	*	£265
1910 P	*	*	*	£265
1910 S	*	*	*	£265

GEORGE V

	F	VF	EF	Unc
1911	*	*	*	£250
1911 proof	*	*	*	£650
1911 C	*	*	£250	£285
1911 M	*	*	*	£250
1911 P	*	*	*	£260
1911 S	*	*	*	£260
1912	*	*	*	£250
1912 M	*	*	*	£260
1912 P	*	*	*	£260
1912 S	*	*	*	£260
1913	*	*	*	£250
1913 C F	*	£400	£1150	*
1913 M	*	*	*	£260
1913 P	*	*	*	£260
1913 S	*	*	*	£260
1914	*	*	*	£250
1914 C	*	£275	£425	£750
1914 M	*	*	*	£260
1914 P	*	*	*	£260
1914 S	*	*	*	£260
1915	*	*	*	£250
1915 M	*	*	*	£260
1915 P	*	*	*	£260
1915 S	*	*	*	£260
1916	*	*	*	£260
1916 C F	*	£6000	£12000	£16500
1916 M	*	*	*	£250
1916 P	*	*	*	£260
1916 S	*	*	*	£260
1917 F	*	£2950	£5000	£8000
1917 C	*	*	£250	£300
1917 M	*	*	*	£260
1917 P	*	*	*	£260
1917 S	*	*	*	£260
1918 C	*	*	£250	£300
1918 I on ground below dragon	*	*	£250	£300
1918 M	*	*	*	£260
1918 P	*	*	*	£260
1918 S	*	*	*	£260
1919 C	*	*	£250	£300
1919 M	*	*	*	£260
1919 P	*	*	*	£260
1919 S	*	*	*	£260
1920 M	£900	£2000	£3750	*
1920 P	*	*	*	£260
1920 S			highest	rarity
1921 M	£2250	£4500	£8750	£15000
1921 P	*	*	*	£260
1921 S	*	£650	£950	£1875
1922 M	£2250	£4000	£7000	£12500
1922 P	*	*	*	£260
1922 S	£3250	£4750	£7000	£12500
1923 M	*	*	*	£295
1923 S	£2250	£3750	£6750	£12000
1923 SA (Pretoria Mint) on ground below dragon	*	£2750	£4250	£6000
1923 SA proof	*	*	*	£1650
1924 M	*	*	*	£295
1924 P	*	*	*	£295
1924 S	*	£475	£900	£1975
1924 SA	*	*	£4250	£6750
1925	*	*	*	£250
1925 M	*	*	*	£260
1925 P	*	*	*	£325
1925 S	*	*	*	£275
1925 SA	*	*	*	£250
1926 M	*	*	*	£300
1926 P	*	£500	£1100	£2000
1926 S	£3950	£7500	£14250	£21500
1926 SA	*	*	*	£250
1927 P	*	*	£260	£425
1927 SA	*	*	*	£250
1928 M	£475	£725	£1500	£2850
1928 P	*	*	*	£295
1928 SA	*	*	*	£250
1929 M	*	£700	£1650	£3250
1929 P	*	*	*	£295
1929 SA	*	*	*	£250
1930 M	*	*	£250	£325
1930 P	*	*	£250	£325
1930 SA	*	*	*	£250
1931 M	*	*	£425	£675
1931 P	*	*	*	£250
1931 SA	*	*	*	£250
1932	*	*	*	£250

GEORGE VI

	F	VF	EF	Unc
1937 proof only	*	*	*	£2000

George VI 1937 proof Sovereign

ELIZABETH II

	F	VF	EF	Unc
1953 proof				ext. rare

	F	VF	EF	Unc
1957	*	*	*	£265
1958	*	*	*	£250
1959	*	*	*	£250
1962	*	*	*	£250
1963	*	*	*	£250
1964	*	*	*	£250
1965	*	*	*	£250
1966	*	*	*	£250
1967	*	*	*	£250
1968	*	*	*	£250
1974	*	*	*	£250
1976	*	*	*	£250
1977	*	*	*	£250
1978	*	*	*	£250
1979	*	*	*	£250
1979 proof				£285
1980	*	*	*	£250
1980 proof				£285
1981	*	*	*	£250
1981 proof				£285
1982	*	*	*	£250
1982 proof				£285
1983 proof				£285
1984 proof				£285
1985 proof				£285
1986 proof				£285
1987 proof				£285
1988 proof				£285
1989 500th anniversary of sovereign, proof				£1100
1990 proof				£285
1991 proof				£285
1992 proof				£285
1993 proof				£285
1994 proof				£285
1995 proof				£285
1996 proof				£285
1997 proof				£285
1998 proof				£285
1999 proof				£285
2000 proof				£285
2000 BU				£285
2001 proof				£285
2001 BU				£285
2002 shield, proof				£300
2002 BU				£285
2003 proof				£285
2003 BU				£285
2004 Proof				£285
2004 BU				BV
2005 proof				£285
2005 BU				BV
2006 proof				£285
2006 BU				BV
2007 proof				£285
2007 BU				BV
2008 BU				BV
2008 proof				£285
2009 BU				BV
2009 proof				£285

2010 proof				£285
2010 BU				BV

■ HALF-SOVEREIGNS

GEORGE III	F	VF	EF	Unc
1817	£150	£225	£425	£750
1818	£165	£300	£585	£1000
1820	£150	£225	£425	£750

GEORGE IV
Laureate hd/ornate shield date

	F	VF	EF	Unc
1821	£400	£1000	£2250	£3500
1821 proof	*	*	£2650	£4000
1823 plain shield	£145	£200	£475	£875
1824	£145	£200	£500	£875
1825	£145	£195	£495	£850

Bare hd, date/shield and full legend

1826	£145	£195	£495	£850
1826 proof	*	*	£1100	£1850
1827	£145	£200	£525	£900
1828	£145	£200	£525	£900

WILLIAM IV

1831 proof	*	*	£1750	£2850
1834 reduced size	£195	£425	£1000	£1850
1835 normal size	£175	£325	£850	£1425
1836 sixpence obv die	£925	£2250	£4250	£6000
1836	£185	£395	£900	£1650
1837	£185	£395	£900	£1650

VICTORIA

1838	*	£150	£585	£1000
1839 proof only	*	*	£1450	£2250
1841	*	£150	£600	£1100
1842	*	£150	£425	£800
1843	*	£150	£550	£900
1844	*	£150	£425	£800
1845	£195	£475	£1875	*
1846	*	£150	£425	£800
1847	*	£150	£425	£800
1848	*	£150	£425	£800
1849	*	£150	£425	£800
1850	£200	£375	£1250	*
1851	*	£150	£425	£775
1852	*	£150	£425	£800
1853	*	£150	£425	£775
1853 proof	*	*	£3000	£5250
1855	*	£150	£425	£800
1856	*	£150	£425	£775
1857	*	£150	£425	£800
1858	*	£150	£425	£800
1859	*	£150	£365	£685
1860	*	£150	£365	£685
1861	*	£150	£365	£685
1862	£500	£1500	£4750	*
1863	*	£150	£365	£650
1863 die no	*	£150	£425	£800
1864 die no	*	£150	£350	£625

	F	VF	EF	Unc
1865 die no	*	£150	£350	£625
1866 die no	*	£150	£350	£625
1867 die no	*	£150	£350	£625
1869 die no	*	£150	£350	£625
1870 die no	*	£150	£325	£500
1871 die no	*	£150	£325	£500
1871 S below shield	£150	£200	£925	*
1872 die no	*	£150	£325	£525
1872 S	£150	£200	£925	*
1873 die no	*	£150	£325	£525
1873 M below shield	£150	£195	£900	*
1874 die no	*	£150	£325	£525
1875 die no	*	£150	£325	£525
1875 S	£165	£225	£1100	*
1876 die no	*	£150	£325	£500
1877 die no	*	£150	£325	£500
1877 M	£165	£225	£1100	*
1878 die no	*	£150	£325	£500
1879 die no	*	£150	£325	£500
1879 S	£165	£225	£1100	*
1880	*	£150	£325	£525
1880 die no	*	£150	£325	£525
1880 S	£165	£225	£1100	*
1881 S	£200	£265	£1450	*
1881 M	£200	£375	*	*
1882 S	£250	£625	£3500	*
1882 M	£150	£200	£825	*
1883	*	£150	£325	£500
1883 S	£150	£200	£825	*
1884	*	£150	£325	£500
1884 M	£165	£225	£1000	*
1885	*	£150	£325	£500
1885 M	£165	£225	£1100	*
1886 S	£150	£200	£825	*
1886 M	£165	£225	£1100	*
1887 S	£150	£200	£825	*
1887 M	£175	£475	*	*

JH/shield

	F	VF	EF	Unc
1887	*	*	£150	£200
1887 proof	*	*	£425	£650
1887 M	*	£150	£400	£1250
1887 S	*	£150	£400	£1250
1889 S	*	£175	£625	*
1890	*	*	£150	£225
1891	*	*	£150	£225
1891 S	£140	£250	£950	*
1892	*	*	£150	£225
1893	*	*	£150	£225
1893 M	*	£195	£600	*

OH/St George and dragon

	F	VF	EF	Unc
1893	*	*	£135	£185
1893 proof	*	*	£500	£825
1893 M				ext. rare
1893 S	*	£175	£450	*
1894	*	*	£135	£185
1895	*	*	£135	£185
1896	*	*	£135	£185
1896 M	*	£175	£485	*
1897	*	*	£135	£185
1897 S	*	£175	£450	*
1898	*	*	£135	£185
1899	*	*	£135	£185
1899 M	£150	£195	£575	*
1899 P proof only	*	*	*ext. rare	
1900	*	*	£135	£185
1900 M	*	£150	£575	*
1900 P	£140	£250	£875	*
1900 S	*	£145	£350	£1100
1901	*	*	£135	£185
1901 P proof only	*	*	*ext. rare	

EDWARD VII

	F	VF	EF	Unc
1902	*	*	£125	£170
1902 proof	*	*	£200	£300
1902 S	*	*	£250	£750
1903	*	*	£125	£170
1903 S	*	*	£275	£825
1904	*	*	£125	£170
1904 P	*	*	*ext.rate	
1905	*	*	£125	£170
1906	*	*	£125	£170
1906 M	*	£295	£1100	*
1906 S	*	*	£185	£650
1907	*	*	£125	£170
1907 M	*	*	£275	£825
1908	*	*	£125	£170
1908 M	*	*	£275	£825
1908 P	*	£275	*	*
1908 S	*	*	£165	£485
1909	*	*	£125	£170
1909 M	*	*	£275	£825
1909 P	*	£285	£825	*
1910	*	*	£125	£170
1910 S	*	*	£150	£475

GEORGE V

	F	VF	EF	Unc
1911	*	*	*	£145
1911 proof	*	*	£285	£395
1911 P	*	*	£145	£265
1911 S	*	*	£125	£150
1912	*	*	*	£145
1912 S	*	*	*	£150
1913	*	*	*	£145
1914	*	*	*	£145
1914 S	*	*	*	£145
1915	*	*	*	£145
1915 M	*	*	*	£150
1915 S	*	*	£125	£265
1915 S	*	*	*	£150
1916 S	*	*	*	£150
1918 P	*	£675	£1500	£3250
1923 SA proof	*	*	*	£625
1925 SA	*	*	*	£145
1926 SA	*	*	*	£145

GEORGE VI

	F	VF	EF	Unc
1937 proof	*	*	*	£525

ELIZABETH II

	Unc
1953 proof	ext. rare
1980 proof	£140
1982 proof	£140
1982 BU	BV
1983 proof	£140
1984 proof	£140
1985 proof	£140
1986 proof	£140
1986 proof	£140
1987 proof	£140
1988 proof	£140
1989 500th anniversary of the sovereign, proof	£450
1990 proof	£140
1991 proof	£140
1992 proof	£140
1993 proof	£140
1994 proof	£140
1995 proof	£140
1996 proof	£140
1997 proof	£140
1998 proof	£140
1999 proof	£140
2000 proof	£140
2000 BU	BV
2001 proof	£140
2001 BU	£BV
2002 shield, proof	£175
2002 BU	BV
2003 proof	£140
2003 BU	BV
2004 proof	£140
2004 BU	£BV
2005 proof	BV
2005 BU	BV
2006 proof	£140
2006 BU	BV
2007 proof	£140
2007 BU	BV
2008 BU	BV
2008 proof	£140
2009 BU	BV
2009 proof	£140
2010 BU	BV
2010 proof	£150

■ CROWNS

CROMWELL

	F	VF	EF
1658	£1850	£2850	£5250
1658 Dutch copy	£1900	£2950	£6850
1658 Tanner's copy	*	£3750	£8000

CHARLES II

	F	VF	EF
1662 1st bust	£225	£750	£5000
1663	£225	£750	£5000
1664 2nd bust	£225	£850	£5500
1665	£825	£2250	*
1666	£250	£750	£4000
1666 eleph	£700	£2650	£11000

	F	VF	EF
1667	£195	£600	£3750
1668	£195	£600	£3750
1668/7	£195	£600	£3750
1668/5			ext. rare
1669	£325	£1200	*
1669/8	£375	£1350	*
1670	£195	£600	£3750
1670/69	£400	£700	*
1671	£195	£600	£3750
1671 3rd bust	£195	£600	£3750
1672	£195	£600	£3750
1673	£195	£600	£3750
1673/2	£195	£600	£3750
1674	*		*ext. rare
1675	£700	£2250	*
1675/3	£600	£1875	*
1676	£195	£600	£3750
1677	£195	£600	£3750
1677/6	£195	£600	£3750
1678/7	£275	£700	*
1679	£195	£600	£3750
1679 4th bust	£195	£600	£3750
1680 3rd bust	£265	£695	£4250
1680/79 3rd bust	£265	£695	£4250
1680 4th bust	£265	£695	£4250
1680/79	£325	£750	*
1681 eleph & castle	£3500	£6250	*
1681	£265	£695	£4250
1682	£265	£695	£4250
1682/1	£265	£695	£4250
1683	£325	£875	*
1684	£295	£775	*

JAMES II

	F	VF	EF
1686 1st bust	£350	£1375	*
1687 2nd bust	£200	£600	£2000
1688	£200	£600	£2000
1688/7	£200	£600	£2000

WILLIAM & MARY

	F	VF	EF
1691	£525	£1350	£3950
1692	£525	£1350	£3950
1692/2 inv QVINTO	£525	£1350	£3950
1692/2 inv QVARTO	£600	£1500	*

WILLIAM III

	F	VF	EF
1695 1st bust	£120	£325	£1475
1696	£110	£325	£1500
1696 GEI error	£425	£900	*
1696/5	£225	£500	*
1696 2nd bust			unique
1696 3rd bust	£120	£325	£1650
1697	£700	£2250	£15000
1700 3rd bust var	£120	£325	£1625

ANNE

	F	VF	EF
1703 1st bust VIGO	£400	£1100	£3650
1705	£600	£1850	£4650
1706	£275	£625	£2500

1707	£275	£625	£2500
1707 2nd bust	£175	£475	£1950
1707 E	£175	£475	£1950
1708	£175	£475	£1950
1708 E	£175	£495	*
1708/7	£175	£500	*
1708 plumes	£275	£625	£2500
1713 3rd bust	£275	£625	£2500

GEORGE I

1716 rev r & p	£375	£925	£3250

George I 1716 Crown

1718	£385	£900	£3500
1718/6	£400	£975	£3750
1720	£400	£975	£3750
1720/18	£385	£900	£3500
1723 SS C	£385	£900	£3500
1726 small r & p	£750	£1500	£4750

GEORGE II

1732 YH	£400	£750	£2650
1732 proof	*	*	£6500
1734	£400	£750	£2650
1735	£400	£750	£2650
1736	£375	£750	£2650
1739	£295	£650	£2150
1741	£375	£675	£2500
1743 OH	£295	£650	£2500

William & Mary 1691 Crown

	F	VF	EF
1746 OH LIMA	£400	£700	£2250
1746 OH proof	*	£3500	£7000
1750	£400	£800	£2500
1751	£425	£825	£2650

GEORGE III	F	VF	EF
Oval counterstamp	£250	£375	£850
Octagonal counterstamp	£550	£900	£1750
1804 Bank of England Dollar	£150	£300	£675

Collectors should beware of contemporary forgeries on these three coins. The counterstamps are usually on Spanish-American dollars.

	F	VF	EF	Unc
1818 LVIII	£30	£65	£325	£650
1818 LVIII error edge	£250	*	*	*
1818 LIX	£30	£65	£325	£650
1819 LIX	£30	£65	£325	£650
1819 LIX no edge stops	£60	£150	£450	*
1819/8 LIX	£45	£165	£475	*
1819 LIX no stop after TUTAMEN	£45	£165	£475	*
1820 LX	*	*	£350	£675
1820/19 LX	£50	£200	£500	*

GEORGE IV

1821 1st hd SECUNDO	£35	£150	£875	£1850

George IV 1821 Crown

1821 SECUNDO proof	*	*	*	£3750
1821 TERTIO error edge	*	*	*	£4250
1822 SECUNDO	£60	£175	£875	£1925
1822 SECUNDO proof	*	*	*	*
1822 TERTIO	£50	£175	£875	£1925
1822 TERTIO proof	*	*	*	£4250
1823 proof only	*	*	*ext. rare	
1826 2nd head proof	*	*	£3000	£5750

	F	VF	EF	Unc
WILLIAM IV proof only				
1831 W.W.	*	*	£8500	£12500
1831 W.WYON	*	*	£9000	£13500
1834 W.W.	*	*	£9750	£16500
VICTORIA				
1839 proof	*	*	£4250	£8250
1844 star stops	£35	£100	£750	£2650
1844 star stops proof	*	*ext. rare		*
1844 cinquefoil stops	£35	£100	£750	£2650
1845	£35	£100	£750	£2650
1845 proof	*	*	*	£10500
1847	£35	£100	£850	£2850

Victoria 1847 Gothic Crown

	F	VF	EF	Unc
1847 Gothic	£475	£650	£1450	£3250
1847 Gothic plain edge	*	£750	£1650	£3650
1853 SEPTIMO	*	*	£5750	£9750
1853 plain	*	*	£6500	£10500
1887 JH	£18	£27	£70	£150
1887 JH proof	*	*	£400	£900
1888 close date	£25	£35	£100	£250
1888 wide date	£65	£195	£450	*
1889	£25	£35	£95	£225
1890	£25	£35	£100	£250
1891	£25	£45	£125	£300
1892	£25	£50	£150	£375
1893 LVI	£25	£35	£165	£350
1893 LVI proof	*	*	£475	£975
1893 LVII	£25	£65	£250	£575
1894 LVII	£25	£45	£225	£450
1894 LVIII	£25	£45	£225	£450
1895 LVIII	£25	£45	£195	£400
1895 LIX	£25	£45	£185	£385
1896 LIX	£35	£45	£295	£595
1896 LX	£25	£45	£225	£450
1897 LX	£25	£45	£185	£425
1897 LXI	£25	£45	£185	£385
1898 LXI	£25	£75	£325	£600
1898 LXII	£25	£45	£225	£450
1899 LXII	£25	£45	£225	£450
1899 LXIII	£25	£45	£225	£500
1900 LXIII	£25	£45	£200	£425

	F	VF	EF	Unc
1900 LXIV	£25	£45	£185	£395
EDWARD VII				
1902	£35	£90	£165	£250
1902 matt proof	*	*	£165	£250
GEORGE V				
1927 proof	*	*	£165	£285
1928	£85	£150	£275	£385
1929	£85	£165	£285	£450
1930	£85	£150	£275	£400
1931	£85	£150	£275	£400
1932	£140	£250	£475	£700
1933	£85	£140	£275	£385
1934	£975	£1975	£3250	£4250
1935	£5	£7	£10	£20
1935 raised edge proof	*	*	*	£425
1935 gold proof	*	*	*	£25000
1935 proof in good silver (.925)	*	*	*	£1750
1935 specimen	*	*	*	£60
1936	£125	£250	£400	£650
GEORGE VI				
1937	*	*	£20	£30
1937 proof	*	*	*	£75
1937 'VIP' proof	*	*	*ext. rare	
1951	*	*	*	£10
1951 'VIP' proof	*	*	*	£6075
ELIZABETH II				
1953	*	*	*	£8
1953 proof	*	*	*	£35
1953 'VIP' proof	*	*	*	£475
1960	*	*	*	£10
1960 'VIP' proof	*	*	*	£500
1960 polished dies	*	*	*	£25
1965 Churchill	*	*	*	£1.00
1965 Churchill 'satin' finish	*	*	*	£1250

For issues from 1972 onwards see under 25 pence in Decimal Coinage section.

George V 1935 raised edge proof Crown

■ DOUBLE-FLORINS

VICTORIA	F	VF	EF	Unc
1887 Roman 'I'	£13	£25	£60	£125
1887 Roman 'I' proof	*	*	£200	£485
1887 Arabic 'I'	£13	£25	£55	£120
1887 Arabic 'I' proof	*	*	£200	£450
1888	£13	£25	£75	£165
1888 inv 'I'	£28	£45	£185	£450
1889	£13	£25	£75	£165
1889 inv 'I'	£28	£45	£185	£450
1890	£13	£25	£75	£165

■ THREE SHILLING BANK TOKENS

Contemporary forgeries of these pieces, as well as of other George III coins, were produced in quite large numbers. Several varieties exist for the pieces dated 1811 and 1812. Prices given here are for the commonest types of these years.

GEORGE III

	F	VF	EF	Unc
1811	£17	£55	£165	£265
1812 draped bust	£17	£55	£165	£265
1812 laureate hd	£17	£55	£165	£265
1813	£17	£55	£165	£265
1814	£17	£55	£165	£265
1815	£17	£55	£165	£265
1816	*	£300	£975	£1650

■ HALFCROWNS

CROMWELL	F	VF	EF
1656	£2650	£4500	£9750
1658	£1100	£1850	£3500

Cromwell 1658 Halfcrown

CHARLES II

	F	VF	EF
1663 1st bust	£275	£725	£4000
1664 2nd bust	£275	£1000	£4950
1666/3 3rd bust	£850	*	*
1666/3 eleph	£1000	£2750	*
1667/4			ext. rare
1668/4	£275	£950	*

	F	VF	EF
1669	£350	£1100	*
1669/4	£250	£750	*
1670	£150	£575	£3000
1671 3rd bust var	£150	£575	£3000
1671/0	£150	£575	£3000
1672	£150	£575	£3000
1672 4th bust	£150	£575	£3000
1673	£150	£575	£3000
1673 plume below	£8750	*	*
1673 plume both sides	£8000	*	*
1674	£150	£575	£3000
1674/3	£265	£750	*
1675	£135	£450	£2750
1676	£135	£450	£2750
1677	£135	£450	£2750
1678	£175	£685	*
1679	£135	£400	£2450
1680	£165	£550	*
1681	£150	£400	£2800
1681/0	£275	£750	*
1681 eleph & castle	£2950	£7500	£22500
1682	£150	£500	£2850
1682/79	£300	£875	*
1683	£150	£425	£3000
1683 plume below	ext. rare	*	*
1684/3	£300	£875	

JAMES II

	F	VF	EF
1685 1st bust	£175	£650	£2850
1686	£195	£600	£2650
1686/5	£250	£850	*
1687	£195	£600	£2650
1687/6	£525	£600	£2650
1687 2nd bust	£175	£600	£2650
1688	£225	£675	£3250

WILLIAM AND MARY

	F	VF	EF
1689 1st busts 1st shield	£95	£395	£1750
1689 1st busts 2nd shield	£95	£395	£1750
1690	£140	£475	£2250

William and Mary 1690 Halfcrown

	F	VF	EF
1691 2nd busts 3rd shield	£110	£400	£1850
1692	£110	£400	£1850
1693	£110	£400	£1850

	F	VF	EF
1693 2nd busts 3rd shield 3 inv	£125	£475	£1950
1693 3 over 3 inv	£110	£400	£1850

WILLIAM III

	F	VF	EF
1696 1st bust large shield early hp	£60	£250	£975
1696 B	£95	£300	£1600
1696 C	£150	£450	£1975
1696 E	£150	£425	£1975
1696 N	£200	£700	*
1696 Y	£110	£375	£1750
1696 y/E			ext. rare
1696 large shield ord hp	£150	£475	£1350
1696 C	£150	£425	£1600
1696 E	£150	£425	£1600
1696 N	£250	£675	*
1696 small shield	£65	£275	£1100
1696 B	£95	£300	£1500
1696 C	£175	£500	£1975
1696 E	£175	£500	£1975
1696 N	£150	£425	£1975
1696 y	£150	£400	£1825
1696 2nd bust			unique
1697 1st bust large shield	£65	£225	£900
1697 B	£110	£300	£1600
1697 C	£110	£295	£1600
1697 E	£110	£275	£1500
1697 E/C	£150	£525	*
1697 N	£110	£300	£1600
1697 y	£110	£275	£1500
1698	£65	£200	£800
1699	£140	£350	£1750
1700	£60	£165	£800
1701	£75	£250	£1150
1701 eleph & castle	£2750	*	*
1701 plumes	£265	£775	£3500

ANNE

	F	VF	EF
1703 plain	£700	£1850	£9000
1703 VIGO	£175	£425	£1650
1704 plumes	£250	£675	£2750
1705	£185	£575	£2250
1706 r & p	£120	£300	£1450
1707	£120	£275	£1375
1707 plain	£75	£200	£975
1707 E	£75	£225	£1375
1708 plain	£75	£200	£750
1708 E	£75	£275	£1500
1708 plumes	£150	£395	£1650
1709 plain	£70	£250	£875
1709 E	£400	*	*
1710 r & p	£120	£300	£1375
1712	£85	£200	£975
1713 plain	£95	£300	£1450
1713 r & p	£85	£275	£1250
1714	£75	£275	£1250
1714/3	£125	£400	£1475

GEORGE I

	F	VF	EF
1715 proof	*	*	£6500

	F	VF	EF
1715 r & p	£225	£575	£2875
1717	£225	£575	£2875
1720	£275	£650	£3250
1720/17	£225	£575	£2875
1723 SS C	£200	£500	£2400
1726 small r & p	£2500	£4500	£12500

George III oval countermarked Spanish 4 Reales (Half-Dollar)

GEORGE II

	F	VF	EF
1731 YH proof	*	£2000	£4500
1731	£150	£425	£1450
1732	£150	£425	£1450
1734	£165	£495	£1650
1735	£150	£425	£1450
1736	£165	£495	£1650
1739	£125	£285	£1100
1741	£125	£285	£1100
1741/39	£100	£300	£1000
1743 OH	£95	£225	£975
1745	£95	£225	£975
1745 LIMA	£70	£175	£725
1746 LIMA	£65	£175	£700
1746 plain, proof	*	*	£4000
1750	£165	£400	£1650
1751	£165	£475	£1750

GEORGE III	F	VF	EF	Unc
Oval counterstamp, usually on Spanish Half-Dollar	£250	£395	£750	*
1816 large hd	£10	£50	£275	£425
1817	£10	£50	£275	£425
1817 small hd	£10	£50	£245	£425
1818	£10	£50	£300	£475
1819	£10	£50	£275	£425
1819/8				ext. rare
1820	£10	£60	£300	£475

Victoria 1839 proof Halfcrown

George IV 1820 Halfcrown

VICTORIA

From time to time Halfcrowns bearing dates ranging from 1861 to 1871 are found (usually worn), but except for rare proofs in 1853, 1862 and 1864, no Halfcrowns were struck between 1850 and 1874, so pieces dated from this period are now considered to be contemporary or later forgeries.

GEORGE IV 1st hd	F	VF	EF	Unc
1820 1st rev	£25	£70	£300	£625
1821	£30	£70	£325	£575
1821 proof	*	*	£925	£2500
1823	£875	£2250	£7250	*
1823 2nd rev	£30	£70	£385	£800
1824	£35	£85	£395	£825
2nd hd				
1824 3rd rev				ext. rare
1825	£30	£70	£265	£550
1826	£30	£70	£265	£550
1826 proof	*	*	£625	£1100
1828	£50	£150	£625	*
1829	£40	£90	£345	£750

WILLIAM IV	F	VF	EF	Unc
1831				ext. rare
1831 proof	*	*	£975	£1875

Young Head	F	VF	EF	Unc
1839 plain and ornate fillets, ww	£825	£1650	£5250	*
1839 plain and ornate fillets, plain edge proof	*	*	£950	2500
1839 plain fillets, ww inc	£825	£1650	£5250	*
1840	£45	£110	£575	£1150
1841	£550	£1100	£3250	*
1842	£45	£110	£495	£1000
1843	£90	£250	£850	£1950
1844	£40	£90	£450	£975
1845	£40	£110	£450	£975
1846	£40	£110	£450	£975
1848	£125	£325	£1200	£2650
1848/6	£150	£450	£1100	*
1849 large date	£55	£165	£675	£1450
1849 small date	£90	£250	£825	£1750
1850	£50	£200	£695	£1500
1853 proof	*	*	*	£3250
1862 proof	*	*	*	£6250
1864 proof	*	*	*	£6250
1874	£18	£48	£185	£485
1875	£18	£48	£195	£525
1876	£18	£48	£200	£550
1876/5	£20	£60	£375	£800
1877	£18	£48	£200	£525
1878	£18	£48	£200	£525
1879	£18	£50	£250	£575
1880	£18	£48	£200	£525
1881	£18	£48	£200	£525
1882	£18	£48	£200	£525
1883	£18	£48	£200	£525
1884	£18	£48	£200	£525
1885	£18	£48	£200	£525
1886	£18	£48	£200	£525

William IV 1831 proof Halfcrown

	F	VF	EF	Unc
1834 ww	£35	£125	£495	£1000
1834 ww in script	£25	£75	£300	£625
1835	£35	£100	£325	£825
1836	£25	£75	£300	£625
1836/5	£45	£150	£525	*
1837	£40	£140	£495	£975

	F	VF	EF	Unc
1887	£18	£48	£200	£550
Jubilee Head				
1887	£8	£15	£35	£70
1887 proof	*	*	£95	£275
1888	£9	£20	£65	£130
1889	£9	£20	£65	£145
1890	£9	£25	£75	£165
1891	£9	£25	£75	£180
1892	£9	£25	£75	£200
Old Head				
1893	£9	£22	£55	£135
1893 proof	*	*	£200	£400
1894	£9	£27	£110	£245
1895	£9	£25	£85	£195
1896	£9	£25	£85	£195
1897	£9	£22	£55	£170
1898	£9	£22	£80	£190
1899	£9	£22	£66	£175
1900	£9	£22	£55	£150
1901	£9	£22	£55	£140

Edward VII 1909 Halfcrown

EDWARD VII	F	VF	EF	Unc
1902	£12	£30	£75	£150
1902 matt proof	*	*	*	£165
1903	£125	£400	£2000	£4000
1904	£50	£225	£800	£1950
1905 F	£400	£1350	£5000	£9000
1906	£15	£45	£225	£650
1907	£15	£45	£225	£650
1908	£20	£60	£425	£1100
1909	£15	£50	£350	£875
1910	£15	£40	£175	£425

GEORGE V				
1911	*	£10	£60	£200
1911 proof	*	*	*	£185
1912	*	£15	£60	£200
1913	*	£15	£70	£245
1914	*	*	£25	£80
1915	*	*	£20	£65
1916	*	*	£20	£65
1917	*	*	£30	£75
1918	*	*	£20	£60

	F	VF	EF	Unc
1919	*	*	£20	£60
1920	*	*	£30	£125
1921	*	*	£40	£100
1922	*	*	£30	£100
1923	*	*	£12	£45
1924	*	*	£30	£100
1925	*	£45	£300	£850
1926	*	*	£45	£135
1926 mod eff	*	*	£60	£165
1927	*	*	£25	£60
1927 new rev, proof only	*	*	*	£70
1928	*	*	£10	£27
1929	*	*	£10	£28
1930	£7	£35	£285	£850
1931	*	*	£12	£45
1932	*	*	£15	£50
1933	*	*	£10	£35
1934	*	*	£35	£125
1935	*	*	£8	£20
1936	*	*	£8	£17

GEORGE VI				
1937	*	*	*	£14
1937 proof	*	*	*	£30
1938	*	*	£4	£35
1939	*	*	*	£17
1940	*	*	*	£14
1941	*	*	*	£14
1942	*	*	*	£12
1943	*	*	*	£14
1944	*	*	*	£12
1945	*	*	*	£12
1946	*	*	*	£10
1947	*	*	*	£10
1948	*	*	*	£10
1949	*	*	*	£17
1950	*	*	*	£24
1950 proof	*	*	*	£25
1951	*	*	*	£24
1951 proof	*	*	*	£25
1952			2 known	

ELIZABETH II				
1953	*	*	*	£12
1953 proof	*	*	*	£15
1954	*	*	£4	£45
1955	*	*	*	£10
1956	*	*	*	£10
1957	*	*	*	£8
1958	*	*	*	£28
1959	*	*	*	£45
1960	*	*	*	£4
1961	*	*	*	£4
1962	*	*	*	£4
1963	*	*	*	£2
1964	*	*	*	£2
1965	*	*	*	£2
1966	*	*	*	£1
1967	*	*	*	£1

■ FLORINS

The first Florins produced in the reign of Victoria bore the legend VICTORIA REGINA and the date, omitting DEI GRATIA or 'By the Grace of God'. They are therefore known as 'godless' Florins.

The date of a Victorian Gothic Florin is shown in Roman numerals in Gothic lettering on the obverse, for example mdcclvii (1857). Gothic Florins were issued between 1851-1887.

VICTORIA	F	VF	EF	Unc
1848 'Godless' proof with milled edge	*	*	*	£2500
1848 'Godless' proof with plain edge	*	*	*	£1350
1849 'Godless' ww obliterated by circle	£25	£60	£225	£475
1849 'Godless' ww inside circle	£18	£45	£150	£365
1851 proof only	*	*	*	£10000
1852	£20	£45	£150	£375
1853	£20	£45	£150	£375
1853 no stop after date	£20	£50	£200	£425
1853 proof	*	*	*	£2750
1854	£500	£1000	£4000	*
1855	£20	£55	£200	£500
1856	£20	£55	£200	£500
1857	£20	£45	£195	£450
1858	£20	£45	£195	£450
1859	£20	£45	£195	£450
1859 no stops after date	£20	£50	£195	£400
1860	£20	£50	£200	£500
1862	£185	£425	£1500	*
1863	£550	£1000	£2750	*
1864	£20	£50	£200	£495
1865	£35	£95	£300	£675
1865 colon after date	*	*		ext. rare
1866	£30	£75	£250	£525
1866 colon after date				ext. rare
1867	£30	£75	£250	£525
1868	£30	£85	£250	£625
1869	£30	£85	£250	£625
1870	£20	£50	£200	£495
1871	£20	£50	£200	£495
1872	£20	£35	£160	£395
1873	£20	£35	£195	£400

	F	VF	EF	Unc
1874	£20	£50	£200	£495
1874 xxiv/iii die	£75	£200	£500	*
1875	£20	£45	£195	£450
1876	£20	£45	£195	£450
1877	£20	£45	£195	£450
1877 no ww	*	*		*ext. rare
1877 42 arcs	£30	£85	£250	£625
1878	£20	£50	£200	£425
1879 die no	*	*		*ext.rare
1879 ww 42 arcs	£85	£195	£575	*
1879 ww 48 arcs	£20	£40	£175	£350
1879 no ww, 38 arcs	£20	£45	£150	£350
1880	£20	£40	£195	£400
1881	£20	£40	£195	£400
1881 xxri error	£25	£70	£225	£400
1883	£20	£40	£150	£350
1884	£20	£40	£150	£350
1885	£20	£40	£150	£350
1886	£20	£40	£150	£350
1887 46 arcs	£30	£75	£250	£525
1887 JH	*	£10	£25	£55
1887 JH proof	*	*	*	£175
1888	*	£15	£40	£110
1889	*	£20	£60	£150
1890	*	£25	£125	£325
1891	£20	£60	£250	£500
1892	£20	£70	£295	£585
1893 OH	*	£15	£50	£110
1893 proof	*	*	*	£275
1894	*	£20	£90	£225
1895	*	£18	£70	£165
1896	*	£18	£70	£165
1897	*	£15	£60	£125
1898	*	£18	£70	£165
1899	*	£18	£70	£165
1900	*	£15	£55	£120
1901	*	£15	£55	£125

EDWARD VII				
1902	*	£12	£55	£110
1902 matt proof	*	*	*	£85
1903	*	£28	£140	£400
1904	*	£40	£185	£500
1905	£60	£175	£750	£1850
1906	*	£28	£125	£400
1907	*	£30	£135	£425
1908	*	£45	£295	£725
1909	*	£40	£245	£650
1910	*	£20	£100	£285

GEORGE V				
1911	*	*	*	£125
1911 proof	*	*	*	£135
1912	*	*	£50	£165
1913	*	*	£70	£200
1914	*	*	£25	£75
1915	*	*	£45	£100
1916	*	*	£28	£70
1917	*	*	£35	£80

Victoria 1871 Gothic Florin

	F	VF	EF	Unc		F	VF	EF	Unc
1918	*	*	£20	£55	1955	*	*	*	£7
1919	*	*	£30	£75	1956	*	*	*	£7
1920	*	*	£35	£110	1957	*	*	*	£45
1921	*	*	£30	£75	1958	*	*	*	£30
1922	*	*	£20	£60	1959	*	*	*	£35
1923	*	*	£18	£50	1960	*	*	*	£4
1924	*	*	£27	£55	1961	*	*	*	£4
1925	*	£35	£165	£485	1962	*	*	*	£2
1926	*	*	£45	£95	1963	*	*	*	£2
1927 proof	*	*	*	£120	1964	*	*	*	£2
1928	*	*	£7	£25	1965	*	*	*	£2
1929	*	*	£7	£30	1966	*	*	*	£1
1930	*	*	£25	£70	1967	*	*	*	£1
1931	*	*	£12	£50					
1932	£15	£60	£285	£725					

■ EIGHTEENPENCE BANK TOKENS

GEORGE III

1811	£12	£25	£95	£175
1812	£12	£25	£95	£175
1812 laureate hd	£12	£25	£100	£165
1813	£12	£25	£110	£185
1814	£12	£25	£110	£185
1815	£12	£25	£110	£185
1816	£12	£25	£110	£185

■ SHILLINGS

George V 1932 Florin

1933	*	*	£12	£45
1935	*	*	£8	£25
1936	*	*	£5	£20

GEORGE VI

1937	*	*	*	£12
1937 proof	*	*	*	£20
1938	*	*	*	£35
1939	*	*	*	£12
1940	*	*	*	£15
1941	*	*	*	£10
1942	*	*	*	£8
1943	*	*	*	£10
1944	*	*	*	£10
1945	*	*	*	£8
1946	*	*	*	£8
1947	*	*	*	£8
1948	*	*	*	£8
1949	*	*	*	£20
1950	*	*	*	£20
1950 proof	*	*	*	£20
1951	*	*	*	£25
1951 proof	*	*	*	£25

ELIZABETH II

1953	*	*	*	£9
1953 proof	*	*	*	£12
1954	*	*	*	£45

Cromwell 1658 Shilling

CROMWELL	F	VF	EF
1658	£750	£1500	£2750
1658 Dutch copy	*	*	*

Charles II 1671 Shilling, plumes both sides

CHARLES II	F	VF	EF
1663 1st bust	£135	£375	£1850
1663 1st bust var	£135	£375	£1850
1666 1st bust	*	*	*
1666 eleph	£450	£1750	£6000
1666 guinea head, eleph	£2750	*	*
1666 2nd bust	£1700	*	*
1668 1st bust var	£400	£1650	*
1668 2nd bust	£135	£375	£1850
1668/7	£150	£450	£1900
1669/6 1st bust var	ext. rare	*	*
1669 2nd bust	ext. rare	*	*
1670	£150	£525	£2000
1671	£150	£525	£2000
1671 plumes both sides	£750	£1750	£4500
1672	£150	£525	£2000
1673	£150	£525	£2000
1673/2	£150	£525	£2000
1673 plumes both sides	£750	£1750	£4500
1674	£150	£525	£2000
1674/3	£150	£525	£2000
1674 plumes both sides	£750	£1750	£4500
1674 plumes rev only	£825	£1875	£4850
1674 3rd bust	£525	£1500	*
1675	£525	£1500	*
1675/3	£525	£1500	*
1675 2nd bust	£275	£675	£2250
1675/4	£275	£675	£2250
1675 plumes both sides	£750	£1750	£4500
1676	£150	£525	£2000
1676/5	£150	£525	£2000
1676 plumes both sides	£750	£1750	£4500
1677	£150	£525	£2000
1677 plumes obv only	£750	£2000	£5250
1678	£150	£525	£2000
1678/7	£150	£525	£2000
1679	£150	£525	£2000
1679/7	£150	£525	£2000
1679 plumes	£750	£1750	£4500
1679 plumes obv only	£800	£1850	£5000
1680 plumes	£800	£1850	£5000
1680/79 plumes	£800	£1850	£5000
1681	£300	£850	*
1681/0	£350	£950	*
1681/0 eleph & castle	£3000	*	*
1682/1	£875	*	*
1683	£875	*	*
1683 4th bust	£275	£675	£2250
1684	£275	£675	£2250

James II 1687 Shilling

JAMES II	F	VF	EF
1685	£200	£525	£2000
1685 no stops on rev	£200	£525	£2250
1685 plume on rev			ext. rare
1686	£200	£525	£2000
1686/5	£200	£525	£2000
1686 V/S	£200	£525	£2250
1687	£200	£525	£2000
1687/6	£200	£525	£2000
1688	£200	£525	£2000
1688/7	£200	£525	£2250

WILLIAM AND MARY			
1692	£225	£650	£2000
1693	£225	£650	£2000

WILLIAM III			
1695 1st bust	£30	£100	£500
1696	£30	£90	£425
1696 no stops on rev	£100	£325	£700
1669 in error	£875	*	*
1696 B	£45	£150	£600
1696 C	£55	£175	£650
1696 E	£55	£175	£650
1696 N	£55	£175	£650
1696 y	£55	£175	£650
1696 Y	£65	£200	£700
1696 2nd bust		unique	
1696 3rd bust C	£145	£375	£1250
1696 E		ext. rare	
1697 1st bust	£35	£90	£400
1697 no stops on rev	£85	£295	£725
1697 B	£60	£150	£600
1697 C	£60	£150	£600

William III 1699 roses Shilling

1697 E	£60	£150	£600
1697 N	£60	£165	£675
1697 y	£60	£145	£600
1697 Y	£75	£200	£875
1697 3rd bust	£30	£100	£400
1697 B	£60	£200	£825
1697 C	£60	£150	£600
1697 E	£60	£200	£875
1697 N	£60	£200	£875
1697 y	£60	£200	£875
1697 3rd bust var	£30	£90	£395
1697 B	£60	£200	£875
1697 C	£120	£325	£1200

	F	VF	EF
1698 plain	£60	£200	£800
1698 plumes	£250	£550	£2250
1698 4th bust	£225	£550	£1750
1699 4th bust	£225	£550	£1750
1699 5th bust	£175	£385	£1250
1699 plumes	£250	£550	£2250
1699 roses	£235	£500	£1850
1700	£30	£90	£400
1700 no stops on rev	£55	£150	£485
1700 plume below bust	£2250	*	*
1701	£75	£275	£800
1701 plumes	£250	£585	£2250

Anne 1702 Shilling

ANNE

	F	VF	EF
1702 1st bust	£80	£275	£900
1702 plumes	£85	£300	£800
1702 VIGO	£80	£275	£750
1703 2nd bust VIGO	£80	£275	£725
1704	£400	£1250	£2750
1704 plumes	£125	£375	£1350
1705	£135	£450	£1500
1705 plumes	£85	£300	£950
1705 r&p	£80	£325	£950
1707 r&p	£125	£375	£1350
1707 E	£75	£265	£900
1707 E*	£90	£265	£1100
1707 E* local dies	£200	£600	*
1707 3rd bust	£25	£145	£400
1707 plumes	£70	£275	£875
1707 E	£65	£225	£775
1707 Edin bust E*	£450	*	*
1708 2nd bust E	£150	£450	*
1708 E*	£225	£575	*
1708/7 E*			ext. rare
1708 r&p	£125	£350	£1100
1708 3rd bust	£30	£100	£400
1708 plumes	£85	£300	£875
1708 r&p	£120	£350	£1200
1708 E	£75	£225	£875
1708/7 E	£100	£300	£925
1708 Edin bust E*	£175	£500	*
1709	£60	£100	£425
1709 Edin bust E	£300	£925	*
1709 Edin bust E*	£100	£350	£1100
1710 3rd bust r&p	£85	£300	£900
1710 4th bust proof			ext. rare
1710 r&p	£65	£200	£775

	F	VF	EF
1711 3rd bust	£175	£475	£1200
1711 4th bust	£35	£90	£375
1712 r&p	£50	£165	£575
1713/2	£65	£195	£675
1714	£55	£165	£575
1714/3	£60	£250	£675

George I 1721/0 roses & plumes Shilling

GEORGE I

	F	VF	EF
1715 1st bust r&p	£60	£195	£750
1716 r&p	£150	£375	£1200
1717 r&p	£85	£265	£775
1718 r&p	£60	£185	£750
1719 r&p	£150	£375	£1200
1720 r&p	£85	£265	£875
1720/18	£150	£475	£1450
1720 plain	£60	£165	£550
1720 large 0	£60	£165	£575
1721 plain	£175	£500	£1300
1721 r&p	£85	£265	£900
1721/0 r&p	£80	£250	£800
1721/19 r&p	£85	£265	£875
1721/18 r&p	ext. rare	*	*
1722 r&p	£85	£265	£875
1723 r&p	£85	£265	£875
1723 SSC	£30	£80	£300
1723 SSC C/SS	£35	£110	£365
1723 SSC French arms at date	£175	£500	£1500
1723 2nd bust SS C	£50	£120	£350
1723 r&p	£80	£250	£800
1723 WCC	£600	£1500	£4250
1724 r&p	£80	£250	£800
1724 WCC	£600	£1500	£4250
1725 r&p	£80	£250	£800
1725 no obv stops	£80	£250	£875
1725 WCC	£600	£1500	£4250
1726 r&p	£500	£1500	*
1726 WCC	£600	£1500	£4250
1727 r&p	£500	£1250	*
1727 r&p no stops on obv	£500	£1200	*

GEORGE II

	F	VF	EF
1727 YH plumes	£100	£350	£1200
1727 r&p	£75	£200	£850
1728	£150	£395	£1200
1728 r&p	£85	£250	£850
1729 r&p	£85	£250	£850
1731 r&p	£65	£200	£750

	F	VF	EF
1731 plumes	£120	£400	£1200
1732 r&p	£85	£250	£850
1734 r&p	£70	£185	£750
1735 r&p	£70	£185	£750
1736 r&p	£70	£185	£750
1736/5 r&p	£85	£250	£850
1737 r&p	£50	£185	£750
1739 r&p roses	£40	£165	£625
1741 roses	£40	£165	£625
1741/39 roses	£100	£300	£1100

George II 1729 young head Shilling

	F	VF	EF
1743 OH roses	£40	£145	£575
1743/1 roses	£65	£175	£675
1745	£30	£110	£485
1745/3 roses	£65	£175	£600
1745 LIMA	£25	£90	£485
1746 LIMA	£80	£200	£675
1746/5 LIMA	£80	£200	£675
1746 proof	*	£800	£1675
1747 roses	£40	£110	£485
1750	£55	£165	£600
1750/6	£70	£185	£675
1751	£80	£225	£750
1758	£15	£45	£125

George III 1763 'Northumberland' Shilling

GEORGE III

	F	VF	EF	Unc
1763 'Northumberland'	*	£450	£900	£1500
1786 proof or pattern	*	*	*	£5500
1787 no hearts	£15	£30	£70	£165
1787 no hearts no stop over head	£20	£45	£100	£225
1787 no hearts no stops at date	£20	£65	£150	£285
1787 no stops on obv	£250	£600	*	*

	F	VF	EF	Unc
1787 hearts	£15	£25	£70	£165
1798 'Dorrien and Magens'	*	£5500	£12000	£16500
1816	*	£10	£85	£150
1817	*	£10	£85	£150
1817 GEOE error	£75	£150	£525	*
1818	£4	£25	£125	£250
1819	*	£10	£90	£175
1819/8	*	*	£120	£275
1820	*	£10	£90	£175

GEORGE IV

	F	VF	EF	Unc
1820 1st head 1st rev pattern or proof	*	*	*	£4750
1821 1st rev	£12	£45	£185	£450
1821 proof	*	*	£500	£975
1823 1st head 2nd rev	£30	£85	£325	£650
1824 2nd rev	£10	£40	£185	£450
1825 2nd rev	£15	£50	£200	£475
1825 2nd head	£10	£25	£150	£325
1826	*	£25	£120	£265

George IV 1824 Shilling

	F	VF	EF	Unc
1826 proof	*	*	£275	£485
1827	£25	£80	£350	£685
1829	*	£40	£200	£525

WILLIAM IV

	F	VF	EF	Unc
1831 proof	*	*	*	£725
1834	£12	£35	£195	£425
1835	£12	£40	£200	£450
1836	£12	£35	£195	£425
1837	£25	£75	£250	£600

William IV 1836 Shilling

VICTORIA

	F	VF	EF	Unc
1838 YH	£20	£25	£175	£425
1839	£25	£50	£250	£575

	F	VF	EF	Unc
1839 2nd YH	£15	£30	£165	£340
1839 proof	*	*	*	£650
1840	£20	£45	£200	£425
1841	£20	£45	£210	£425
1842	£15	£30	£150	£325
1843	£25	£45	£210	£425
1844	£20	£30	£150	£325
1845	£20	£30	£135	£375
1846	£10	£30	£150	£325
1848/6	£60	£125	£600	£1100
1849	£12	£30	£135	£375
1850	£350	£1000	£2500	*
1850/49	£425	£1100	£2750	*
1851	£40	£150	£475	£975
1852	£12	£20	£110	£265
1853	£12	£20	£110	£265
1853 proof	*	*	*	£800
1854	£75	£350	£1200	£2250
1855	£12	£20	£110	£265
1856	£12	£20	£110	£265
1857	£12	£20	£110	£265
1857 F:G:	£250	£575	*	*
1858	£12	£20	£110	£265
1859	£12	£20	£110	£265
1860	£12	£25	£150	£325
1861	£12	£25	£150	£325
1862	£22	£50	£225	£450

Victoria 1860 Shilling

	F	VF	EF	Unc
1863	£40	£100	£400	£875
1863/1	£60	£200	£675	*
1864	£12	£25	£120	£265
1865	£12	£25	£120	£265
1866	£12	£25	£120	£265
1866 BBRITANNIAR error	£80	£225	£750	*
1867	£12	£25	£120	£265
1867 3rd YH, die no	£195	£385	£1200	*
1868	£10	£25	£120	£265
1869	£15	£40	£150	£325
1870	£10	£25	£120	£265
1871	£10	£20	£120	£265
1872	£10	£20	£120	£265
1873	£10	£20	£120	£265
1874	£10	£20	£120	£265
1875	£10	£20	£120	£265
1876	£10	£25	£120	£265
1877	£10	£20	£120	£265

	F	VF	EF	Unc
1878	£12	£28	£150	£325
1879 no die		ext. rare		
1879 4th YH	£10	£20	£120	£265
1880	£10	£15	£80	£195
1880 longer line below SHILLING	*	*	*	*
1881	£10	£20	£95	£195
1881 longer line below SHILLING	£10	£20	£95	£195
1881 longer line below SHILLING, large rev lettering	£10	£20	£95	£195
1882	£15	£20	£120	£235
1883	£10	£20	£70	£195
1884	£10	£20	£70	£195
1885	£10	£20	£70	£195
1886	£10	£20	£70	£195
1887	£10	£25	£110	£265
1887 JH	*	£5	£12	£35
1887 proof	*	*	*	£150
1888/7	*	£8	£45	£90
1889	£40	£100	£425	*
1889 large JH	*	£8	£50	£120
1890	*	£8	£50	£120
1891	*	£8	£50	£135
1892	*	£8	£50	£145
1893 OH	£4	£12	£35	£85
1893 proof	*	*	*	£165
1893 small obv letters	*	*	£40	£80
1894	*	£8	£45	£110
1895	*	*	£40	£120
1896	*	*	£40	£100

Victoria 1896 Shilling

	F	VF	EF	Unc
1897	*	£8	£40	£90
1898	*	£8	£40	£90
1899	*	£8	£40	£100
1900	*	£8	£40	£90
1901	*	£8	£40	£90

EDWARD VII

1902	*	*	£45	£75
1902 matt proof	*	*	£50	£80
1903	*	£20	£150	£425
1904	*	£15	£110	£325
1905	£70	£200	£1250	£2850
1906	*	*	£65	£185
1907	*	*	£70	£200

	F	VF	EF	Unc
1908	£8	£20	£175	£525
1909	£8	£20	£175	£525
1910	*	*	£45	£125

GEORGE V

	F	VF	EF	Unc
1911	*	*	£25	£60
1911 proof	*	*	*	£70
1912	*	*	£30	£80
1913	*	*	£65	£160
1914	*	*	£25	£55
1915	*	*	£20	£50
1916	*	*	£20	£50
1917	*	*	£25	£75
1918	*	*	£20	£50
1919	*	*	£25	£70
1920	*	*	£20	£70
1921	*	*	£25	£100
1922	*	*	£20	£70
1923	*	*	£20	£55
1923 nickel	*	*	*	£1200
1924	*	*	£25	£60
1924 nickel	*	*	*	£1200
1925	*	*	£45	£120
1926	*	*	£25	£70
1926 mod eff	*	*	£18	£48
1927	*	*	£20	£50
1927 new type	*	*	£12	£40
1927 new type proof	*	*	*	£60
1928	*	*	*	£25
1929	*	*	£8	£25
1930	*	*	£25	£85
1931	*	*	£8	£30
1932	*	*	£8	£30
1933	*	*	£8	£30
1934	*	*	£13	£45
1935	*	*	£4	£20
1936	*	*	£4	£20

GEORGE VI

	F	VF	EF	Unc
1937 Eng	*	*	*	£9
1937 Eng proof	*	*	*	£12
1937 Scot	*	*	*	£9
1937 Scot proof	*	*	*	£12
1938 Eng	*	*	£5	£30
1938 Scot	*	*	£5	£25
1939 Eng	*	*	*	£10
1939 Scot	*	*	*	£10
1940 Eng	*	*	*	£10
1940 Scot	*	*	*	£10
1941 Eng	*	*	£2	£12
1941 Scot	*	*	£2	£12
1942 Eng	*	*	*	£10
1942 Scot	*	*	*	£10
1943 Eng	*	*	*	£10
1943 Scot	*	*	*	£10
1944 Eng	*	*	*	£8
1944 Scot	*	*	*	£9
1945 Eng	*	*	*	£6
1945 Scot	*	*	*	£6

	F	VF	EF	Unc
1946 Eng	*	*	*	£6
1946 Scot	*	*	*	£6
1947 Eng	*	*	*	£6
1947 Scot	*	*	*	£6
1948 Eng	*	*	*	£7
1948 Scot	*	*	*	£7
1949 Eng	*	*	*	£20
1949 Scot	*	*	*	£20
1950 Eng	*	*	*	£17
1950 Eng proof	*	*	*	£20
1950 Scot	*	*	*	£17
1950 Scot proof	*	*	*	£20
1951 Eng	*	*	*	£17
1951 Eng proof	*	*	*	£20
1951 Scot	*	*	*	£17
1951 Scot proof	*	*	*	£20

ELIZABETH II

	F	VF	EF	Unc
1953 Eng	*	*	*	£5
1953 Eng proof	*	*	*	£10
1953 Scot	*	*	*	£5
1953 Scot proof	*	*	*	£10
1954 Eng	*	*	*	£5
1954 Scot	*	*	*	£5
1955 Eng	*	*	*	£5
1955 Scot	*	*	*	£5
1956 Eng	*	*	*	£10
1956 Scot	*	*	*	£9
1957 Eng	*	*	*	£4
1957 Scot	*	*	*	£20
1958 Eng	*	*	*	£50
1958 Scot	*	*	*	£4
1959 Eng	*	*	*	£4
1959 Scot	*	*	*	£70
1960 Eng	*	*	*	£2
1960 Scot	*	*	*	£3
1961 Eng	*	*	*	£2
1961 Scot	*	*	*	£10
1962 Eng	*	*	*	£1
1962 Scot	*	*	*	£1
1963 Eng	*	*	*	£1
1963 Scot	*	*	*	£1
1964 Eng	*	*	*	£1
1964 Scot	*	*	*	£1
1965 Eng	*	*	*	£1
1965 Scot	*	*	*	£1
1966 Eng	*	*	*	£1
1966 Scot	*	*	*	£1

■ SIXPENCES

CROMWELL	F	VF	EF
1658		highest rarity	
1658 Dutch copy	*	£4000	£6500

CHARLES II	F	VF	EF
1674	£50	£225	£750
1675	£50	£245	£785

	F	VF	EF
1675/4	£50	£245	£785
1676	£50	£250	£825
1676/5	£50	£250	£825
1677	£50	£225	£750
1678/7	£50	£245	£785
1679	£50	£250	£825
1680	£70	£250	£825
1681	£50	£245	£785
1682	£65	£285	£875
1682/1	£50	£245	£785
1683	£50	£225	£750
1684	£65	£245	£750

James II 1686 Sixpence

JAMES II

	F	VF	EF
1686 early shields	£100	£350	£900
1687 early shields	£100	£350	£900
1687/6	£100	£350	£900
1687 later shields	£100	£350	£900
1687/6	£100	£375	£1000
1688	£100	£375	£1000

WILLIAM AND MARY

	F	VF	EF
1693	£110	£375	£950

William and Mary 1693 Sixpence

	F	VF	EF
1693 3 upside down	£125	£425	£1000
1694	£140	£400	£1000

WILLIAM III

	F	VF	EF
1695 1st bust early hp	£30	£95	£375
1696	£25	£70	£200
1696 no obv stops	£40	£125	£450
1696/5	£30	£100	£450
1696 B	£30	£80	£350
1696 C	£35	£100	£450
1696 E	£35	£100	£450
1696 N	£35	£100	£450
1696 y	£30	£95	£425

	F	VF	EF
1696 Y	£40	£100	£425
1696 1st bust later hp	£50	£135	£400
1696 B	£75	£200	*
1696 C	£60	£225	£500
1696 N	£70	£225	£525
1696 2nd bust	£185	£500	£1750
1696 3rd bust, early hp, E			ext. rare
1696 3rd bust, early hp, y			ext. rare
1697 1st bust early hp	£25	£60	£275
1697 B	£40	£100	£425
1697 C	£60	£150	£500
1697 E	£40	£110	£425
1697 N	£40	£110	£425
1697 y	£40	£110	£425
1697 2nd bust	£145	£395	£1200
1697 3rd bust later hp	£25	£75	£250
1697 B	£40	£100	£425
1697 C	£60	£185	£650
1697 E	£65	£120	£450
1697 Y	£60	£150	£500
1698	£45	£95	£300
1698 plumes	£80	£175	£575
1699	£85	£200	£625
1699 plumes	£70	£165	£500
1699 roses	£75	£185	£585

William III 1699 plumes Sixpence

	F	VF	EF
1700	£25	£60	£225
1700 plume below bust	£2750	*	*
1701	£40	£85	£325

ANNE

	F	VF	EF
1703 VIGO	£40	£110	£325
1705	£60	£185	£525
1705 plumes	£50	£165	£475
1705 r&p	£45	£150	£450
1707	£40	£140	£425
1707 plain	£25	£75	£275
1707 E	£25	£100	£385
1707 plumes	£35	£100	£375

Anne 1707 plumes Sixpence

	F	VF	EF
1708 plain	£30	£95	£285
1708 E	£35	£110	£450
1708/7 E	£60	£165	£525
1708 E*	£40	£150	£500
1708/7 E*	£60	£185	£550
1708 Edin bust E*	£60	£185	£550
1708 plumes	£45	£125	£450
1710 r&p	£45	£135	£450
1711	£20	£75	£200

George I 1726 roses and plumes Sixpence

GEORGE I

	F	VF	EF
1717 r&p	£50	£175	£575
1720/17 r&p	£50	£175	£575
1723 SS C, small letters on obv	£25	£85	£250
1723 SS C, large letters on both sides	£25	£85	£250
1726 small r&p	£35	£200	£625

George II 1728 roses and plumes Sixpence

GEORGE II

	F	VF	EF
1728 YH	£65	£225	£550
1728 plumes	£45	£150	£450
1728 YH r&p	£25	£110	£400
1731	£25	£110	£400
1732	£25	£110	£400
1734	£35	£125	£465
1735	£35	£125	£425
1735/4	£35	£125	£485
1736	£30	£125	£400
1739 roses	£25	£100	£325
1739 O/R	£60	£185	£475
1741	£25	£110	£325
1743 OH roses	£25	£110	£325
1745	£25	£110	£325
1745/3	£30	£125	£350
1745 LIMA	£20	£85	£225
1746	£20	£85	£225
1746 plain proof	*	*	£900

	F	VF	EF
1750	£35	£135	£325
1751	£35	£175	£400
1757	£10	£20	£60
1757	£10	£20	£60
1758/7	£15	£35	£70

GEORGE III

	F	VF	EF	Unc
1787 hearts	£10	£20	£50	£100
1787 no hearts	£10	£20	£50	£100
1816	£8	£12	£60	£110
1817	£8	£12	£60	£110
1818	£8	£18	£65	£140
1819	£8	£15	£60	£130
1819/8	£8	£15	£60	£130
1819 small 8	£10	£20	£100	£150
1820	£8	£15	£60	£120
1820 I inv	£30	£100	£375	£600

GEORGE IV

	F	VF	EF	Unc
1820 1st head 1st rev pattern or proof	*	*	*	£2500
1821	£8	£20	£125	£300
1821 BBITANNIAR error	£100	£250	£675	*
1824 1st head 2nd rev	£8	£20	£120	£325
1825	£8	£20	£120	£325
1826	£20	£60	£285	£550
1826 2nd head 3rd rev	£5	£14	£100	£285
1826 proof	*	*	*	£375
1827	£15	£45	£325	£550
1828	£8	£20	£185	£425
1829	£6	£20	£110	£300

William IV 1831 proof Sixpence

WILLIAM IV

	F	VF	EF	Unc
1831	£10	£20	£110	£250
1831 proof	*	*	*	£375
1834	£10	£30	£120	£250
1835	£10	£20	£120	£250
1836	£15	£35	£175	£325
1837	£12	£30	£175	£325

VICTORIA

	F	VF	EF	Unc
1838 1st YH	£7	£17	£100	£220
1839	£8	£17	£100	£220
1839 proof	*	*	*	£485
1840	£8	£18	£125	£265
1841	£8	£20	£145	£300
1842	£8	£18	£125	£265
1843	£8	£18	£125	£265

	F	VF	EF	Unc
1844	£8	£18	£125	£265
1845	£8	£18	£110	£265
1846	£8	£18	£125	£265
1848	£30	£110	£465	£875
1848/6	£25	£100	£425	£800
1850	£12	£18	£125	£265
1850 5/3	£17	£45	£200	£400
1851	£8	£18	£125	£265
1852	£8	£18	£125	£265
1853	£6	£17	£95	£180
1853 proof	*	*	*	£650
1854	£100	£375	£800	*
1855	£8	£15	£110	£240
1855/3	£10	£17	£120	£285
1856	£8	£15	£110	£240
1857	£8	£15	£110	£240
1858	£8	£15	£110	£240
1859	£8	£15	£110	£240
1859/8	£8	£20	£110	£250
1860	£8	£17	£110	£240
1862	£50	£110	£475	£975
1863	£40	£85	£365	£775
1864	£8	£15	£110	£240
1865	£8	£15	£110	£240
1866	£7	£15	£110	£240
1866 no die no				ext. rare
1867	£10	£20	£125	£275
1868	£10	£20	£125	£275
1869	£12	£18	£125	£265
1870	£12	£25	£150	£325

Victoria 1871 proof Sixpence

	F	VF	EF	Unc
1871	£7	£12	£90	£225
1871 no die no	£7	£15	£95	£250
1872	£7	£15	£95	£250
1873	£7	£12	£85	£215
1874	£7	£12	£85	£215
1875	£7	£12	£85	£215
1876	£9	£20	£120	£295
1877	£7	£12	£80	£215
1877 no die no	£5	£12	£70	£200
1878	£7	£10	£80	£215
1878/7	£40	£115	£600	*
1878 DRITANNIAR error	£65	£185	£750	*
1879 die no	£10	£20	£110	£295
1879 no die no	£7	£15	£95	£225
1880 2nd YH	£7	£15	£80	£215
1880 3rd YH	£5	£8	£70	£125
1881	£5	£10	£60	£110
1882	£8	£25	£100	£285

	F	VF	EF	Unc
1883	£5	£10	£70	£125
1884	£5	£10	£45	£110
1885	£5	£10	£45	£110
1886	£5	£10	£45	£110
1887	£5	£10	£45	£110
1887 JH shield rev	£2	£5	£10	£28
1887 proof	*	*	*	£110
1887 new rev	£2	£5	£10	£30
1888	£3	£5	£28	£75
1889	£3	£7	£28	£75
1890	*	£8	£28	£75
1891	*	£8	£35	£85
1892	*	£10	£40	£100
1893	£250	£650	£2150	*
1893 OH	*	£5	£20	£60
1893 proof	*	*	*	£150
1894	*	£7	£35	£100
1895	*	£7	£32	£75
1896	*	£7	£30	£65
1897	*	£7	£30	£65
1898	*	£7	£30	£65
1899	*	£7	£30	£65
1900	*	£7	£25	£65
1901	*	£7	£25	£55

EDWARD VII

	F	VF	EF	Unc
1902	*	£8	£35	£65
1902 matt proof	*	*	*	£65
1903	*	£10	£45	£110
1904	*	£20	£80	£195
1905	*	£20	£90	£200
1906	*	£10	£45	£100
1907	*	£10	£45	£110
1908	*	£15	£55	£125
1909	*	£10	£45	£110
1910	*	£7	£35	£75

GEORGE V

	F	VF	EF	Unc
1911	*	*	£15	£45
1911 proof	*	*	*	£65
1912	*	*	£28	£70
1913	*	*	£35	£75
1914	*	*	£12	£40
1915	*	*	£12	£45
1916	*	*	£12	£35
1917	*	*	£35	£100
1918	*	*	£12	£30
1919	*	*	£15	£50
1920	*	*	£12	£55
1920 debased	*	*	£12	£55
1921	*	*	£12	£50
1922	*	*	£12	£50
1923	*	*	£15	£50
1924	*	*	£12	£50
1925	*	*	£12	£35
1925 new rim	*	*	£12	£30
1926	*	*	£12	£35
1926 mod eff	*	*	£9	£30
1927	*	*	£10	£28

	F	VF	EF	Unc
1927 new rev proof	*	*	*	£40
1928	*	*	£7	£20
1929	*	*	£7	£20
1930	*	*	£8	£25
1931	*	*	£8	£25
1932	*	*	£12	£40
1933	*	*	£8	£25
1934	*	*	£10	£35
1935	*	*	£5	£15
1936	*	*	£5	£15

GEORGE VI
	F	VF	EF	Unc
1937	*	*	£1	£7
1937 proof	*	*	*	£10
1938	*	*	£4	£15
1939	*	*	£2	£10
1940	*	*	£2	£10
1941	*	*	£2	£10
1942	*	*	£1	£7
1943	*	*	£1	£7
1944	*	*	£1	£7
1945	*	*	£1	£7
1946	*	*	£1	£7
1947	*	*	*	£7
1948	*	*	£1	£5
1949	*	*	£1	£8
1950	*	*	£1	£8
1950 proof	*	*	*	£10
1951	*	*	£1	£12
1952	*	£5	£20	£95

ELIZABETH II
	F	VF	EF	Unc
1953	*	*	*	£5
1953 proof	*	*	*	£7
1954	*	*	*	£5
1955	*	*	*	£3
1956	*	*	*	£4
1957	*	*	*	£3
1958	*	*	*	£6
1959	*	*	*	£2
1960	*	*	*	£4
1961	*	*	*	£4
1962	*	*	*	£1
1963	*	*	*	£1
1964	*	*	*	£1
1965	*	*	*	£1
1966	*	*	*	£1
1967	*	*	*	£1

■ GROATS 'BRITANNIA' TYPE

Earlier dates are included in Maundy sets (see p136).

WILLIAM IV
	F	VF	EF	Unc
1836	*	*	£45	£100
1836 proof	*	*	*	£625
1837	*	*	£60	£120
1837 proof	*	*	*	£825

VICTORIA	F	VF	EF	Unc
1838	*	£5	£40	£110
1838 8/8 on side	*	£15	£60	£165
1839	*	£8	£40	£110
1839 proof	*	*	*	£400
1840	*	£10	£40	£110
1840 narrow 0	*	£12	£40	*
1841	*	£10	£50	£125
1841 1 for last 1	*	*	*	*
1842	*	£8	£50	£125
1842/1	*	£15	£70	£180
1843	*	£5	£50	£125
1843 4/5	*	£15	£65	£185
1844	*	£8	£50	£125
1845	*	£8	£50	£125
1846	*	£8	£50	£125
1847/6	£25	£70	£325	*
1848	*	£8	£45	£120
1848/6	£10	£25	£75	*
1848/7	*	£20	£90	£265
1849	*	£10	£45	£120
1849/8	*	£10	£50	£125
1851	£20	£95	£350	*
1852	£45	£185	£500	*

Victoria 1852 Groat

	F	VF	EF	Unc
1853	£45	£195	£475	*
1853 proof	*	*	*	£650
1854	*	£8	£45	£120
1854 5/3	*	£20	£85	*
1855	*	£8	£45	£120
1857 proof	*	*	*	£1150
1862 proof	*	*	*	£1750
1888 JH	*	£20	£40	£90

■ SILVER THREEPENCES

Earlier dates are included in Maundy sets.

WILLIAM IV
	F	VF	EF	Unc
1834	*	£12	£70	£195
1835	*	£12	£65	£175
1836	*	£12	£70	£195
1837	*	£20	£85	£200

Victoria 1866 Threepence

VICTORIA	F	VF	EF	Unc
1838	*	£15	£50	£165
1839	*	£20	£85	£225
1840	*	£15	£60	£165
1841	*	£15	£85	£175
1842	*	£15	£85	£175
1843	*	£15	£55	£165
1844	*	£15	£85	£200
1845	*	£12	£60	£135
1846	*	£20	£95	£275
1847	£45	£125	£400	£800
1848	£35	£100	£400	£750
1849	*	£15	£85	£175
1850	*	£10	£50	£95
1851	*	£12	£55	£150
1852	£45	£175	£450	*
1853	*	£20	£85	£275
1854	*	£10	£60	£150
1855	*	£15	£85	£180
1856	*	£10	£60	£150
1857	*	£15	£70	£180
1858	*	£12	£50	£165
1858 BRITANNIAB error	ext. rare			
1858/6	£10	£25	£150	£275
1859	*	£8	£50	£125
1860	*	£15	£60	£165
1861	*	£8	£50	£110
1862	*	£8	£50	£110
1863	*	£10	£80	£150
1864	*	£10	£50	£100
1865	*	£10	£70	£150
1866	*	£8	£50	£100
1867	*	£8	£50	£100
1868	*	£8	£50	£100
1868 RRITANNIAR error	ext. rare			
1869	£10	£30	£100	£250
1870	*	£6	£50	£95
1871	*	£7	£60	£110
1872	*	£5	£55	£110
1873	*	£5	£35	£75
1874	*	£5	£35	£75
1875	*	£5	£35	£75
1876	*	£5	£35	£75
1877	*	£5	£35	£75
1878	*	£5	£35	£75
1879	*	£5	£35	£75
1880	*	£6	£40	£70
1881	*	£6	£40	£70
1882	*	£8	£45	£100
1883	*	£5	£30	£60
1884	*	£5	£30	£55
1885	*	£5	£25	£55
1886	*	£5	£25	£50
1887 YH	*	£6	£35	£65
1887 JH	*	£2	£5	£15
1887 proof	*	*	*	£45
1888	*	£2	£12	£35
1889	*	£2	£10	£30
1890	*	£2	£10	£30
1891	*	£2	£10	£30

	F	VF	EF	Unc
1892	*	£3	£12	£30
1893	£12	£40	£100	£275
1893 OH	*	*	£6	£20
1893 proof	*	*	*	£75
1894	*	£2	£10	£30
1895	*	£2	£10	£30
1896	*	£2	£10	£30
1897	*	*	£5	£25
1898	*	*	£5	£30
1899	*	*	£5	£30
1900	*	*	£5	£18
1901	*	*	£5	£20
EDWARD VII				
1902	*	*	£7	£15
1902 matt proof	*	*	*	£20
1903	*	£2	£15	£40
1904	*	£6	£25	£80
1905	*	£6	£25	£70
1906	*	£3	£20	£70
1907	*	£2	£15	£40
1908	*	£2	£12	£35
1909	*	£2	£25	£50
1910	*	£2	£10	£30
GEORGE V				
1911	*	*	£6	£17
1911 proof	*	*	*	£30
1912	*	*	£6	£17
1913	*	*	£6	£17
1914	*	*	£4	£15
1915	*	*	£4	£20
1916	*	*	£3	£12
1917	*	*	£3	£12
1918	*	*	£3	£12
1919	*	*	£3	£12
1920	*	*	£3	£17
1920 debased	*	*	£3	£17
1921	*	*	£3	£20
1922	*	*	£10	£45
1925	*	£1	£10	£45
1926	*	£3	£15	£60
1926 mod eff	*	£1	£8	£30
1927 new rev proof	*	*	*	£95
1928	*	£2	£15	£45
1930	*	£1	£8	£30
1931	*	*	£1	£9
1932	*	*	£1	£9
1933	*	*	£1	£9
1934	*	*	£1	£9
1935	*	*	£1	£9
1936	*	*	£1	£9
GEORGE VI				
1937	*	*	£2	£5
1937 proof	*	*	*	£10
1938	*	*	£2	£6
1939	*	£1	£5	£20
1940	*	*	£2	£8

	F	VF	EF	Unc
1941	*	*	£2	£12
1942	*	£2	£6	£35
1943	*	£3	£17	£55
1944	*	£6	£28	£80
1945	*	*	*	*

Some of the Threepences were issued for use in the Colonies. Note: all specimens of 1945 were probably melted down but it appears that one or two still exist.

■ SMALL SILVER FOR COLONIES

These tiny coins were struck for issue in some of the Colonies but they were never issued for circulation in Britain. However, they are often included in collections of British coins, so we have given the prices.

Twopences

Other dates are included in Maundy sets.

VICTORIA	F	VF	EF	Unc
1838	*	£5	£20	£45
1838 2nd 8 like S	*	£8	£30	£75
1848	*	£5	£20	£50

Threehalfpences

WILLIAM IV				
1834	*	£5	£40	£75
1835	*	£5	£65	£165
1835/4	*	£10	£40	£95
1836	*	£5	£35	£60
1837	£10	£25	£100	£265

VICTORIA				
1838	*	£8	£25	£65
1839	*	£8	£25	£65
1840	*	£15	£65	£135
1841	*	£8	£30	£80
1842	*	£8	£30	£80
1843	*	£8	£20	£60
1843/34	£5	£20	£65	£150
1860	£4	£15	£45	£110
1862	£4	£15	£45	£110
1870 proof				£750

■ NICKEL-BRASS THREEPENCES

Edward VIII 1937 Threepence, extremely rare

The 1937 Edward VIII threepences, struck in 1936 ready for issue, were melted after Edward's abdication.

A few, however, escaped into circulation to become highly prized collectors' pieces.

George VI 1937 threepences were struck in large numbers, and are consequently worth much less.

EDWARD VIII	F	VF	EF	BU
1937	*	*	£35000	*

GEORGE VI				
1937	*	*	£1	£6
1938	*	*	£3	£28
1939	*	*	£6	£50
1940	*	*	£2	£20
1941	*	*	£1	£8
1942	*	*	£1	£8
1943	*	*	£1	£8
1944	*	*	£1	£8
1945	*	*	£1	£12
1946	*	£15	£165	£585
1948	*	*	£5	£45
1949	*	£15	£100	£450
1950	*	*	£15	£85
1951	*	*	£25	£110
1952	*	*	*	£12

ELIZABETH II				
1953	*	*	*	£5
1953 proof	*	*	*	£8
1954	*	*	*	£5
1955	*	*	*	£7
1956	*	*	*	£7
1957	*	*	*	£4
1958	*	*	*	£10
1959	*	*	*	£3
1960	*	*	*	£3
1961	*	*	*	£1
1962	*	*	*	£1
1963	*	*	*	£1
1964	*	*	*	£1
1965	*	*	*	£1
1966	*	*	*	£1
1967	*	*	*	*

■ COPPER TWOPENCE

GEORGE III				
1797	£20	£75	£375	*

■ COPPER PENNIES

GEORGE III				
1797 10 leaves	£5	£35	£250	*
1797 11 leaves	£5	£45	£250	*
1806	£3	£8	£90	£300
1806 no incuse curl	£3	£8	£90	£325
1807	£3	£8	£90	£350

George III 1806 Penny

GEORGE IV

	F	VF	EF	BU
1825	£5	£25	£175	£485
1826	£3	£12	£150	£300
1826 Proof	*	*	£300	£500
1826 thin line down				
St Andrew's cross	£5	£25	£175	£485
1826 thick line	£5	£40	£225	*
1827	£200	£550	£3000	*

William IV 1831

WILLIAM IV

1831	£10	£50	£285	£1000
1831 Proof	*	*	*	£675
1831 .ww inc				ext. rare
1831 w.w inc	£15	£75	£375	*
1834	£15	£75	£365	£1375
1837	£20	£90	£600	£2000

Victoria 1841 Penny

VICTORIA

	F	VF	EF	BU
1839 proof	*	*	*	£1100
1841	£20	£60	£300	£800
1841 no colon after REG	£3	£15	£65	£275
1843	£90	£300	£1650	£3500
1843 no colon after REG	£65	£200	£1350	£3000
1844	£3	£20	£100	£375
1845	£8	£20	£145	£525
1846 DEF far colon	£3	£15	£110	£395
1846 DEF close colon	£3	£15	£135	£425
1847 DEF close colon	£3	£15	£95	£275
1847 DEF far colon	£3	£15	£85	£250
1848	£3	£15	£95	£300
1848/6	£15	£75	£475	*
1848/7	£3	£15	£95	£300
1849	£100	£350	£1650	£2850
1851 DEF far colon	£3	£18	£125	£475
1851 DEF close colon	£4	£15	£110	£385
1853 OT	£2	£10	£80	£215
1853 PT	£2	£10	£85	£285
1854 PT	£2	£10	£80	£215
1854/3	£15	£40	£165	£395
1854 OT	£2	£10	£80	£215
1855 OT	£2	£10	£80	£215
1855 PT	£2	£10	£80	£215
1856 PT	£50	£175	£600	£2000
1856 OT	£60	£225	£750	£2250
1857 OT	£2	£10	£80	£215
1857 PT	£2	£10	£80	£215
1857 small date	£2	£10	£85	£285
1858	£2	£10	£65	£195
1858 small date	£3	£10	£85	£285
1858/3	£20	£65	£350	*
1858/7	£2	£5	£85	£285
1858 no ww	£2	£5	£65	£250
1858 no ww				
(large 1 and 5, small 8s)	£3	£8	£65	£250
1859	£3	£10	£85	£285
1859 small date	£4	£15	£100	£295
1860/59	£325	£875	£2650	*

■ BRONZE PENNIES

For fuller details of varieties in bronze pennies see *English Copper, Tin and Bronze Coins in the British Museum 1558-1958* by C W Peck, *The Bronze Coinage of Great Britain* by M J Freeman and *The British Bronze Penny 1860-1970* by Michael Gouby.

The die pairings used below are from the latter publication, a must for the penny collector. There are a large number of varieties and die combinations for this series, and only the more significant of these are listed below.

VICTORIA

	F	VF	EF	BU
1860 BB, dies C/a	£100	£300	£700	*
1860 BB dies C/b	£40	£100	£245	£500
1860 BB rev rock to				
left of lighthouse, dies C/c	£80	£200	£750	*
1860 obv BB/rev				
TB, dies C/d	£400	£750	£1500	£3000

Victoria 1860 bronze Penny

	F	VF	EF	BU
1860 obv TB/rev BB, dies D/b	£300	£625	£2000	*
1860 TB, signature on cape, dies D/d	*	£15	£60	£235
1860 TB, rev L.C.W. inc below foot, dies E/e	£300	£575	£1000	£2500
1860 TB, rev L.C.W inc below shield, dies F/d	*	£15	£90	£225
1860 TB obv, no signature on cape, dies H/d	*	£150	£400	£800

1861 bronze Penny

	F	VF	EF	BU
1861 signature on cape, rev LCW below shield, dies D/d	£80	£225	£450	£1500
1861 signature on cape, rev no signature, dies D/g	£80	£225	£450	£1500
1861 signature below cape, L.C.W. below shield, dies F/d	*	£10	£90	£300
1861 signature below cape, rev no signature, dies F/g	£80	£350	£850	*
1861 obv no signature, L.C.W. below shield, dies H/d	*	£20	£100	£300
1861 date: 6 over 8	£400	£1250	£2500	*
1861 no signature either side, dies J/g	*	£12	£75	£275
1862 obv signature, rev no LCW, dies D/g	£450	£875	£1875	*
1862 obv no signature dies J/g	*	£10	£75	£275
1862 date: small figures (½d size)	£475	£1500	£2750	*
1863 dies J/g	*	£10	£60	£200

	F	VF	EF	BU
1863 die no 2 below date	£2000	*	*	*
1863 die no 3 below date	£1450	£3000	*	*
1863 die no 4 below date	£1350	*	*	*
1863 die no 5 below date	unique			
1864 upper serif to 4 in date		£20	£135	£1000	*
1864 crosslet serif to 4 in date	£25	£150	£1450	£4000
1865	*	£25	£150	£525
1865/3	£40	£125	£525	£1450
1866	*	£15	£90	£425
1867	£10	£35	£200	£750
1868	£10	£40	£225	£875
1869	£150	£450	£2250	£4000
1870	£10	£40	£200	£575
1871	£30	£85	£525	£1500
1872	*	£12	£85	£300
1873	*	£12	£85	£350
1874	*	£20	£125	£400
1874 H dies J/g	*	£12	£80	£325
1874 rev lighthouse tall and thin, dies J/j	£20	£95	£300	£600
1874 H dies J/j	£25	£95	£250	£675
1874 obv, aged portrait, dies K/g	*	£20	£85	£325
1874 H	*	£20	£85	£325
1875 dies L/k	*	£15	£80	£285
1875 H	£30	£200	£875	£2250
1876 H	*	£15	£85	£275
1877	*	£8	£75	£225
1878	*	£35	£175	£500
1879	*	*	£75	£200
1880 no rock to left of lighthouse, dies M/k	£12	£35	£125	£375
1880 rocks to left of lighthouse, dies M/n	£12	£45	£150	£495
1881	*	*	£200	£575
1881 new obv, dies P/k	£45	£145	£350	*
1881 H	*	*	£65	£285
1882 H	*	*	£65	£235
1882 no H	£575	£1000	*	*
1883	*	*	£60	£225
1884	*	*	£50	£165
1885	*	*	£50	£165
1886	*	*	£50	£165
1887	*	*	£45	£140
1888	*	*	£50	£165
1889 14 leaves	*	*	£45	£140
1889 15 leaves	*	*	£50	£165
1890	*	*	£40	£125
1891	*	*	£40	£125
1892	*	*	£40	£145
1893	*	*	£40	£125
1894	*	*	£60	£225
1895 2mm	*	£50	£325	£750

	F	VF	EF	BU
1895	*	*	£15	£65
1896	*	*	£12	£60
1897	*	*	£12	£60
1897 higher horizon	£40	£120	£450	*
1898	*	*	£15	£65
1899	*	*	£15	£60
1900	*	*	£12	£55
1901	*	*	£10	£35

EDWARD VII

	F	VF	EF	BU
1902 low horizon	*	£15	£100	£275
1902	*	*	£10	£45
1903	*	*	£20	£70
1904	*	*	£35	£140
1905	*	*	£30	£95
1906	*	*	£20	£75
1907	*	*	£20	£80
1908	*	*	£17	£75
1909	*	*	£20	£80
1910	*	*	£17	£65

George V 1933 Penny

GEORGE V

	F	VF	EF	BU
1911	*	*	£12	£45
1912	*	*	£12	£50
1912 H	*	*	£55	£185
1913	*	*	£15	£55
1914	*	*	£12	£50
1915	*	*	£12	£50
1916	*	*	£12	£50
1917	*	*	£12	£50
1918	*	*	£12	£50
1918 H	*	£35	£250	£525
1918 KN	*	£45	£375	£800
1919	*	*	£12	£45
1919 H	*	£35	£325	£725
1919 KN	*	£75	£600	*
1920	*	*	£12	£45
1921	*	*	£12	£45
1922	*	*	£12	£45
1922 rev as 1927	ext. rare			
1926	*	*	£20	£80
1926 mod eff	*	£50	£800	£2000
1927	*	*	£7	£30
1928	*	*	£7	£28

	F	VF	EF	BU
1929	*	*	£7	£30
1930	*	*	£10	£35
1931	*	*	£10	£30
1932	*	*	£20	£75
1933		highest rarity		
1934	*	*	£15	£40
1935	*	*	£4	£15
1936	*	*	£4	£15

Edward VIII proof Penny

EDWARD VIII

proof penny			highest rarity	

GEORGE VI

	F	VF	EF	BU
1937	*	*	*	£5
1938	*	*	*	£5
1939	*	*	£1	£6
1940	*	*	£7	£35
1944	*	*	£5	£20
1945	*	*	£4	£15
1946	*	*	*	£9
1947	*	*	*	£4
1948	*	*	*	£5
1949	*	*	*	£5
1950	*	£7	£20	£60
1951	*	£7	£28	£45
1952 proof				unique

George VI 1952 Penny, unique

	F	VF	EF	BU
ELIZABETH II				
1953	*	£1	£2	£15
1953 proof	*	*	*	£20
1954		unique		
1961	*	*	*	£2
1962	*	*	*	£1
1963	*	*	*	£1
1964	*	*	*	£0.50
1965	*	*	*	£0.50
1966	*	*	*	£0.50
1967	*	*	*	£0.25

■ COPPER OR TIN HALFPENNIES

Charles II 1675 Halfpenny

CHARLES II	Fair	F	VF	EF
1672	£8	£45	£225	£1350
1672 CRAOLVS error		ext. rare		*
1673	£8	£45	£200	£1350
1673 CRAOLVS error		ext. rare		*
1673 no stops on rev	£10	£65	£325	*
1673 no stops on obv	£12	£60	£300	*
1675	£10	£50	£200	£1475
1675 no stops on obv	£10	£60	£300	*
1675 5/3	£35	£120	£400	*

JAMES II				
1685 tin	£65	£250	£550	£3250
1686 tin	£70	£250	£600	*
1687 tin	£65	£250	£550	*
1687 D/D	*	*	*	*

WILLIAM AND MARY				
1689 tin, ET on right	£650	£1250	£2500	*
1689 tin, ET on left	*	*	*	*

	Fair	F	VF	EF
1690 tin, date on edge	£65	£200	£525	£2750
1691 tin, date in exergue and on edge	£65	£200	£525	£2750
1691/2 tin, 1691 in exergue 1692 on edge		ext. rare		*
1692 tin, date in exergue and on edge	£65	£75	£450	*
1694 copper	£12	£50	£250	£1350
1694 GVLIEMVS error	£150	*	*	*
1694 no stop after MARIA	£25	£65	£300	£1400
1694 BRITANNIA with last I/A	£30	£125	£350	*
1694 no stop on rev	£20	£60	£300	£1350

William III 1696 Halfpenny

WILLIAM III
Type 1, date in exergue

	Fair	F	VF	EF
1695	£10	£35	£175	£1250
1695 BRITANNIA, A's unbarred	£50	£175	*	*
1695 no stop on rev	£10	£50	£225	*
1696	£10	£35	£175	£1250
1696 GVLIEMVS, no stop on rev		ext. rare		*
1696 TERTVS error	£85	£200	*	*
1697	£10	£45	£175	£1250
1697 no stops	£35	£150	*	*
1697 I/E on TERTIVS	£35	£150	*	*
1697 GVLILMVS no stop on rev		ext. rare		*
1697 no stop after TERTIVS	£15	£40	£150	£1250
1698	£15	£45	£200	*

Type 2, date in legend

1698	£10	£45	£225	£1250
1699	£10	£30	£225	£1100
1699 BRITANNIA, A's unbarred	£35	£150	*	*
1699 GVLIEMVS error	£35	£150	*	*

Type 3, Britannia's hand on knee, date in exergue

1699	£10	£30	£200	£1150
1699 stop after date	£35	£150	*	*

	Fair	F	VF	EF
1699 BRITANNIA, A's unbarred	£20	£70	£250	*
1699 GVILELMVS	£50	£225	*	*
1699 TERTVS	£50	£225	*	*
1699 no stop on rev	£35	£150	*	*
1699 no stops on obv	£15	£60	£250	*
1699 no stops after GVLIELMVS	£15	£60	£250	*
1700	£8	£20	£200	£1100
1700 no stops on obv	£20	£70	£250	*
1700 no stops after GVLIELMVS	£20	£70	£250	*
1700 BRITANNIA, A's unbarred	£8	£20	£200	£1100
1700 no stop on reverse	£8	£25	£200	£1100
1700 GVLIELMS error	£20	£70	£250	*
1700 GVLIEEMVS error	£12	£45	£185	*
1700 TER TIVS error	£8	£20	£200	£1100
1700 I/V on TERTIVS	£50	£225	*	*
1701 BRITANNIA, A's unbarred	£8	£20	£200	£1100
1701 no stops on obv	£50	£225	*	*
1701 GVLIELMVS TERTIVS, V's inverted A's	£12	£45	£225	*

GEORGE I
Type 1

	Fair	F	VF	EF
1717	£10	£35	£250	£875
1717 no stops on obv	£15	£65	£475	*

George I 1717 Halfpenny

	Fair	F	VF	EF
1718	£10	£30	£225	£800
1718 no stop on obv	£15	£65	£475	*
1719 on large flan of type 2	£250	*	*	*
1719 on large flan of type 2, edge grained			ext. rare	*

Type 2

	Fair	F	VF	EF
1719 both shoulder straps ornate	£5	£25	£150	£825
1719 both shoulder straps ornate, edge grained			ext. rare	*
1719 bust with left strap plain	£5	£25	£150	£800
1720	£5	£25	£150	£750
1721	£5	£25	£150	£725
1721/0	£5	£25	£150	£725

	Fair	F	VF	EF
1721 stop after date	£5	£25	£150	£725
1722	£5	£25	£150	£725
1722 GEORGIVS, V inverted A	£15	£90	£300	*
1723	£5	£25	£150	£725
1723 no stop on reverse	£15	£90	£300	*
1724	£5	£25	£150	£650

George II 1733 Halfpenny

GEORGE II
Young Head

	Fair	F	VF	EF
1729	*	£20	£85	£400
1729 no stop on rev	*	£25	£90	£425
1730	*	£20	£85	£375
1730 GEOGIVS, no stop on reverse	*	£25	£110	£450
1730 stop after date	£5	£20	£85	£375
1730 no stop after REX or on rev	*	£25	£110	£450
1731	*	£20	£85	£365
1731 rev no stop	*	£25	£100	£400
1732	*	£20	£75	£350
1732 rev no stop	*	£25	£100	£400
1733	*	£18	£70	£350
1734	*	£18	£70	£350
1734/3	*	£25	£150	*
1734 no stops on obv	*	£25	£150	*
1735	*	£18	£70	£350
1736	*	£18	£75	£350
1737	*	£18	£75	£350
1738	*	£18	£70	£325
1739	*	£18	£70	£325

Old Head

	Fair	F	VF	EF
1740	*	£7	£55	£285
1742	*	£7	£55	£285
1742/0	*	£10	£80	£325
1743	*	£7	£55	£285
1744	*	£7	£55	£285
1745	*	£7	£55	£285
1746	*	£7	£55	£285
1747	*	£7	£55	£285
1748	*	£7	£55	£285
1749	*	£7	£55	£285
1750	*	£7	£55	£295
1751	*	£7	£55	£275

	Fair	F	VF	EF
1752	*	£7	£55	£275
1753	*	£7	£55	£275
1754	*	£7	£55	£275

George II 1777 Halfpenny

GEORGE III

	F	VF	EF	BU
1770	£5	£45	£200	£700
1771	£5	£45	£200	£700
1771 no stop on rev	£7	£45	£200	£700
1771 ball below spear head	£5	£45	£200	£700
1772	£5	£45	£200	£700
1772 GEORIVS error	£10	£80	£275	*
1772 ball below spear head	£5	£45	£200	£700
1772 no stop on rev	£5	£45	£200	£700
1773	£5	£45	£200	£700
1773 no stop after REX	£5	£45	£200	£700
1773 no stop on reverse	£5	£45	£200	*
1774	£5	£45	£200	£700
1775	£5	£45	£200	£850
1799 five inc gunports	*	£8	£60	£175
1799 six relief gunports	*	£8	£60	£175
1799 nine relief gunports	*	£8	£60	£200
1799 no gunports	*	£8	£60	£185
1799 no gunports and raised line along hull	*	£8	£60	£185
1806 no berries on olive branch	*	£8	£55	£175
1806 line under SOHO three berries	*	£8	£55	£175
1807	*	£8	£45	£175

GEORGE IV

1825	*	£30	£135	£350
1826 Proof	*	*	*	£385
1826 two inc lines down cross	*	£15	£85	£250
1826 raised line down centre of cross	*	£20	£100	£275
1827	*	£15	£85	£250

WILLIAM IV

1831	*	£20	£110	£275
1831 Proof	*	*	*	£400
1834	*	£20	£110	£275
1837	*	£15	£100	£265

VICTORIA

	F	VF	EF	BU
1838	£3	£8	£50	£175
1839 proof	£1	*	*	£395
1839 proof, rev inv	£1	*	*	£395
1841	£3	£8	£50	£175
1843	£15	£45	£150	£475
1844	£3	£8	£55	£175
1845	£75	£185	£875	*
1846	£3	£8	£50	£175
1847	£3	£8	£50	£175
1848	£5	£30	£125	£325
1848/7	£5	£20	£95	£200
1851	£3	£8	£50	£175
1851 seven inc dots on and above shield	£2	£5	£35	£175
1852	£3	£8	£50	£175
1852 seven inc dots on and above shield	£2	£8	£50	£175
1853 proof	*	*	*	£425
1853/2	£4	£25	£110	£295
1854	£3	£5	£45	£130

Victoria 1853 proof Halfpenny

1855	£2	£5	£45	£135
1856	£3	£8	£50	£185
1857	£2	£5	£45	£135
1857 seven inc dots on and above shield	£1	£5	£35	£135
1858	£2	£5	£45	£135
1858/6	£3	£10	£45	£150
1858/7	£2	£5	£45	£150
1858 small date	£1	£5	£35	£150
1859	£2	£5	£50	£160
1859/8	£6	£12	£85	£200
1860 proof only	*	*	*	£6750

■ BRONZE HALFPENNIES

For fuller details of varieties in bronze Halfpennies and Farthings see *English Copper, Tin and Bronze Coins in the British Museum 1558-1958* by C W Peck and *The Bronze Coinage of Great Britain* by M J Freeman. There are a large number of varieties and die combinations for this series, only the more significant are listed below.

Victoria 1860 bronze Halfpenny

	F	VF	EF	BU
1875	*	£5	£50	£165
1875 H	*	£5	£60	£190
1876 H	*	£5	£50	£165
1877	*	£5	£50	£165
1878	*	£15	£90	£385
1879	*	£5	£45	£150
1880	*	£4	£45	£165
1881	*	£4	£45	£165
1881 H	*	£4	£40	£165
1882 H	*	£4	£40	£165
1883	*	£4	£40	£165
1884	*	£2	£35	£145
1885	*	£2	£35	£145
1886	*	*	£35	£145
1887	*	*	£35	£145
1888	*	*	£35	£145
1889	*	*	£35	£145
1889/8	*	£20	£110	£325
1890	*	*	£35	£120
1891	*	*	£35	£120
1892	*	*	£35	£120
1893	*	*	£35	£120
1894	*	£5	£50	£185
1895 OH	*	*	£5	£60
1896	*	*	£5	£45
1897 normal horizon	*	*	£5	£45
1897 higher horizon	*	*	£5	£45
1898	*	*	£6	£45
1899	*	*	£5	£45
1900	*	*	£2	£25
1901	*	*	£2	£20

VICTORIA

	F	VF	EF	BU
1860 BB	*	£5	£40	£145
1860 rev TB/obv BB		ext. rare		*
1860 TB, 4 berries	*	£5	£50	£175
1860 TB, double inc leaf veins	*	£15	£80	£265
1861 obv 5 berries	*	£30	£100	£325
1861 obv 4 berries, rev L.C.W. on rock	*	£20	£95	£265
1861 rev no signature	£12	£50	£150	*
1861 rev no signature, breastplate has inc lines	*	£30	£100	£325
1861 obv 4 double incuse leaf veins, rev no signature, breastplate has inc lines	*	£20	£95	£265
1861 same obv, rev L.C.W. on rock	*	£5	£50	£175
1861 obv 7 double incuse leaf veins, rev L.C.W. on rock	*	£5	£60	£185
1861 rev no signature	*	£5	£40	£125
1861 obv 16 leaves, rev rounded to top lighthouse	*	£20	£95	£265
1861 rev pointed top to lighthouse	*	£5	£50	£175
1861 no signature	*	£8	£50	£150
1861 HALP error	£185	£475	*	*
1861 6/8	£200	£525	*	*
1862	*	£5	£35	£150
1862 letter A left of lighthouse base	£395	£750	£2000	*
1862 letter B left of lighthouse base	£550	*	*	*
1862 letter C left of lighthouse base	£650	*	*	*
1863	*	£5	£55	£185
1864	*	£6	£100	£275
1865	*	£10	£85	£395
1865/3	£30	£90	£285	£775
1866	*	£8	£65	£245
1867	*	£8	£80	£300
1868	*	£8	£75	£265
1869	£20	£65	£295	£825
1870	*	£5	£55	£195
1871	£20	£65	£295	£825
1872	*	£5	£55	£175
1873	*	£8	£65	£225
1874	*	£15	£100	£395
1874 H	*	£5	£50	£160

EDWARD VII

	F	VF	EF	BU
1902 low horizon	*	£25	£100	£275
1902	*	*	£8	£25
1903	*	*	£10	£50
1904	*	*	£15	£75
1905	*	*	£12	£60
1906	*	*	£12	£50
1907	*	*	£9	£50
1908	*	*	£9	£50
1909	*	*	£12	£60
1910	*	*	£9	£50

GEORGE V

	F	VF	EF	BU
1911	*	*	£7	£30
1912	*	*	£8	£40
1913	*	*	£8	£40
1914	*	*	£8	£45
1915	*	*	£8	£45
1916	*	*	£5	£45
1917	*	*	£5	£30
1918	*	*	£5	£30
1919	*	*	£5	£30
1920	*	*	£5	£35
1921	*	*	£5	£30
1922	*	*	£5	£40
1923	*	*	£5	£35
1924	*	*	£5	£35

	F	VF	EF	BU
1925	*	*	£5	£35
1925 mod eff	*	*	£5	£45
1926	*	*	£5	£35
1927	*	*	£3	£30
1928	*	*	£3	£20
1929	*	*	£3	£20
1930	*	*	£3	£20
1931	*	*	£3	£20
1932	*	*	£3	£20
1933	*	*	£3	£20
1934	*	*	£3	£25
1935	*	*	£3	£20
1936	*	*	£3	£15

GEORGE VI

1937	*	*	*	£5
1938	*	*	*	£9
1939	*	*	*	£16
1940	*	*	*	£16
1941	*	*	*	£6
1942	*	*	*	£4
1943	*	*	*	£4
1944	*	*	*	£5
1945	*	*	*	£4
1946	*	*	*	£12
1947	*	*	*	£6
1948	*	*	*	£6
1949	*	*	*	£8
1950	*	*	*	£8
1951	*	*	*	£17
1952	*	*	*	£5

ELIZABETH II

1953	*	*	*	£2
1954	*	*	*	£5
1955	*	*	*	£4
1956	*	*	*	£5
1957	*	*	*	£2
1958	*	*	*	£2
1959	*	*	*	£1
1960	*	*	*	£1
1962	*	*	*	*
1963	*	*	*	*
1964	*	*	*	*
1965	*	*	*	*
1966	*	*	*	*
1967	*	*	*	*

■ COPPER FARTHINGS

OLIVER CROMWELL	Fair	F	VF	EF
Patterns only	*	£2500	£5000	£7500

CHARLES II

1671 patterns only	*	*	£350	£750
1672	£2	£35	£175	£625
1672 no stop on obv	£5	£45	£250	£750
1672 loose drapery				

at Britannia's elbow	£4	£35	£200	£775
1673	£1	£35	£175	£650
1673 CAROLA error	£30	£125	£400	*
1673 BRITINNIA error			ext. rare	
1673 no stops on obv	£30	£125	*	*
1673 rev no stop	£25	£125	*	*
1674	*	£35	£175	£675
1675	*	£35	£175	£650
1675 no stop after CAROLVS	£45	£165	*	*
1679	*	£25	£175	£700
1679 no stop on rev	£7	£75	£300	*
1694 tin, various edge readings	£35	£175	£550	£3000
1685 tin		ext. rare	*	*

James II 1685 tin Farthing

JAMES II

1684 tin		ext. rare		*
1685 tin, various edge readings	£60	£165	£600	£2650
1686 tin, various edge readings	£70	£185	£600	£3000
1687 tin, draped bust, various readings		ext. rare	*	*

WILLIAM AND MARY

1689 tin, date in exergue and on edge, many varieties	£250	£500	*	*
1689/90 tin, 1689 in exergue, 1690 on edge	*	*	*	*
1689/90 tin, 1690 in exergue, 1689 on edge	*	*	*	*
1690 tin, various types	£40	£150	£475	£2650
1691 tin, small and large figures	£40	£150	£475	£2650
1692 tin	£40	£150	£475	£2650
1694 copper, many varieties	£10	£50	£165	£800

William and Mary 1694 Farthing

WILLIAM III	Fair	F	VF	EF
Type 1, date in exergue				
1695	£2	£40	£160	£725
1695 GVLIELMV error	£60	£185	*	*
1696	*	£40	£145	£700
1697	*	£40	£145	£700
1698	£50	£175	£450	*
1699	£2	£40	£150	£700
1700	£2	£40	£145	£700
Type 2, date in legend				
1698	£5	£45	£175	£750
1699	£5	£45	£185	£775
ANNE				
1714 patterns F	*	*	£475	£875

George I 1717 'dump' Farthing

GEORGE I
Smaller flan, 'dump type'

	Fair	F	VF	EF
1717	*	£150	£375	£875
1718	unique			
1718 silver proof	*	*	*	£1750

Larger flan

	Fair	F	VF	EF
1719 large lettering on obv	£3	£35	£200	£600
1719 small lettering on obv	£3	£35	£200	£625
1719 last A over I in BRITANNIA	£10	£60	£295	*

George I 1721 Farthing

	Fair	F	VF	EF
1719 legend continuous over bust	£20	£60	*	*
1720 large lettering on obv	£20	£60	£275	*
1720 small lettering on obv	£2	£20	£110	£525
1721	£2	£20	£110	£500
1721/0	£5	£40	£125	£525
1722 large lettering on obv	*	£25	£125	£550

	Fair	F	VF	EF
1722 small lettering on obv	*	£20	£110	£500
1723	*	£20	£125	£525
1723 R/R REX	£12	£75	£150	£650
1724	£5	£25	£125	£550
GEORGE II				
1730	*	£10	£55	£285
1731	*	£10	£55	£285
1732	*	£12	£60	£325
1733	*	£10	£50	£285
1734	*	£10	£55	£325
1734 no stops on obv	*	£12	£70	£375
1735	*	£10	£40	£265
1735 3/3	*	£12	£70	£375
1736	*	£10	£50	£285
1736 triple tie-riband	*	£15	£70	£375
1737 small date	*	£10	£45	£265
1737 large date	*	£10	£45	£265
1739	*	£10	£45	£285
1739/5	*	£10	£55	£325
1741 OH	*	£10	£45	£200
1744	*	£10	£55	£250
1746	*	£10	£45	£200
1746 V/U	ext. rare		*	*
1749	*	£10	£45	£175
1750	*	£10	£55	£200
1754/0	*	£20	£80	£265
1754	*	£8	£40	£125

GEORGE III	F	VF	EF	BU
1771	£5	£45	£200	£550
1773	£5	£30	£175	£400
1774	£5	£30	£175	£400
1775	£5	£30	£175	£400
1799	*	*	£50	£110
1806	*	£3	£50	£115
1807	*	£4	£50	£120
GEORGE IV				
1821	*	£8	£45	£130
1822	*	£8	£45	£130
1823	*	£8	£45	£130
1825	*	£8	£45	£130
1825 D/U in DEI	*	£50	£175	*
1826 date on rev	*	£10	£60	£150
1826 date on obv	*	£9	£50	£135
1826 1 for I in date	£15	£65	£300	£575
1827	*	£9	£50	£140
1828	*	£9	£55	£135
1829	*	£10	£60	£180
1830	*	£9	£50	£135
WILLIAM IV				
1831	*	£7	£55	£150
1831 Proof	*	*	*	£375
1834	*	£7	£55	£150
1835	*	£7	£50	£165
1836	*	£7	£50	£165
1837	*	£7	£55	£165

VICTORIA	F	VF	EF	BU
1838	*	£5	£35	£150
1839	*	£5	£35	£145
1839 Proof	*	*	*	£425
1840	*	£5	£35	£145
1841	*	£5	£35	£145
1842	*	£35	£100	£350
1843	*	£5	£40	£145
1843 I for I	£40	£200	£575	*
1844	£35	£100	£600	£2000
1845	*	£6	£30	£130
1846	*	£6	£60	£150
1847	*	£5	£40	£130
1848	*	£6	£40	£130
1849	*	£50	£325	*
1850	*	£5	£35	£130
1851	*	£15	£50	£165
1851 D/D sideways	£10	£75	£300	£850
1852	*	£12	£55	£165
1853 Proof	*	*	*	£500
1853 w.w. raised	*	£5	£35	£120
1853 w.w. inc	*	£20	£85	£275
1854	*	£5	£35	£95
1855	*	£6	£45	£130
1855 w.w. raised	*	£6	£40	£130
1856 w.w. inc	*	£7	£55	£165
1856 R/E in VICTORIA	£10	£50	£275	*
1857	*	£5	£40	£120
1858	*	£5	£40	£120
1859	*	£15	£50	£195
1860 proof	*	*	*	£7000

Victoria 1859 copper Farthing

■ BRONZE FARTHINGS

VICTORIA

VICTORIA	F	VF	EF	BU
1860 BB	*	£2	£20	£85
1860 TB/BB (mule)	£100	£200	£450	*
1860 TB	*	£1	£15	£75
1861	*	£1	£12	£75
1862 small 8	*	£1	£12	£65
1862 large 8	£40	£100	£225	*
1863	£20	£40	£150	£375
1864	*	£3	£30	£110
1865	*	£3	£25	£85
1865-5/2	*	£5	£35	£135
1866	*	£2	£20	£80
1867	*	£3	£30	£100
1868	*	£3	£30	£100

	F	VF	EF	BU
1869	*	£8	£40	£125
1872	*	£2	£20	£80
1873	*	£3	£20	£80
1874 H	*	£5	£30	£90
1874 H G sideways/Gs	£65	£175	£475	*
1875 large date	*	£10	£35	£125
1875 small date	£8	£20	£90	£300
1875 older features	*	£20	£80	£250
1875 H	*	£2	£15	£70
1875 H older features	£60	£175	£300	*
1876 H	*	£10	£35	£120
1877 proof only				£5000
1878	*	£2	£10	£75
1879	*	£2	£20	£80
1879 large 9	*	£1	£12	£90
1880	*	£2	£25	£95
1881	*	£5	£20	£75
1881 H	*	£2	£20	£75
1882 H	*	£2	£20	£75
1883	*	£5	£35	£110
1884	*	*	£12	£50
1886	*	*	£12	£50
1887	*	*	£20	£75
1890	*	*	£12	£55
1891	*	*	£12	£55
1892	*	£9	£35	£120
1893	*	*	£10	£60
1894	*	*	£12	£70
1895	*	£15	£60	£200
1895 OH	*	*	£3	£25
1896		*	£5	£30
1897 bright finish	*	*	£3	£30
1897 black finish higher horizon	*	*	£2	£30
1898	*	*	£3	£30
1899	*	*	£2	£30
1900	*	*	£2	£30
1901	*	*	£2	£15

EDWARD VII	F	VF	EF	BU
1902	*	*	£3	£20
1903 low horizon	*	*	£4	£20
1904	*	*	£4	£20
1905	*	*	£4	£20
1906	*	*	£4	£20
1907	*	*	£4	£20
1908	*	*	£4	£20
1909	*	*	£4	£20
1910	*	*	£8	£25

GEORGE V	F	VF	EF	BU
1911	*	*	£4	£15
1912	*	*	£4	£15
1913	*	*	£4	£15
1914	*	*	£4	£15
1915	*	*	£4	£15
1916	*	*	£4	£15
1917	*	*	£4	£10
1918 black finish	*	*	£6	£20

	F	VF	EF	BU
1919 bright finish	*	*	£3	£9
1919	*	*	£3	£10
1920	*	*	£3	£10
1921	*	*	£3	£10
1922	*	*	£3	£10
1923	*	*	£3	£10
1924	*	*	£3	£10
1925	*	*	£3	£10
1926 mod eff	*	*	£2	£6
1927	*	*	£2	£6
1928	*	*	*	£3
1929	*	*	*	£3
1930	*	*	*	£3
1931	*	*	*	£3
1932	*	*	*	£3
1933	*	*	*	£3
1934	*	*	*	£5
1935	*	*	£1	£7
1936	*	*	*	£2

GEORGE VI

	F	VF	EF	BU
1937	*	*	*	£2
1937 Proof	*	*	*	£6
1938	*	*	*	£7
1939	*	*	*	£3
1940	*	*	*	£3
1941	*	*	*	£3
1942	*	*	*	£3
1943	*	*	*	£3
1944	*	*	*	£3
1945	*	*	*	£3
1946	*	*	*	£3
1947	*	*	*	£3
1948	*	*	*	£3
1949	*	*	*	£3
1950	*	*	*	£3
1950 Proof	*	*	*	£6
1951	*	*	*	£3
1951 Proof	*	*	*	£6
1952	*	*	*	£3

ELIZABETH II

	F	VF	EF	BU
1953	*	*	*	£2
1954	*	*	*	£2
1955	*	*	*	£2
1956	*	*	*	£4

■ FRACTIONS OF FARTHINGS

Copper Half-Farthings

GEORGE IV

	F	VF	EF	BU
1828 Britannia breaks legend	£5	£20	£100	£275
1828 Britannia below legend	£8	£35	£110	£300
1830 trident breaks legend	£5	£25	£100	£275
1830 trident to base of legend	£20	£60	£225	*

	F	VF	EF	BU
WILLIAM IV				
1837	£40	£125	£300	*
VICTORIA				
1839	*	£6	£40	£100
1842	*	£6	£40	£100
1843	*	*	£15	£70
1844	*	*	£15	£70
1844 E/N	£3	£12	£75	£250
1847	*	£5	£20	£85
1851	*	£5	£40	£100
1852	*	£5	£40	£100
1853	*	£8	£45	£125
1853 proof				£325
1854	*	£20	£80	£200
1856	*	£20	£80	£200
1856 large date	£40	£95	£300	*
1868 bronze proof	*			£475
1868 copper-nickel proof	*			£600

Copper Third-Farthings

	F	VF	EF	BU
GEORGE IV				
1827	*	£10	£55	£150
WILLIAM IV				
1835	*	£12	£85	£200
VICTORIA				
1844	*	£25	£85	£300
1844 RE for REG	£25	£60	£325	*

Bronze Third-Farthings

	F	VF	EF	BU
VICTORIA				
1866	*	*	£15	£60
1868	*	*	£15	£60
1876	*	*	£15	£65
1878	*	*	£15	£60
1881	*	*	£15	£65
1884	*	*	£10	£60
1885	*	*	£10	£60
EDWARD VII				
1902	*	*	£8	£28
GEORGE V				
1913	*	*	£8	£28

Copper Quarter-Farthings

	F	VF	EF	BU
VICTORIA				
1839	£8	£15	£40	£125
1851	£8	£15	£40	£145
1852	£8	£15	£40	£110
1853	£8	£18	£50	£125
1853 proof	*	*	*	£550
1868 bronze-proof	*	*	*	£400
1868 copper-nickel proof	*	*	*	£475

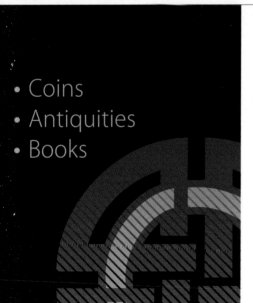

MAUNDY SETS

These sets are given out by the monarch each year on Maundy Thursday, the day before Good Friday.

The number of recipients and the amount they receive matches the sovereign's age that year.

Maundy coins are newly minted every year, and are legal tender.

The ceremony has been known in England since about 600. The first recorded occasion when the sovereign distributed alms at a Maundy service was in 1210, when King John did so at Knaresborough.

Extremely Fine prices are for evenly matched sets.

CHARLES II	F	VF	EF
Undated	£165	£285	£600
1670	£150	£265	£575
1671	£150	£265	£550
1672	£150	£265	£550
1673	£150	£265	£550
1674	£150	£265	£550
1675	£150	£265	£550
1676	£150	£265	£575
1677	£150	£265	£575
1678	£165	£285	£600
1679	£150	£265	£550
1680	£150	£265	£550
1681	£150	£265	£575
1682	£150	£265	£550
1683	£150	£265	£550
1684	£150	£300	£650

JAMES II	F	VF	EF
1686	£185	£365	£750
1687	£185	£365	£750
1688	£185	£365	£750

WILLIAM AND MARY	F	VF	EF
1689	£475	£1250	*
1691	£145	£295	£750
1692	£150	£295	£750
1693	£150	£295	£750
1694	£145	£285	£650

WILLIAM III	F	VF	EF
1698	£150	£325	£650
1699	£150	£325	£675
1700	£150	£325	£675
1701	£150	£250	£650

ANNE	F	VF	EF
1703	£150	£250	£625
1705	£150	£275	£600
1706	£150	£235	£575
1708	£150	£250	£575
1709	£150	£235	£575
1710	£195	£275	£750
1713	£150	£250	£575

GEORGE I	F	VF	EF
1723	£140	£235	£565
1727	£140	£235	£565

GEORGE II	F	VF	EF
1729	£125	£225	£465
1731	£125	£225	£450
1732	£125	£225	£450
1735	£125	£225	£365
1737	£125	£225	£365
1739	£125	£225	£365
1740	£125	£225	£400
1743	£125	£225	£425
1746	£125	£225	£400
1760	£125	£225	£425

GEORGE III		F	VF	EF
1763		*	£150	£300
1766		*	£150	£300
1772		*	£150	£300
1780		*	£150	£300
1784		*	£150	£300
1786		*	£150	£300
1792 wire type		*	£225	£450
1795		*	£150	£300
1800		*	£150	£300
	Fair	F	VF	EF
1817	*	£85	£245	£385
1818	*	£85	£245	£400
1820	*	£65	£185	£325

GEORGE IV	Fair	F	VF	EF
1822	*	*	£225	£350
1823	*	*	£225	£350
1824	*	*	£225	£350
1825	*	*	£225	£350
1826	*	*	£225	£350
1827	*	*	£225	£350
1828	*	*	£225	£350
1829	*	*	£225	£350
1830	*	*	£225	£350

George III Maundy set, 1818

WILLIAM IV	Fair	F	VF	EF
1831	*	*	£225	£365
1831 proof	*	*	*	£600
1831 gold proof	*	*	*	£30000
1832	*	*	£195	£325
1832	*	*	£195	£325
1834	*	*	£195	£325
1835	*	*	£195	£325
1836	*	*	£195	£325
1837	*	*	£225	£375

Maundy Groat 1831

VICTORIA	EF	Unc
1838	£200	£450
1839	£190	£400
1839 proof	*	£775
1840	£225	£465
1841	£150	£365
1842	£190	£400
1843	£190	£400
1844	£225	£465
1845	£185	£385
1846	£250	£575
1847	£225	£500
1848	£225	£465
1849	£225	£465
1850	£200	£450
1851	£190	£400
1852	£225	£465
1853	£225	£465
1853 proof	*	£850
1854	£190	£400
1855	£190	£400
1856	£175	£300
1857	£175	£300
1858	£160	£275
1859	£160	£275
1860	£160	£275
1861	£160	£275
1862	£160	£275
1863	£160	£275
1864	£160	£275
1865	£160	£275
1866	£160	£275
1867	£160	£275
1868	£160	£275
1869	£160	£275
1870	£160	£275
1871	£150	£265
1872	£150	£265
1873	£150	£265
1874	£150	£265

1875	£150	£265
1876	£150	£265
1877	£150	£265
1878	£150	£275
1879	£150	£265
1880	£150	£265
1881	£150	£265
1882	£150	£265
1883	£150	£265
1884	£150	£265
1885	£150	£265
1886	£150	£265
1887	£150	£285
1888 JH	£110	£150
1889	£110	£150
1890	£110	£150
1891	£110	£150
1892	£110	£150
1893 OH	£90	£130
1894	£90	£135
1895	£90	£135
1896	£90	£135
1897	£90	£135
1898	£90	£135
1899	£90	£135
1900	£90	£135
1901	£90	£135

EDWARD VIII		
1902	£80	£110
1902 matt proof	*	£125
1903-08	£85	£120
1909-10	£100	£165

GEORGE V		
1911	£90	£125
1911 proof	*	£135
1912-36	£90	£140

GEORGE VI		
1937	£90	£120
1938-52	£90	£140

ELIZABETH II		
1953	*	£650
1954-69	*	£130
1970-99	*	£130
2000	*	£130
2001	*	£130
2002	*	£130
2002 gold from set	*	£1650
2003	*	£130
2004	*	£130
2005	*	£130
2006	*	£130
2007	*	£130
2008	*	£130
2009	*	£135
2010	*	£165
2011	*	£200

DECIMAL COINAGE

■ BRITANNIAS

A United Kingdom gold bullion coin, introduced in the autumn of 1987, which contains one ounce of 22ct gold and has a face value of £100. There are also ½ ounce, ¼ ounce and 1/10 ounce versions, with face values of £50, £25 and £10 respectively. The ½ and ¼ oz are issued only in sets. All are legal tender.

The coins bear a portrait of the Queen on the obverse and the figure of Britannia on the reverse.

BV indicates bullion value, at the time of going to press gold is approximately £1000 per troy ounce and platinum is approximately £1100 per troy ounce.

1987-2005 1oz, proof	*
1987-2005 1/10 oz, proof	*
1987-2005 ½ oz, proof	*
1987-2005 ¼ oz, proof	*

To commemorate the 10th anniversary of the first Britannia issue, new reverse designs were introduced for the gold coins. A series of four silver coins with denominations from £2 to 20 pence was issued as well. The silver coins were issued only in proof condition in 1997.

1997 1oz, ¼oz and 1/10oz issued individually; all coins issued in 4-coin sets
1997 1oz, ¼ oz silver coins issued individually; all coins issued in 4-coin sets
1998 gold and silver coins issued with new portrait of HM the Queen and first reverse design
2001 new reverse designs introduced

■ FIVE POUNDS

Crown sized.

1990 Queen Mother's 90th birthday, gold, proof	BV
1990 silver, proof	£48
1990 cu-ni, BU	£6
1990 cu-ni, specimen	£7
1993 40th Anniversary of the Coronation, gold, proof	BV
1993 silver, proof	£28
1993 cu-ni, specimen	£8
1993 cu-ni, BU	£5
1993 cu-ni, proof, originally issued in a Royal Mint set	£8
1996 Queen's 70th Birthday, gold, proof	BV
1996 silver, proof	£40
1996 cu-ni, BU	£7
1996 cu-ni, proof, originally issued in a Royal Mint set	£7
1996 cu-ni, specimen	£8
1997 Golden Wedding, gold, proof	BV
1997 silver, proof	£40
1997 cu-ni, BU	£7
1997 cu-ni, proof, originally issued in a Royal Mint set	£7

1997 cu-ni, specimen	£9
1998 Prince Charles 50th Birthday, gold, proof	BV
1998 silver, proof	£55
1998 cu-ni, BU	£7
1998 cu-ni, proof, originally issued in a Royal Mint set	£10
1998 cu-ni, specimen	£8
1999 Diana Memorial, gold, proof	BV
1999 silver, proof	£47
1999 cu-ni, proof, originally issued in a Royal Mint set	£10
1999 cu-ni, BU	£7
1999 cu-ni, specimen	£8
1999 Millennium, gold, proof	BV
1999 silver, proof	£40
1999 cu-ni, BU	£6
1999 cu-ni, specimen	£8
2000 gold, proof	BV
2000 silver with 22 carat gold, proof	£40
2000 cu-ni, BU	£6
2000 cu-ni, specimen	£13
2000 cu-ni, proof, originally issued in a Royal Mint set	£12
2000 cu-ni, specimen, Dome mintmark	£15
2000 silver, proof	£48
2000 Queen Mother commemorative, gold, proof	BV
2000 silver, proof	£45
2000 silver piedfort	£55
2000 cu-ni, BU	£6
2000 cu-ni, proof, originally issued in a Royal Mint set	£7
2001 Victorian Era anniversary, gold, proof	BV
2001 gold, proof with reverse frosting	BV
2001 silver, proof	£40
2001 silver, proof with reverse frosting	£85
2001 cu-ni, BU	£6
2001 cu-ni, proof, originally issued in a Royal Mint set	£10
2001 cu-ni, specimen	£8
2002 Golden Jubilee, gold proof	BV
2002 silver, proof	£45
2002 cu-ni, BU	£5
2002 cu-ni, proof, originally issued in a Royal Mint set	£9
2002 cu-ni, specimen	£8
2002 Queen Mother memorial, gold, proof	BV
2002 silver, proof	£45
2002 cu-ni, BU	£7
2002 cu-ni proof, originally issued in a Royal Mint set	£12
2003 Coronation commemorative, gold proof	BV
2003 silver, proof	£45
2003 cu-ni, BU	£6
2003 cu-ni, proof, originally issued in a Royal Mint set	£8
2003 cu-ni, specimen	£9
2004 Entente Cordiale, gold, proof	BV
2004 platinum, piedfort, proof	BV
2004 silver piedfort, proof	£110
2004 silver, proof	£45
2004 Entente Cordiale, cu-ni, proof	£14
2004 specimen	£10
2004 BU	£5
2005 Trafalgar, gold, proof	BV
2005 silver piedfort, proof	£55
2005 silver, proof	£40
2005 cu-ni, proof, originally issued in a Royal Mint set	£8
2005 specimen	£8

2005 BU	£5
2005 Nelson, gold, proof	BV
2005 platinum, piedfort, proof	BV
2005 silver piedfort, proof	£55
2005 silver, proof	£40
2005 cu-ni, proof, originally issued in a Royal Mint set	£8
2005 BU	£5
2005 specimen	£8
2006 Queen's 80th Birthday, gold, proof	BV
2006 platinum, piedfort, proof	BV
2006 silver piedfort, proof	£55
2006 silver, proof	£40
2006 cu-ni, proof, originally issued in a Royal Mint set	£8
2006 specimen	£8
2006 BU	£5
2007 Diamond Wedding, gold, proof	BV
2007 silver piedfort, proof	£85
2007 silver, proof	£45
2007 cu-ni, proof, originally issued in a Royal Mint set	£12
2008 Elizabeth I, platinum, piedfort, proof	BV
2008 gold, proof	BV
2008 silver piedfort, proof	£85
2008 silver, proof	£45
2008 BU	£5
2009 Henry VIII, gold, proof	BV
2009 silver piedfort, proof	£99
2009 silver, proof	£54
2009 Countdown to London gold proof	BV
2009 silver piedfort, proof	£99
2010 Restoration of Monarchy gold proof	BV
2010 silver, proof	£55
2010 Countdown to London silver, piedforf, proof	£99
2010 silver, proof	£55
2010 BU	£5

■ TWO POUNDS

1986 Commonwealth Games, proof gold	BV
1986 silver, proof	£25
1986 silver unc	£12
1986 proof, nickel brass, originally issued in a Royal Mint set	£5
1986 specimen	£4
1986 unc	£3
1989 Bill of Rights, silver piedfort, proof, originally issued in a Royal Mint set	£45
1989 silver, proof	£25
1989 proof, nickel brass, originally issued in a Royal Mint set	£7
1989 specimen	£4
1989 unc	£3
1989 Claim of Rights, silver piedfort proof, originally issued in a Royal Mint set	£45
1989 silver, proof	£25
1989 proof, nickel brass, originally issued in a Royal Mint set	£7
1989 specimen	£4
1989 unc	£3

1994 Bank of England, gold, proof	BV
1994 gold 'mule', proof	BV
1994 silver piedfort, proof	£45
1994 silver, proof	£25
1994 proof, nickel brass, originally issued in a Royal Mint set	£5
1994 specimen	£4
1994 in folder, BU	£3
1995 50th Anniversary of end of Second World War, gold, proof	BV
1995 silver piedfort, proof	£45
1995 silver, proof	£25
1995 proof, nickel brass, originally issued in a Royal Mint set	£5
1995 specimen	£4
1995 BU	£3
1995 50th Anniversary of United Nations, gold, proof	BV
1995 silver piedfort, proof	£45
1995 silver, proof	£25
1995 specimen	£4
1995 BU	£3
1996 European Football, gold, proof	BV
1996 silver piedfort, proof	£45
1996 silver, proof	£25
1996 proof, nickel brass, originally issued in a Royal Mint set	£5
1996 specimen	£4
1996 BU	£3
1997 Iron Age, bimetal, gold, proof	BV
1997 silver piedfort, proof	£45
1997 silver, proof	£25
1997 proof, originally issued in a Royal Mint set	£5
1997 specimen	£4
1997 BU	£3
1997 Britannia chariot, proof 1 oz fine silver	£35
1998 bimetal, silver, proof	£27
1998 silver piedfort	£40
1998 proof, originally issued in a Royal Mint set	£6
1998 in folder, BU	£6
1998 Britannia standing, proof, 1 oz fine silver	£15
1998 unc	£10
1999 Rugby World Cup, gold, proof	BV
1999 silver piedfort, proof	£30
1999 silver, proof	£150
1999 proof, originally issued in a Royal Mint set	£5
1999 BU	£3
2000 bimetal, silver, proof, originally issued in a Royal Mint set	£20
2000 proof, originally issued in a Royal Mint set	£5
2000 Britannia standing, unc, 1 oz fine silver	£10
2001 Marconi commemorative, gold, proof	BV
2001 silver piedfort, proof	£35
2001 silver, proof	£25
2001 with reverse frosting, silver, proof	£40
2001 proof, originally issued in a Royal Mint set	£7
2001 specimen	£5
2001 BU	£3
2002 Iron Age, gold proof	BV
2002 Commonwealth Games, gold,	

proof, four different reverses	*
2002 Commonwealth Games,	
silver, proof, four different reverses	*
2002 Commonwealth Games,	
piedfort, four different reverses	*
2002 Commonwealth Games, BU,	
four different reverses	*
2002 Britannia standing, unc,	
1 oz fine silver	£10
2003 DNA gold bi-metal proof	BV
2003 silver piedfort, proof	£40
2003 silver, proof	£20
2003 specimen	£5
2003 proof, originally issued in a Royal Mint set	£6
2003 BU	£3
2003 Britannia helmeted, silver, proof	£25
2003 silver	£12
2004 Locomotive, gold, proof	BV
2004 silver piedfort, proof	£40
2004 silver, proof	£20
2004 BU, silver	£12
2004 proof, originally issued in a Royal Mail set	£6
2004 specimen	£6
2004 BU	£3
2004 Britannia standing, proof, 1 oz fine silver	£25
2004 unc	£15
2005 400th Gunpowder Plot gold, proof	BV
2005 silver piedfort, proof	£50
2005 silver, proof	£30
2005 proof, originally issued in a Royal Mint set	£6
2005 specimen	£5
2005 BU	£3
2005 World War II, gold proof	BV
2005 silver, proof, piedfort	£45
2005 silver, proof	£25
2005 specimen	£5
2005 BU	£3
2005 Britannia seated, silver, proof	£30
2005 silver, unc	£14
2006 Brunel the Man, gold, proof	BV
2006 silver, proof, piedfort	£40
2006 silver, proof	£25
2006 proof, originally issued	
in a Royal Mint set	£7
2006 specimen	£8
2006 BU	£3
2006 Britannia seated, silver, proof	£30
2007 Abolition of the Slave Trade,	
gold, proof	BV
2007 silver, proof	£29
2007 Act of Union, silver, proof	£29
2007 Britannia, silver	£17
2008 Olympiad London, gold, proof	BV
2008 silver, proof, piedfort	£49
2008 silver, proof	£30
2008 specimen	£8
2009 BU	face
2009 Burns, cu-ni, BU	£3
2010 BU	face
2010 Nightingale, cu-ni, BU	£3

■ ONE POUND

1983	£3
1983 specimen	£4
1983 proof, originally issued in a Royal Mint set	£4
1983 silver, proof	£35
1983 silver, proof, piedfort	£125
1984 Scottish reverse	£3
1984 specimen	£4
1984 proof, originally issued in a Royal Mint set	£4
1984 silver, proof	£20
1984 silver, proof, piedfort	£40
1985 new portrait, Welsh reverse	£4
1985 specimen	£4
1985 proof, originally issued in a Royal Mint set	£4
1985 silver, proof	£20
1985 silver, proof, piedfort	£50
1986 Northern Ireland reverse	£5
1986 specimen	£4
1986 proof, originally issued in a Royal Mint set	£4
1986 silver, proof	£20
1986 silver, proof, piedfort	£4
1987 English reverse	£4
1987 specimen	£4
1987 proof, originally issued in a Royal Mint set	£4
1987 silver, proof	£20
1987 silver, proof, piedfort	£45
1988 Royal Arms reverse	£5
1987 specimen	£4
1987 proof, originally issued in a Royal Mint set	£4
1987 silver, proof	£20
1987 silver, proof, piedfort	£45
1989 Scottish reverse as 1984	£4
1987 proof, originally issued in a Royal Mint set	£4
1987 silver, proof	£20
1990 Welsh reverse as 1985	£5
1990 proof, originally issued in a Royal Mint set	£4
1990 silver, proof	£30
1991 Northern Ireland reverse as 1986	£4
1991 proof, originally issued in a Royal Mint set	£4
1991 silver, proof	£25
1992 English reverse as 1987	£4
1987 proof, originally issued in a Royal Mint set	£4
1987 silver, proof	£20
1993 Royal coat of arms reverse as 1983	£3
1993 proof, originally issued in a Royal Mint set	£4
1993 silver, proof	£20
1993 silver, proof, piedfort	£50
1994 Scottish Lion	£4
1994 specimen	£4
1994 proof, originally issued in a Royal Mint set	£5
1984 silver, proof	£20
1994 silver, proof, piedfort	£45
1995 Welsh dragon	£4
1995 specimen, English version	£4
1995 specimen, Welsh version	£7
1995 proof, originally issued in a Royal Mint set	£5
1985 silver, proof	£20
1995 silver, proof, piedfort	£45
1996 Northern Ireland Celtic Ring	£4

1996 specimen	£4
1996 proof, originally issued in a Royal Mint set	£5
1985 silver, proof	£20
1995 silver, proof, piedfort	£40
1997 English Lions	£5
1997 specimen	£4
1997 proof, originally issued in a Royal Mint set	£5
1997 silver, proof	£20
1997 silver, proof, piedfort	£40
1998 Royal coat of arms reverse as 1983	£4
1998 proof, originally issued in a Royal Mint set	£5
1998 silver, proof	£20
1998 silver, proof, piedfort	£35
1999 Scottish Lion reverse as 1984	£3
1999 specimen	£4
1999 proof, originally issued in a Royal Mint set	£5
1999 silver, proof	£20
1999 with reverse frosting	£30
1999 silver, proof, piedfort	£35
2000 Welsh Dragon reverse as 1995	£3
2000 proof, originally issued in a Royal Mint set	£5
2000 silver, proof	£20
2000 silver, proof, with reverse frosting	£30
2000 silver, proof, piedfort	£35
2001 Northern Ireland reverse as 1996	£4
2001 proof, originally issued in a Royal Mint set	£5
2001 silver, proof	£20
2001 silver, proof, with reverse frosting	£45
2001 silver, proof, piedfort	£37
2002 English design, reverse as 1997	£4
2002 gold proof, originally issued in a Royal Mint set	£625
2002 proof, originally issued in a Royal Mint set	£5
2002 silver, proof	£20
2002 silver, proof, with reverse frosting	£40
2002 silver, proof, piedfort	£39
2003 Royal Arms	£45
2003 proof, originally issued in a Royal Mint set	£5
2003 silver, proof	£20
2003 silver, proof, piedfort	£39
2003 Forth Rail Bridge, 'pattern', silver, proof, originally issued in a Royal Mint set	*
2003 gold proof, originally issued in a Royal Mint set	£625
2003 Menai Bridge, 'pattern', silver, proof, originally issued in a Royal Mint set	*
2003 gold proof, originally issued in a Royal Mint set	£625
2003 Egyptian Arch, 'pattern', silver, proof, originally issued in a Royal Mint set	*
2003 gold proof, originally issued in a Royal Mint set	£625
2003 Millennium Bridge, 'pattern', silver, proof, originally issued in a Royal Mint set	*
2003 gold proof, originally issued in a Royal Mint set	£625
2004 Dragon, 'pattern', silver, proof, originally issued in a Royal Mint set	*
2004 gold proof, originally issued in a Royal Mint set	£625
2004 Unicorn, 'pattern', silver, proof, originally issued in a Royal Mint set	*
2004 gold proof, originally issued in a Royal Mint set	£625
2004 Stag, 'pattern', silver, proof, originally issued in a Royal Mint set	*
2004 gold proof, originally issued in a Royal Mint set	£625

2004 Lion, 'pattern', silver, proof, originally issued in a Royal Mint set	*
2004 gold proof, originally issued in a Royal Mint set	£625
2004 Forth Rail Bridge	£625
2004 specimen	£5
2004 proof, originally issued in a Royal Mint set	£5
2004 silver, proof	£20
2004 silver, proof, piedfort	£39
2004 gold, proof	£625
2005 Menai Bridge	£4
2005 specimen	£5
2005 proof, originally issued in a Royal Mint set	£5
2005 silver, proof	£20
2005 silver, proof, piedfort	£39
2005 gold, proof	£625
2006 Egyptian Arch	£4
2006 specimen	£5
2006 proof, originally issued in a Royal Mint set	£7
2006 silver, proof	£25
2006 silver, proof, piedfort	£40
2006 gold, proof	£625
2007 Forth, Menai, Egyptian Arch and Millennium Bridges, gold proof, originally issued in a Royal Mint set	£625
2007 silver, proof, originally issued in a Royal Mint set	£625
2007 Millennium Bridge, BU	£7
2008 Royal Arms, gold, proof	BV
2008 silver, proof	£30
2009 Shoulders of Giants, proof	£17
2009 BU	£5
2009 Darwin, proof	£23
2009 BU	£5
2009 Burns, proof	£21
2009 BU	£5
2010 Nightingale, proof	£23
2010 BU	£5
2010 Shoulders of Giants, proof	£18
2010 BU	£5

Note that the edge inscriptions on £2 and £1 appear either upright or inverted in relation to the obverse.

■ FIFTY PENCE

1969 unc	£2
1970 unc	£3
1971 proof, originally issued in a Royal Mint set	£3
1972 proof, originally issued in a Royal Mint set	£4
1973 EEC proof, originally issued in a Royal Mint set	£3
1973 silver, proof VIP	ext. rare
1973 unc	£1
1974 proof, originally issued in a Royal Mint set	£3
1975 proof, originally issued in a Royal Mint set	£3
1976 proof, originally issued in a Royal Mint set	£2
1976 unc	£1
1977 proof, originally issued in a Royal Mint set	£2
1977 unc	£1
1978 proof	£2
1978 unc	£1
1979 proof, originally issued in a Royal Mint set	£2

1979 unc	£1
1980 proof, originally issued in a Royal Mint set	£2
1980 unc	£1
1981 proof, originally issued in a Royal Mint set	£2
1981 unc	£1
1982 proof, originally issued in a Royal Mint set	£2
1982 unc	£1
1983 proof, originally issued in a Royal Mint set	£2
1983 unc	£1
1984 proof, originally issued in a Royal Mint set	£2
1984 unc	£3
1985 proof, originally issued in a Royal Mint set	£2
1985 unc	£4
1986 proof, originally issued in a Royal Mint set	£2
1986 unc	£2
1987 proof, originally issued in a Royal Mint set	£3
1987 unc	£2
1988 proof, originally issued in a Royal Mint set	£3
1988 unc	£2
1989 proof, originally issued in a Royal Mint set	£2
1989 unc	£3
1990 proof, originally issued in a Royal Mint set	£4
1990 unc	£3
1991 proof, originally issued in a Royal Mint set	£4
1991 unc	£2
1992 proof	£4
1992 unc	£2
1992 European Community	£5
1992 specimen	£2
1992 proof, originally issued in a Royal Mint set	£7
1992 silver, proof	£20
1992 silver, proof, piedfort	£750
1992 gold, proof	BV
1993 proof	£3
1993 unc	£3
1994 Normandy Landings	£2
1994 specimen	£2
1994 proof, originally issued in a Royal Mint set	£4
1994 silver, proof	£25
1994 silver, proof, piedfort	£40
1994 gold, proof	£750
1995 proof	£3
1995 unc	£2
1996 proof	£3
1996 unc	£2
1996 silver, proof	£15
1997 unc	£2
1997 proof	£3
1997 silver, proof	£2
1997 new size (27.3mm diameter), unc	£2
1997 proof, originally issued in a Royal Mint set	£4
1997 silver, proof	£18
1997 silver, proof, piedfort	£35
1998 proof, originally issued in a Royal Mint set	£2
1998 unc	£1
1998 European Presidency	£2
1998 specimen	£2
1998 silver, proof	£20
1998 silver, proof, piedfort	£40
1998 gold, proof	£600

1998 NHS, unc	£2
1998 proof, originally issued in a Royal Mint set	£2
1998 silver, proof	£25
1998 silver piedfort	£45
1998 gold, proof	£600
1999 proof, originally issued in a Royal Mint set	£2
1999 unc	face
2000 proof, originally issued in a Royal Mint set	£2
2000 unc	face
2000 silver, proof	£15
2000 Library Commemorative, unc	£2
2000 specimen	£5
2000 proof, originally issued in a Royal Mint set	£2
2000 silver, proof	£25
2000 silver, proof, piedfort	£47
2000 gold, proof	£650
2002 gold proof, originally issued in a Royal Mint set	£650
2003 Suffragette, unc	£1
2003 proof, originally issued in a Royal Mint set	£4
2003 specimen	£3
2003 silver, proof	£20
2003 silver, proof, piedfort	£40
2003 gold, proof	£600
2004 Roger Bannister, unc	£1
2004 specimen	£4
2004 proof, originally issued in a Royal Mint set	£4
2004 silver, proof	£20
2004 silver, proof piedfort	£25
2005 Samuel Johnson, unc	£1
2005 proof, originally issued in a Royal Mint set	£4
2005 silver, proof	£4
2005 silver, proof, piedfort	£40
2005 gold proof	£600
2006 Victoria Cross, unc	£1
2006 proof, originally issued in a Royal Mint set	£4
2006 specimen	£3
2006 silver, proof	£20
2006 silver, proof, piedfort	£40
2006 gold, proof	£600
2007 Scouting Centenary, gold, proof	£600
2007 silver, proof	£39
2007 silver piedfort, proof	£79
2008 issued in sets only	*
2009 gold, proof	£700
2009 silver, proof	£40
2009 unc	£1
2010 England, gold, proof	£700
2010 silver piedfort, proof	£54
2010 silver, proof	£32
2010 Northern Ireland, gold, proof	£700
2010 silver piedfort, proof	£54
2010 silver, proof	£32
2010 Shield, silver proof	£29

■ TWENTY-FIVE PENCE (crown)

1972 Silver Wedding	£1
1972 proof, originally issued in a Royal Mint set	£4
1972 silver, proof	£20

1977 Jubilee	£1
1977 proof, originally issued in a Royal Mint set	£4
1977 specimen	£2
1977 silver, proof	£20
1980 Queen Mother 80th Birthday	£1
1980 specimen	£2
1980 silver, proof	£40
1981 Royal Wedding	£1
1981 specimen	£3
1981 silver, proof	£25

■ TWENTY PENCE

1982-1997	face
1982 proof, originally issued in a Royal Mint set	£2
1982 silver, proof, piedfort	£40
1983-1997 proof, originally issued in a Royal Mint set	£3
1998-2008	face
1998-2008 proof, originally issued in a Royal Mint set	£3
2000 silver, proof, originally issued in a Royal Mint set	*
2002 gold proof, originally issued in a Royal Mint set	£275
2006-2010 silver, proof, originally issued in a Royal Mint set	*
2009 error, obverse of 2008, no date	£45

■ TEN PENCE

1968-1981 new pence	face
1972 & 1981 proof, originally issued in a Royal Mint set	£2
1982-1984 Pence, unc & proof, originally issued in a Royal Mint set	£2
1985-1992 unc & proof, originally issued in a Royal Mint set	£2
1992 silver, proof, originally issued in a Royal Mint set	£10
1992-1997 new size: 24.5mm diameter, 1993 & 1994 issued in sets only	face
1992-1997 proof, originally issued in a Royal Mint set	£2
1992 silver, proof	£10
1992 silver, proof, piedfort	£20
1996 silver, proof	£10
1998-2007, 1998, 1999 & 2007 issued in sets only	face
1998-2010 proof, originally issued in a Royal Mint set	£2
2002 gold proof, originally issued in a Royal Mint set	£225
2006-2010 silver, proof, originally issued in a Royal Mint set	*

■ FIVE PENCE

1968-81, 1972-74, 1976 & 1981 issued in sets only	£0.25
1971-1981 proof, originally issued in a Royal Mint set	£1
1982-1984 proof, unc, originally issued in a Royal Mint set	£1
1985-1990, 1985, 1996 & 1990 issued in sets only	face
1985-1990 proof, originally issued in a Royal Mint set	£2
1990-1997	face
1990-1997 proof, originally issued in a Royal Mint set	£2

1990 silver, proof, originally issued in a Royal Mint set	£10
1990 piedfort	£20
1996 silver, proof	£10
1998-2008, 2007-8 issued in sets only	face
1998-2010 proof, originally issued in a Royal Mint set	£3
2000 silver, proof	*
2002 gold proof, originally issued in a Royal Mint set	£175
2006-2010 silver, proof	*

■ TWO PENCE

1971-1981, 1972 & 1974 issued in sets only	face
1971-1981 proof, originally issued in a Royal Mint set	£1
1982-1984 new reverse	face
1983, mule, old reverse issued in sets	ext. rare
1982-1984 proof, originally issued in a Royal Mint set	£1
1985-1992 1992 issued in sets only	face
1985-1992 proof, originally issued in a Royal Mint set	£1
1992-1997	face
1993-1997 proof, originally issued in a Royal Mint set	£1
1996 silver, proof, originally issued in a Royal Mint set	£10
2002 gold proof. originally issued in a Royal Mint set	£250
1998-2010	face
1998-2010 proof, originally issued in a Royal Mint set	£1

■ ONE PENNY

1971-1981, 1972 issued in sets only	face
1971-1981 proof, originally issued in a Royal Mint set	£1
1982-1984 new reverse, proof, unc, originally issued in a Royal Mint set	£1
1985-1992, 1992 issued in sets only	face
1985-1992 proof, originally issued in a Royal Mint set	£1
1992-1997	face
1993-1997 proof, originally issued in a Royal Mint set	£1
1996 silver, proof, originally issued in a Royal Mint set	£10
2002 gold proof, originally issued in a Royal Mint set	£175
1998-2010	face
1998-2010 proof, originally issued in a Royal Mint set	£1

■ HALF PENNY

1971-1981	£0.10
1971-1981 proof, originally issued in a Royal Mint set	£1
1982-1984 new reverse	face
1982-1984 proof, originally issued in a Royal Mint set	£1

"THE I.A.P.N. dealer, your guide to the world of numismatics"

"More than one hundred of the world's most respected coin dealers are members of the I.A.P.N. (International Association of Professional Numismatists). I.A.P.N. members offer the collector an exceptional selection of quality material, expert cataloguing, outstanding service, and realistic pricing. The I.A.P.N. also maintain the International Bureau for the Suppression of Counterfeit Coins (I.B.S.C.C.) which, for a fee can provide expert opinions on the authenticity of coin submitted to it. A booklet listing the name, address and specialities of all I.A.P.N. members is available without charge by writing to the I.A.P.N. Secretariat". Jean-Luc Van der Schueren, 14, Rue de la Bourse, B-1000, Bruxelles.
Tel: +32-2-513 3400   Fax: +32-2-512 2528   E-mail: iapnsecret@compuserve.com   Web site: http://www.iapn-coins.org

AUSTRALIA
DOWNIES COINS Pty Ltd, PO Box 888, Abbotsford, VIC. 3067
NOBLE NUMISMATICS Pty Ltd, 169 Macquarie Street, SYDNEY NSW 2000

AUSTRIA
HERINEK, Gerhard, Josefstädterstrasse 27, A-1082 WIEN
CHRISTINE MOZELT NUMISMATIK, Postfach 19, A-1043 WIEN

BELGIUM
FRANCESCHI & Fils, B, 10, Rue Croix-de-Fer, B-1000 BRUXELLES
VAN DER SCHUEREN, Jean-Luc, 14, Rue de la Bourse, B-1000 BRUXELLES

CANADA
WEIR LTD., Randy, PO Box 64577, UNIONVILLE, Ontario, L3R 0M9

EGYPT
BAJOCCHI JEWELLERS, 45 Abdel Khalek Sarwat Street, 11511 CAIRO

FRANCE
BOURGEY, Sabine, 7, Rue Drouot, F-75009 PARIS
BURGAN NUMISMATIQUE—Maison Florange, 8, Rue du 4 Septembre, F-75002, PARIS
LA PARPAIOLLE, 10 rue Bernex – B. P. 30006, F-13191, Cedex 20, MARSEILLE
MAISON PLATT SA, 49, Rue de Richelieu, F-75001, PARIS
NUMISMATIQUE et CHANGE DE PARIS, 3, Rue de la Bourse, F-75002 PARIS
O.G.N., 64, Rue de Richelieu, F-75002 PARIS
POINSIGNON-NUMISMATIQUE, 4, Rue des Francs Bourgeois, F-67000 STRASBOURG
SAIVE NUMISMATIQUE, 18, rue Dupont des Loges, F-57000, METZ
SILBERSTEIN, Claude, Comptoir de Numismatique, 39, Rue Vivienne, F-75002 PARIS
VINCHON-NUMISMATIQUE, 77, Rue de Richelieu, F-75002 PARIS

GERMANY
DILLER, Johannes, Postfach 70 04 29, D-81304 MÜNCHEN
FRITZ RUDOLF KÜNKER GmbH & Co. KG, Gutenbergstrasse 23, D-49076 OSNABRUCK
GORNY & MOSCH, GIESSENER MÜNZHANDLUNG GmbH, Maximiliansplatz 20, D-80333 MÜNCHEN
GERHARD HIRSCH Nachfolger, Promenadeplatz 10/II, D-80333 MÜNCHEN
JACQUIER,Paul-Francis, Honsellstrasse 8, D-77694 KEHL am RHEIN
KAISER MÜNZFACHGESCHAFT, Mittelweg 54, D-60318 FRANKFURT
KRICHELDORF Nachf., H. H. Günter-stalstrasse 16, D-79100 FREIBURG i.Br.
KURPFÄLZISCHE MÜNZENHANDLUNG—KPM, Augusta-Anlage 52, D-68165 MANNHEIM,
LEIPZIGER Münzhandlung und Auktion (Heidrun HOHN), Nikolaistrasse 25, D-04109, LEIPZIG
MANFRED OLDING MÜNZEN-HANDLUNG, Goldbreede 14, D-49078, OSNABRÜCK
MEISTER MÜNZENHANDLUNG, Moltkestrasse 6, D-71634 LUDWIGSBURG
MÜNZEN-UND MEDAILLEN-HANDLUG STUTTGART, Charlottenstrasse 4, D-70182 STUTTGART
NEUMANN GmbH, Ernst, Watteplatz 6, D-89312, GÜNZBURG
NUMISMATIK LANZ, Luitpoldblock-Maximiliansplatz 10, D-80333 MÜNCHEN
PEUS NACHF., Dr. Busso Bornwiesenweg 34, D-60322 FRANKFURT/M,
Münzhandlung RITTER GmbH Postfach 24 01 26, D-40090 DÜSSELDORF
TIETJEN + CO, Spitalerstrasse 30, D-20095 HAMBURG
WESFÄLISCHE AUKTIONSGESELLSCHAFT oHG, Nordring 22, D-59821, ARNSBERG

HUNGARY
NUMISMATICA EREMBOLT, Vörösmarty Tèr 6, HG-1051, BUDAPEST

ITALY
BARANOWSKY s.a.s, Via del Corso 184, I-00187, ROMA
CRIPPA NUMISTMATIQUE s.a.s., Via Cavalieri del S. Sepolcro 10, I-20121 MILANO
DE FALCO, Corso Umberto 24, I-80138 NAPOLI
FALLANI, Via del Babuino 58a, I-00187, ROMA
GIULIO BERNARDI, Casella Postale 560, I-34 121 TRIESTE
PAOLUCCI NUMISMATICA s.a.s., Via San Francesco 154, I-35121 PADOVA
RANIERI Numismatica srl, Sign. Marco Ranieri, I-BOLOGNA
RINALDI & Figlio, O.,Via Cappello 23 (Casa di Giulietta), I-37121 VERONA
VARESI Numismatica s.a.s., Alberto Varesi, Via Robolini 1, I-2-7100, PAVIA

JAPAN
DARUMA INTERNATIONAL GALLERIES, 2-16-32-701, Takanawa, Minato-ku, JP-TOKYO 108-0074
WORLD COINS, 1-15-5, Hamamatsu-cho, Minato-Ku, TOKYO 105-0013

MONACO
EDITIONS VICTOR GADOURY, 57 rue Grimaldi, "Le Panorama", MC-98000

THE NETHERLANDS
LAURENS SCHULMAN BV, Willemslaan 34, NL-1406 LZ BUSSUM
MEVIUS NUMISBOOKS Int. BV Oosteinde 97, NL 7671 VRIEZENVEEN
SCHULMAN BV, PO Box 346, NL-1400 AH BUSSUM
VERSCHOOR MUNTHANDEL, Postbus 5803, 3291 AC STRIJEN
WESTERHOF, Trekpad 38–40, NL–8742 KP, Burgwerd

NORWAY
OSLO MYNTHANDEL AS, Postboks 2745, Solli, N-0204, OSLO

PORTUGAL
NUMISPORTO LDA, Av. Combatentes Grande Cuerra 610 1.J6, P-4200-186 PORTO

SPAIN
AUREO & CALICO, Plaza del Angel 2, E-08002 BARCELONA
CAYON, JANO S.L., Calle Orfila 10, E-28010 MADRID
SEGARA, Plaza Mayor 26, E-28012, MADRID
Jesús VICO S.A., Jorge Juan n-83, Duplicado, E - 28009 MADRID

SWEDEN
NORDLINDS MYNTHANDEL AB, ULF, Karlavagen 46, PO Box 5132, S-102 43 STOCKHOLM

SWITZERLAND
ADOLPH HESS A. G Postfach 7070, CH-8023, ZÜRICH
HESS—DIVO AG, Ulf Künker, Postfach 7070, CH-8023, ZÜRICH
LHS NUMISMATIK, Post-fach 2553, CH - 8022, ZÜRICH
NUMISMATICA ARS CLASSICA AG, Postfach 2655, CH-8022 ZÜRICH
NUMISMATICA GENEVENSIS SA, 1 Rond-point de Plainpalais, CH-1205 GENEVE

THAILAND
HOUSE OF THE GOLDEN COIN, 193/119 Moo 10, South Pattaya Road, Nongprue Banglamung, CHONBURI 20230

UNITED KINGDOM
BALDWIN & SONS LTD., A.H., 11 Adelphi Terrace, LONDON WC2N 6BJ
PAUL DAVIES LTD, PO Box 17, ILKLEY, West Yorkshire LS29 8TZ
DIX NOONAN WEBB, 16 Bolton Street, Piccadilly, LONDON W1J 8BQ
CHRISTOPHER EIMER, PO Box 352, LONDON NW11 7RF
FORMAT OF BIRMINGHAM LTD Burlington Court, 18 Lower Temple Street, BIRMINGHAM B2 4JD
KNIGHTSBRIDGE COINS, 43 Duke Street. St. James's, LONDON SW1Y 6DD
LUBBOCK & SON LTD, PO Box 35732, LONDON, W14 7WB
RASMUSSEN Mark, PO Box 42, BETCHWORTH RH3 7YR
RUDD , Chris, PO Box 222. Aylsham, NORFOLK NR11 6TY
SAVILLE, Douglas, Chiltern Thameside, 37c St Peters Avenue, Caversham, READING RG4 7DH
SPINK & SON LTD, 69, Southampton Row, Bloomsbury, LONDON WC1B 4ET
WILKES, Tim, PO Box 150, Battle, TN33 0FA

UNITED STATES OF AMERICA
BASOK, Alexander, 1954 First Street #186, HIGHLAND PARK, IL 60035
BERK, LTD., 31 North Clark Street, CHICAGO, IL. 60602
BULLOWA, C.E. COINHUNTER, Suite 2112, 1616 Walnut Street, PHILADELPHIA, PA 19103
CENDERLIND Tom, P. O. BOX 1963, PORTLAND, OR 97207
CLASSICAL NUMISMATIC GROUP INC, PO Box 479, LANCASTER, PA 17608
COIN AND CURRENCY INSTITUTE INC, PO Box 1057, CLIFTON, NJ 07014
DAVISSON'S LTD, COLD SPRING, MN 56320-1050
DUNIGAN, Mike, 5332 Birchman, Fort Worth, TX 76107
FREEMAN & SEAR, PO Box 641352, LOS ANGELES, CA 90064-6352
FROSETH INC., K.M., PO Box 23116, MINNEAPOLIS, MN 55423
GILLIO INC. - GOLDMÜNZEN INTERNATIONAL 8 West Figueroa Street, SANTA BARBARA, CA. 93101
HARVEY, Stephen, PO Box 3778, BEVERLEY HILLS, CA 90212
JENCEK, John, 205 De Anza Blvd. No. 119, SAN MATEO, CA 94402
KERN, Jonathan K. Co., 441, S. Ashland Avenue, LEXINGTON, KY 40502-2114
KOLBE, George Frederick, PO Drawer 3100, CRESTLINE, CA 92325-3100
KOVACS, Frank L., PO Box 7150, CORTE MADERA, CA 94976
KREINDLER, B&H, 236 Altessa Blvd, MELVILLE, NY 11747
MALTER GALLERIES Inc., 17003 Ventura Blvd., ENCINO, CA 91316
MARGOLIS, Richard, PO Box 2054, TEANECK, NJ 07666
DMITRY MARKOV COINS & MEDALS, PO Box 950, NEW YORK, NY 10272
MILCAREK, Dr. Ron, PO Box 1028, GREENFIELD, MA 01302
PEGASI Numismatics, PO. Box 131040 ANN ARBOR, MI. 48113
PONTERIO & ASSOCIATES, Inc, 1818 Robinson Ave., SAN DIEGO, CA 92103
RARCOA INC, 6262 South Route 83, WILLOWBROOK, IL 60514
WILLIAM M. ROSENBLUM RARE COINS, PO Box 785, LITTLETON, CO. 80160-0785
STEPHENS Inc., Karl, PO Box 3038, FALLBROOK, CA 92088
SUBAK Inc., 79 West Monroe Street, Room 1008, CHICAGO, IL 60603
TELLER NUMISMATIC ENTERPRISES 16055 Ventura Blvd., Suite 635, ENCINO, CA 91436
WADDELL, Ltd., Edward J., PO Box 3759, FREDERICK, MD 21705-3759
WORLD-WIDE COINS OF CALIFORNIA, PO Box 3684, SANTA ROSA, CA 95402

VENEZUELA
NUMISMATICA GLOBUS, Apartado de Correos 50418, CARACAS 1050-A

~ Visit our website at www.iapn-coins.org ~

PROOF & SPECIMEN SETS

Proof or specimen sets have been issued since 1887 by the Royal Mint. Before then sets were issued privately by the engraver.

Some sets are of currency coins, easily distinguishable from proofs, which have a vastly superior finish. The two 1887 sets frequently come on to the market, hence their place in this list.

The 1953 'plastic' set, though made up of currency coins, is official and was issued in a plastic packet, hence the name. Sets are proof sets unless stated.

	FDC
GEORGE IV	
1826 new issue, £5-farthing (11 coins)	**£45000**
WILLIAM IV	
1831 Coronation, £2-farthing (14 coins)	**£35000**
VICTORIA	
1839 young head, 'Una and the Lion'	
£5, sovereign-farthing (15 coins)	**£75000**
1853 sovereign-half farthing,	
inc Gothic crown (16 coins)	**£45000**
1887 Jubilee head, £5-threepence ('full set': 11 coins)	**£14500**
1887 currency set, unofficial	**£3000**
1887 crown-threepence ('short set': 7 coins)	**£2500**
1887 currency set, unofficial	**£350**
1893 old head, £5-threepence ('full set': 10 coins)	**£15250**
1893 Crown-threepence ('short set': 6 coins)	**£3000**
EDWARD VII	
1902 Coronation, £5-Maundy penny,	
matt proofs (13 coins)	**£4000**
1902 sovereign-Maundy penny, matt proofs (11 coins)	**£1350**
GEORGE V	
1911 Coronation, £5-Maundy penny (12 coins)	**£5250**
1911 sovereign-Maundy penny (10 coins)	**£1600**
1911 halfcrown-Maundy penny (8 coins)	**£725**
1927 new types, crown-threepence (6 coins)	**£525**
GEORGE VI	
1937 Coronation, gold set, £5-half sovereign (4 coins)	**£4750**
1937 silver and bronze set, crown-farthing	
including Maundy money (15 coins)	**£350**
1950 mid-century, halfcrown-farthing (9 coins)	**£150**
1951 Festival of Britain, crown-farthing (10 coins)	**£175**
ELIZABETH II	
1953 Coronation, crown-farthing (10 coins)	**£100**
1953 currency, official, known as the 'plastic' set,	
halfcrown-farthing (9 coins)	**£20**
Specimen decimal set, 1968 10p, 5p;	
1971 2p, 1p, ½p in wallet (5 coins)	**£1**
1970 last £sd coins, (issued 1971-73),	
halfcrown-halfpenny (8 coins)	**£18**
1971 decimal (issued 1973),	

50p, 10p, 5p, 2p, 1p, ½p (6 coins)	**£12**
1972 decimal 50p, Silver Wedding	
25p, 10p, 5p, 2p, 1p, ½p (7 coins)	**£17**
1973-76 decimal, 50p-½p (6 coins)	**£13**
1977 decimal 50p-½p and Jubilee crown (7 coins)	**£13**
1978 decimal, 50p-½p (6 coins)	**£13**
1979 decimal, 50p-½p (6 coins)	**£13**
1980 decimal, 50p-½p (6 coins)	**£13**
1980 gold, £5, £2, sovereign, half sovereign (4 coins)	**BV**
1981 commemorative, £5, sovereign,	
Royal Wedding silver crown, 50p-½p (9 coins)	**£1350**
1981 commemorative, sovereign and	
Royal Wedding silver crown (2 coins)	**£250**
1982 decimal, 50p-½p (6 coins)	**£13**
1982 gold, £5, £2, sovereign, half sovereign (4 coins)	**BV**
1982 decimal, 50p-½p including 20p (7 coins)	**£13**
1982 uncirculated decimal,	
50p-½p including 20p (7 coins)	**£6**
1983 gold, £2, sovereign, half sovereign (3 coins)	**BV**
1983 decimal, £1-½p (8 coins)	**£15**
1983 uncirculated decimal, £1-½p (8 coins)	**£13**
1984 gold £5, sovereign, half sovereign (3 coins)	**BV**
1984 decimal, £1 Scottish rev-½p (8 coins)	**£16**
1984 uncirculated decimal, £1 Scottish rev-½p (8 coins)	**£10**
1985 gold, new portrait, £5, £2,	
sovereign, half sovereign (4 coins)	**BV**
1985 decimal, £1 Welsh	
rev-1p (7 coins) in deluxe case	**£20**
1985 in standard case	**£13**
1985 uncirculated decimal, £1 Welsh rev-1p (7 coins)	**£10**
1986 gold Commonwealth Games,	
£2, sovereign, half sovereign (3 coins)	**BV**
1986 decimal, Commonwealth Games £2,	
Northern Ireland £1.50-1p	
(8 coins) in deluxe case	**£25**
1986 in standard case	**£19**
1986 uncirculated decimal, in folder	**£10**
1987 gold Britannia, £100-£10 (4 coins)	**BV**
1987 decimal, £25, £10 (2 coins)	**BV**
1987 gold, £2, sovereign, half sovereign (3 coins)	**BV**
1987 decimal, £1 English rev-1p (7 coins) in deluxe case	**£25**
1987 in standing case	**£17**
1987 uncirculated decimal, 1987, in folder	**£8**
1988 gold Britannia, £100-£10 (4 coins)	**BV**
1988 £25, £10 (2 coins)	**BV**
1988 £2, sovereign, half sovereign (3 coins)	**BV**
1988 £1 Royal Arms rev-1p (7 coins) in deluxe case	**£24**
1988 in standard case	**£14**
1988 uncirculated decimal, in folder	**£9**
1989 gold Britannia, £100-£10 (4 coins)	**BV**
1989 £25, £10 (2 coins)	**BV**
1989 gold 500th anniversary of the sovereign,	
£5, £2, sovereign, half sovereign (4 coins)	**£3650**
1989 gold 500th anniversary of the sovereign,	
£2, sovereign, half sovereign (3 coins)	**£2000**
1989 decimal, Bill of Rights £2, Claim of Right	
£2, £1 Scottish rev, 50p-1p (9 coins) in deluxe case	**£35**
1989 in standard case	**£23**
1989 silver, Bill of Rights £2,	
Claim of Right £2 (2 coins)	**£50**

1989 silver piedfort, 1989, £2 as above (2 coins)	**£80**	1997 gold Britannia, £100-£10 (4 coins)	**BV**
1989 uncirculated, in folder	**£12**	1996 uncirculated decimal, £2-1p (8 coins)	**£8**
1989 uncirculated decimal set,		1997 gold, £5, £2 bimetal, sovereign,	
£1 Scottish rev-1p (7 coins)	**£18**	half sovereign (4 coins)	**BV**
1990 gold Britannia, £100-£10 (4 coins)	**BV**	1997 £2 bimetal, sovereign, half sovereign (3 coins)	**BV**
1990 gold, £5, £2, sovereign, half sovereign (4 coins)	**BV**	1997 silver Britannia, £2-20p	**£100**
1990 £2, sovereign, half sovereign (3 coins)	**BV**	1997 decimal, fifty pence, large and small size	**£55**
1990 silver, 5p (large and small size)	**£28**	1997 Golden Wedding £5, £2 bimetal, £1 English rev-1p	
1990 decimal, £1 Welsh rev-1p including large		with new 50p in deluxe case	**£33**
and small 5p (8 coins) in deluxe case	**£30**	1997 in standard case	**£28**
1990 in standard case	**£20**	1997 uncirculated decimal, £2 bimetal,	
1990 uncirculated decimal, £1 Welsh rev as 1985-1p		£1 English rev-1p with new 50p (9 coins)	**£9**
including large and small 5p (8 coins)	**£17**	1998 gold Britannia, £100-£10 (4 coins)	**BV**
1991 gold Britannia, £100-£10 (4 coins)	**BV**	1998 silver Britannia, £2-20p	**£100**
1991 gold, £5, £2, sovereign, half sovereign (4 coins)	**BV**	1998 gold, £5-half sovereign	**BV**
1991 £2, sovereign, half sovereign (3 coins)	**BV**	1998 £2-half sovereign	**BV**
1991 decimal, £1-1p (7 coins) in deluxe case	**£34**	1998 decimal, Prince Charles, £5-1p in deluxe case	**£35**
1991 in standard case	**£25**	1998 in standard case	**£27**
1991 uncirculated decimal, 1991 (7 coins)	**£16**	1998 uncirculated, as above, £2-1p (9 coins)	**£11**
1991 gold Britannia, £100-£10 (4 coins)	**BV**	1998 silver, EU and NHS 50p (2 coins)	**£40**
1992 gold, £5, £2, sovereign, half sovereign (4 coins)	**BV**	1999 gold Britannia, £100-£10 (4 coins)	**BV**
1992 £2, sovereign, half sovereign (3 coins)	**BV**	1999 £5, £2 Rugby World Cup,	
1992 silver, ten pence, large and small size	**£30**	sovereign, half sovereign	**BV**
1992 decimal, £1 English rev-1p including		1999 £2 Rugby World Cup,	
two 50p, new 10p (9 coins) in deluxe case	**£30**	sovereign, half sovereign	**BV**
1992 in standard case	**£26**	1999 decimal, Diana £5-1p in deluxe case	**£35**
1992 uncirculated decimal, 1992	**£17**	1999 in standard case	**£28**
1993 gold Britannia, £100-£10 (4 coins)	**BV**	1999 uncirculated, £2-1p (8 coins)	**£11**
1993 gold, £5, £2, sovereign, half sovereign (4 coins)	**BV**	2000 gold Britannia, £100-£10 (4 coins)	**BV**
1993 £2, sovereign, half sovereign (3 coins)	**BV**	2000 gold, £5-half sovereign	**BV**
1993 Coronation Anniversary £5,		2000 £2-half sovereign	**BV**
£1-1p (8 coins), deluxe case	**£37**	2000 decimal, £5-1p Maundy coins (13 coins)	**£250**
1993 in standard case	**£30**	2000 executive (10 coins)	**£55**
1993 uncirculated decimal,		2000 deluxe (10 coins)	**£32**
with two 50p, no £5 (8 coins)	**£20**	2000 standard (10 coins)	**£24**
1994 gold Britannia, £100-£10 (4 coins)	**BV**	2001 gold Britannia, £100-£10 (4 coins)	**BV**
1994 gold, £5, £2 Bank of England, sovereign,		2001 gold, £5, £2 Marconi Commemorative,	
half sovereign (4 coins)	**BV**	sovereign, half sovereign (4 coins)	**BV**
1994 £2 Bank of England, sovereign,		2001 £2 Marconi commemorative, sovereign,	
half sovereign (3 coins)	**BV**	half sovereign (3 coins)	**BV**
1994 decimal, £2 Bank of England, £1 Scottish rev,		2001 silver Britannia, new reverse designs, £2-20p	**£80**
50p D Day-1p (8 coins) in deluxe case	**£34**	2001 decimal, executive (10 coins)	**£45**
1994 in standard case	**£28**	2001 deluxe (10 coins)	**£32**
1994 uncirculated decimal, 1994	**£11**	2001 gift (10 coins)	**£32**
1995 gold Britannia, £100-£10 (4 coins)	**BV**	2001 standard (10 coins)	**£27**
1996 gold, £5, £2 Peace, sovereign,		2001 uncirculated, as above but no £5 (9 coins)	**£12**
half sovereign (4 coins)	**BV**	2002 gold, £5-half sovereign, new reverse design	**BV**
1996 gold, £2 Peace, sovereign,		2002 £2-half sovereign, new reverse design	**BV**
half sovereign (3 coins)	**BV**	2002 Golden Jubilee £5, £2 bimetal, £1 (English rev)-1p	
1996 decimal, £2 Peace, £1 Welsh		plus Maundy coins (13 coins)	**£4750**
rev-1p (8 coins), deluxe case	**£35**	2002 Commonwealth Games £2, four reverses: England,	
1996 in standard case	**£28**	Northern Ireland, Scotland and Wales	**BV**
1996 uncirculated decimal	**£10**	2002 silver, Commonwealth Games, four reverses,	
1996 gold Britannia, £100-£10 (4 coins)	**BV**	£2 England, Northern Ireland, Scotland and Wales	**£98**
1996 gold, £5, £2, sovereign, half sovereign (4 coins)	**BV**	2002 gold Britannia, £100-£10 (4 coins)	**BV**
1996 gold, £2, sovereign, half sovereign (3 coins)	**BV**	2002 silver piedfort, Commonwealth	
1996 silver decimal, £1-1p (7 coins)	**£85**	Games £2, four reverses: England,	
1996 decimal, £5 60th Birthday, £2 Football,		Northern Ireland, Scotland and Wales	**£195**
£1 Northern Irish rev-1p in deluxe case (9 coins)	**£30**	2002 decimal, Executive, Golden Jubilee £5,	
1996 in standard case	**£28**	£2 bimetal, £1 English rev-1p (9 coins)	**£58**

2002 deluxe (9 coins)	£37
2002 gift (9 coins)	£32
2002 standard (9 coins)	£25
2002 uncirculated, 2002, £2 bimetal, £1 English rev-1p (8 coins)	£14
2002 uncirculated, Commonwealth Games £2, reverses: England, Northern Ireland, Scotland and Wales	£12
2003 gold, £5-half sovereign	BV
2003 £2 DNA-half sovereign	BV
2003 pattern set gold pounds (4 coins)	BV
2003 pattern set silver pounds (4 coins)	£80
2003 gold Britannia £100-£10 (4 coins)	BV
2003 silver Britannia £2-20p	£75
Gold set, mixed dates £100 (4 coins)	BV
Silver set, mixed dates £2 (4 coins)	£40
Silver set, mixed dates £2 (4 coins)	£40
Silver set, £5 (2 coins) different types	£50
2003 Silver set, £5-50p Coronation-Suffragette (5 coins)	£120
2003 decimal, executive (11 coins)	£55
2003 deluxe (11 coins)	£37
2003 standard (11 coins)	£28
2003 uncirculated (10 coins)	£11
2004 gold £5-half sovereign (4 coins)	BV
2004 gold, £2-half sovereign (3 coins)	BV
2004 pattern set, gold pounds (4 coins)	BV
2004 pattern set, silver pounds (4 coins)	£80
2004 silver set, £5-50p Entente Cordiale-Bannister (5 coins)	£125
2004 silver piedfort set, £2-50p Penydarren engine-Bannister (3 coins)	£120
2004 gold Britannia, £100-£10 (4 coins)	BV
2004 £50-£10	BV
2004 uncirculated set, 'new coin pack' (10 coins)	£9
2004 deluxe (10 coins)	£23
2004 executive (10 coins)	£42
2004 standard (10 coins)	£18
2005 gold, £5-half sovereign (4 coins)	BV
2005 £2-half sovereign (3 coins)	BV
2005 silver piedfort set, £2-50p Gunpowder Plot-Johnson's Dictionary (4 coins)	£140
2005 silver piedfort set, £5 (2 coins)	£110
2005 decimal, 2005, Executive (12 coins)	£65
2005 deluxe (12 coins)	£40
2005 standard (12 coins)	£30
2005 uncirculated (10 coins)	£12
2005 gold Britannia, £100-£10 (4 coins)	BV
2005 £50-£10 (3 coins)	BV
2005 silver Britannia, £2-20p (4 coins)	£80
2006 gold, £5-half sovereign (4)	BV
2006 £2-half sovereign (3 coins)	BV
2006 gold Britannia, £100-£10 (4 coins)	BV
2006 silver Britannia £2 gold plated, 5 different (5 coins)	£225
2006 gold, Brunel £2 (2 coins)	BV
2006 Victoria Cross 50p (3 coins)	BV
2006 silver, 80th Birthday (13 coins)	£275
2006 silver Britannia (5 coins)	£275
2006 Brunel £2 (2 coins)	£60
2006 silver piedfort, Brunel £2 (2 coins)	£80
2006 silver, 50p, Victoria Cross & Wounded Soldier (2 coins)	£50
2006 silver piedfort, 50 pence (2 coins)	£50
2006 silver piedfort, £5-50p 80th Birthday-Wounded Soldier (6 coins)	£275
2006 executive (13 coins)	£70
2006 deluxe (13 coins)	£45
2006 standard (13 coins)	£35
2007 gold, £5-half sovereign (4 coins)	BV
2007 £2-half sovereign (3 coins)	BV
2007 'Bridge' series (4 coins)	BV
2007 sovereign and half sovereign (2 coins)	BV
2007 platinum Britannia, £100-£10 (4 coins)	£BV
2007 silver 'Bridge' series (4 coins)	£115
2007 decimal executive (12 coins)	£79
2007 deluxe (12 coins)	£50
2007 standard (12 coins)	£39
2007 uncirculated (9 coins)	£14
2008 gold Britannia, £100-£10 (4 coins)	BV
2008 gold, £5-half sovereign (4 coins)	BV
2008 gold £2-half sovereign (3 coins)	BV
2008 gold, sovereign and half sovereign (2 coins)	BV
2008 platinum Britannia, £100-£10 (4 coins)	BV
2008 platinum Royal Shield (7 coins)	BV
2008 platinum Emblems of Britain (7 coins)	BV
2008 platinum Double set (14 coins)	BV
2008 gold Royal shield (7 coins)	BV
2008 gold Emblems of Britain (7 coins)	BV
2008 gold Double set (14 coins)	BV
2008 silver Britannia, £100-£10 (4 coins)	BV
2008 silver Piedfort Royal Shield (6 coins)	£249
2008 silver Royal Shields (6 coins)	£149
2008 silver Emblems of Britain (6 coins)	£149
2008 silver Double set (12 coins)	£275
2008 Family (5 coins)	£150
2008 commemorative piedfort (4)	£200
2008 decimal Royal Shields (6 coins)	BV
2008 decimal executive (11 coins)	£60
2008 deluxe (11 coins)	£40
2008 standard (11 coins)	£30
2008 uncirculated (9 coins)	£15
2008 uncirculated Emblems of Britain (9 coins)	£9
2008 Royal Shields (6 coins)	£30
2008 standard royal shields (6 coins)	£9
2008 double set (12 coins)	£18
2009 gold Britannia, £100-£10 (4 coins)	BV
2009 gold, £5-half sovereign (4 coins)	BV
2009 gold £2-half sovereign (3 coins)	BV
2009 silver Britannia, £2-20p	£100
2009 gold, sovereign and half sovereign (2 coins)	BV
2009 silver 50th Anniversary Mini (4 coins)	£150
2009 silver piedfort collection (4 coins)	£225
2009 silver family collection (6 coins)	£150
2009 silver set (12 coins)	£225
2009 decimal executive (12 coins)	£60
2009 deluxe (12 coins)	£40
2009 standard (12 coins)	£32
2009 uncirculated (11 coins)	£16

Sets beyond 2009 are not listed in this guide.

SCOTTISH COINS

■ MINTS IN OPERATION IN SCOTLAND

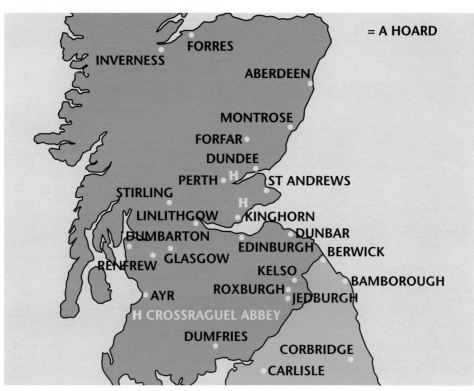

= A HOARD

FORRES
INVERNESS
ABERDEEN
MONTROSE
FORFAR
DUNDEE
PERTH H ST ANDREWS
STIRLING
LINLITHGOW KINGHORN
DUMBARTON DUNBAR
EDINBURGH BERWICK
GLASGOW
RENFREW KELSO
BAMBOROUGH
AYR ROXBURGH JEDBURGH
H CROSSRAGUEL ABBEY
DUMFRIES
CORBRIDGE
CARLISLE

The mints of the first coinage of Alexander III were the greatest number working together in Scotland, and therefore this area attracts collectors of the different mint issues.

For his reign, we give a price for issues of each mint town, but not for any other reign. From the reign of Mary, all Scottish coins were struck at Edinburgh.

MINT TOWN	KING
Aberdeen	Alexander III, David II, Robert III, James I, II, III
Ayr	Alexander III
Bamborough	Henry
Berwick	David I, Malcolm IV, William I, Alexander II, III, Robert Bruce, James III
Carlisle	David I, Henry
Corbridge	Henry
Dumbarton	Robert III
Dumfries	Alexander III
Dunbar	William I?, Alexander III

MINT TOWN	KING
Dundee	William I?, Alexander III
Dunfermline	William I
Forfar	Alexander III
Forres	Alexander III
Glasgow	Alexander III
Inverness	Alexander III
Jedburgh	Malcolm IV
Kelso	Alexander II
Kinghorn	Alexander III
Lanark	Alexander III
Linlithgow	James I, II
Montrose	Alexander III
Perth	William I, Alexander III, Robert II-James II
Renfrew	Alexander III
Roxburgh	Alexander III
St Andrews	Alexander III
Stirling	Alexander III, James I, II, Mary Stuart

Prices are for the commonest coins in each case. For further details see *The Scottish Coinage*, by I Stewart (Spink, 1967, reprint 1975) and *Coins of Scotland, Ireland and The Islands*, (Spink 2003).

DAVID I 1124-53

	F	VF
Silver Pennies	£1000	£2500

Four different groups; struck at the mints of Berwick, Carlisle, Roxborough and Edinburgh.

HENRY 1136-52

Earl of Huntingdon and Northumberland

	F	VF
Silver Pennies	£2750	£6500

Three types; struck at the mints of Corbridge, Carlisle and Barnborough.

MALCOLM IV 1153-65

	F	VF
Silver Pennies	£5500	£12000

Five types; struck at the mints of Roxburgh and Berwick.

William the Lion Penny, Edinburgh

WILLIAM THE LION 1165-1214

	F	VF
Silver Pennies	£185	£500

Three issues; struck at the mints of Roxburgh, Berwick, Edinburgh, Dun (Dunfermline?), Perth.

ALEXANDER II 1214-49

	F	VF
Silver Pennies	£875	£2500

Mints of Berwick and Roxburgh, varieties of bust

Alexander III first coinage Halfpenny

ALEXANDER III 1249-86
First coinage silver Pennies 1250-80

	F	VF
Aberdeen	£200	£450
Ayr	£225	£500
Berwick	£140	£250
'DUN'	£250	£550
Edinburgh	£175	£350
Forfar	£425	£850
Fres	£385	£800
Glasgow	£225	£450
Inverness	£325	£725
Kinghorn	£450	£1000
Lanark	£350	£825

	F	VF
Montrose	£775	£1750
Perth	£140	£295
Renfrew	£585	£1500
Roxburgh	£140	£295
St Andrews	£285	£650
Stirling	£195	£475
'WILANERTER'	£500	£1100

Alexander III second coinage Halfpenny

Second coinage c1280

	F	VF
Silver Pennies	£45	£110
Halfpennies	£100	£250
Farthings	£350	£750

Many types and varieties

JOHN BALLIOL 1292-6
First coinage, rough surface issue

	F	VF
Silver Pennies	£130	£365
Halfpennies	£325	£775

Second coinage, smooth surface issue

	F	VF
Silver Pennies	£145	£400
Halfpennies	£200	£575

ROBERT BRUCE 1306-29

	F	VF
Silver Pennies	£750	£1750
Halfpennies	£950	£3500
Farthings	£1750	£4000

Probably all struck at Berwick.

David II Halfgroat

DAVID II 1329-71

		ext. rare
Gold Nobles		
Silver Groats	£125	£350
Halfgroats	£110	£325
Pennies	£50	£150
Halfpennies	£375	£950
Farthings	£675	£1500

Three issues, but these denominations were not struck for all issues. Edinburgh and Aberdeen mints.

ROBERT II 1371-90

	F	VF
Silver Groats	£100	£300
Halfgroats	£125	£350
Pennies	£125	£295
Halfpennies	£135	£365

Some varieties. Struck at Dundee, Edinburgh and Perth.

ROBERT III 1390-1406

	F	VF
Gold Lion or Crowns	£1325	£3250
Demy-lions or Halfcrowns	£950	£2650
Silver groats	£125	£325
Halfgroats	£165	£385
Pennies	£385	£750
Halfpennies	£400	£850

Three issues, many varieties. Struck at mints of Edinburgh, Aberdeen, Perth and Dumbarton.

James I Demy

JAMES I 1406-37

	F	VF
Gold Demies	£975	£2150
Half-demies	£1350	£2850
Silver Groats	£200	£500
Billon Pennies	£225	£500
Billon Halfpennies	£485	£1100

Mints: Aberdeen, Edinburgh, Inverness, Linlithgow, Perth and Stirling.

JAMES II 1437-60

	F	VF
Gold Demies from	£975	£2200
Lions from	£1950	£4750
Half lions		ext. rare
Silver Groats	£245	£675
Halfgroats	£725	*
Billon Pennies	£250	£650

Two issues, many varieties. Mints: Aberdeen, Edinburgh, Linlithgow, Perth, Roxburgh and Stirling.

ECCLESIASTICAL ISSUES c1452-80

	F	VF
Bishop Kennedy copper Pennies	£95	£295
Copper Farthings	£195	£525

Different types and varieties.

JAMES III 1460-88

		F	VF
Gold Riders	from	£2250	£4850
Half-riders		£2500	£5750
Quarter-riders		£4750	*
Unicorns		£1950	£4850
Silver Groats	from	£275	£550

James III Groat

		F	VF
Halfgroats	from	£495	£1250
Pennies	from	£385	£750
Billon Placks	from	£100	£275
Half-Placks	from	£100	£300
Pennies	from	£100	£295
Copper Farthings	from	£325	*

Many varieties. Mints: Aberdeen, Berwick and Edinburgh.

James IV Unicorn

JAMES IV 1488-1513

	F	VF
Gold Unicorns	£1650	£4250
Half-unicorns	£1375	£3250
Lions or Crowns	£2000	£4500
Half-lions	£2650	£6500
Pattern Angel		unique
Silver Groats from	£500	£1200
Halfgroats	£575	£1500
Pennies, light coinage	ext. rare	*
Billon Placks	£40	£100
Half-placks	£125	£400
Pennies	£70	£165

Different types and varieties. Mint: Edinburgh.

James V 1540 'Bonnet' piece

JAMES V 1513-42		F	VF
Gold Unicorns		£2350	£4850
Half-unicorns		£2950	£6250
Crowns		£1500	£2850
'Bonnet' pieces or Ducats		£4250	£8500
Two-thirds ducats		£3250	£7500
One-third ducats		£3850	*
Silver Groats	from	£225	£575
One-third groats		£185	£525

James V Groat

	F	VF
Billon Placks	£25	£85
Bawbees	£25	£80
Half-bawbees	£75	£225
Quarter-bawbees		unique

Different issues and varieties. Mint: Edinburgh.

MARY 1542-67

First period 1542-58

	F	VF
Gold Crown	£2250	£4750
Twenty Shillings	£3000	£6250
Lions or Forty-four Shillings	£1850	£3500

Mary three pound piece or ryal

	F	VF
Half-lions or Twenty-two shillings	£1650	£3250
Ryals or Three Pound pieces, 1555, 1557, 1558	£4500	£8750
Half-ryals 1555, 1557, 1558	£5000	£10000
Portrait Testoons, 1553	£4500	£9000
Non-portrait Testoons, 1555-58	£325	£850
Half-testoons, 1555-58	£295	£725
Billon Bawbees	£45	£125
Half-bawbees	£65	£175
Pennies, facing bust	£225	£650
No bust 1556	£165	£495
Lions, 1555, 1558	£30	£125
Placks, 1557	£45	£125

Second period, Francis and Mary, 1558-60	F	VF
Gold Ducats or Sixty shillings		ext. rare
Non-portrait Testoons, 1558-61	£350	£850
Half-testoons, 1558-60	£275	£625
Twelvepenny groats, Nonsunt, 1558-9	£75	£225
Lions, 1559-60	£30	£95

Third period, widowhood, 1560-5	F	VF
Gold Crown 1562		ext. rare
Portrait Testoons, 1561-2	£2500	£6250
Half-testoons, 1561-2	£2750	£7000

Fourth period, Henry and Mary, 1565-7	F	VF
Portrait Ryals, 1565		ext.rare
Non-portrait Ryals, 1565-7	£500	£1375

Mary and Henry Darnley 1566 Ryal

	F	VF
Two-third ryals, 1565-7	£350	£825
Two-third ryals, undated	£975	£2500
One-third ryals, 1565-6	£365	£875
Testoon, 1565		ext. rare

Fifth period, 2nd widowhood, 1567	F	VF
Non-portrait Ryals, 1567	£525	£1400
Two-thirds ryal, 1567	£350	£800
One-thirds ryals, 1566-7	£475	£1100

Mints: Edinburgh, Stirling (but only for some bawbees)

JAMES VI

Before English accession 1567-1603

First coinage 1567-71

	F	VF
Ryals 1567-71	£425	£925
Two-third ryals	£375	£825
One-third ryals	£400	£950

Second coinage 1571-80

	F	VF
Gold Twenty Pounds pieces	£35000	£60000
Silver Nobles, 1572-77, 1580	£90	£250
Half nobles	£70	£225

	F	VF
Two merks, 1578-80	£1950	£4750
Merks, 1579-80	£3250	*

Third coinage 1580-81

Gold Ducats, 1580	£5850	£10500
Sixteen shillings, 1581	£2500	£5250
Eight shillings, 1581	£1500	£3750
Four shillings, 1581	£3500	*
Two shillings, 1581		ext. rare

Fourth coinage 1582-88

Gold Lion Nobles	£4500	£9750
Two-third lion nobles	£5250	£12000
One-third lion nobles	£4750	£11000
Silver Forty shillings, 1582	£6500	£15500
Thirty shillings, 1582-86	£425	£1375
Twenty shillings, 1582-85	£395	£1350
Ten shillings, 1582-84	£295	£1000

James VI 1582 Ten Shillings

Fifth coinage 1588

Gold Thistle nobles	£2750	£5750

Sixth coinage 1591-93

Gold Hat pieces, 1591-93	£4500	£10000
Silver Balance half-merks, 1591-93	£350	£750
Balance quarter merks, 1591	£600	£1350

Severnth coinage 1594-1601

Gold Riders	£850	£2250
Half Riders	£875	£1750
Silver Ten Shillings, 1593-95, 1598-1601	£135	£375
Five shillings, 1593-5, 1598-1601	£110	£325

James VI seventh coinage 1593 Five shillings

	F	VF
Thirty-pence pieces 1595-6, 1598-9, 1601	£150	£375
Twelve-pence piece 1594-6	£135	£275

James VI 1603 Sword and Sceptre piece

Eighth coinage 1601-4

Gold Sword and Sceptre pieces	£500	£1250
Half sword and sceptre pieces	£425	£975
Silver thistle-merks, 1601-4	£75	£225
Half thistle-merks	£65	£185
Quarter thistle-merks	£60	£175
Eighth thistle-merks, 1601-3	£45	£125

Billon and copper issues

Billon Placks or Eightpenny groats	£20	£90
Half-placks	£135	£350
Hardheads	£25	£100
Saltire Placks	£200	£495
Copper Twopence 1597	£95	£250
Penny 1597	£600	*

After English accession 1603-25

Gold Units	£875	£1975
Double Crowns	£1450	£3250
Britain Crowns	£700	£1650
Halfcrowns	£575	£1375
Thistle Crowns	£400	£975
Silver Sixty shillings	£400	£975
Thirty shillings	£125	£325
Twelve shillings	£135	£400
Six shillings	£475	£1200
Two shillings	£40	£110
One shilling	£65	£165
Sixpences	*	*
Copper Twopences	£20	£60
Pennies	£135	£375

CHARLES 1625-49
First coinage 1625-36

Gold Units	£1100	£3000
Double Crowns	£1250	£3500
Britain Crowns		ext. rare
Silver Sixty shillings	£875	£2950
Thirty shillings	£150	£450
Twelve shillings	£285	£725
Six shillings	£375	£1000
Two shillings	£65	£165
One shilling	£85	£250

Second coinage 1636

	F	VF
Half-merks	£60	£150
Forty-pence pieces	£50	£135
Twenty-pence pieces	£65	£150

Third coinage 1637-42

	F	VF
Gold Units	£1500	£2950
Half-units	£1250	£2750
Britain Crowns	£1100	£2750
Britain Halfcrowns	£500	£1000
Silver Sixty shillings	£525	£1500
Thirty shillings	£125	£325

Charles II first coinage 1669 Merk

	F	VF
1668	£225	£575
1669	£80	£300
1670	£80	£300
1671	£80	£300
1672	£90	£325
1673	£80	£300
1674	£150	£475
1674 F below bust	£120	£375
1675 F below bust	£120	£375
1675	£225	£575
Half-merks, 1664	£175	£500
1665	£150	£475
1666	£225	£700
1667	£225	£700
1668	£150	£475
1669	£90	£350
1670	£90	£350
1671	£100	£325
1672	£100	£325
1673	£120	£400
1675 F below bust	£110	£375
1675	£120	£400

Charles I third coinage Briot's issue Twelve shillings

	F	VF
Twelve shillings	£110	£300
Six shillings	£90	£225
Half-merks	£90	£225
Forty-pence piece	£35	£100
Twenty-pence piece	£30	£80
Three shillings	£65	£175
Two shillings	£50	£125
Copper twopences, lion	£20	£50
Pennies	£300	*
Twopences, CR crowned	£15	£35
Twopences, Stirling turners	£15	£35

CHARLES II 1660-85
First coinage

	F	VF
Silver Four merks, 1664 thistle above bust	£850	£1850
1664 thistle below bust	£800	£1650
1665	£1500	*
1670	£900	*
1673	£800	£1750
1674 F below bust	£800	£1800
1675	£800	£1800
Two merks, 1664 thistle above bust	£475	£1300
1664 thistle below bust	£350	£950
1670	£525	£1300
1673	£325	£950
1673 F below bust	£325	£950
1674	£325	£950
1674 F below bust	£325	£950
1675	£325	£950
Merks, 1664	£110	£375
1665	£125	£425
1666	£275	£750

Charles II second coinage 1676 Dollar

Second coinage

	F	VF
Silver Dollars, 1676	£425	£1450
1679	£475	£1500
1680	£485	£1750
1681	£485	£1650
1682	£425	£1350
Half-dollars, 1675	£450	£1200
1676	£525	£1600

	F	VF
1681	£450	£1350
Quarter-dollars, 1675	£135	£475
1676	£120	£350
1677	£120	£375
1678	£125	£450
1679	£135	£475
1680	£120	£375
1681	£120	£375
1682	£125	£425
Fighth-dollars, 1676	£85	£300
1677	£85	£300
1678/7	£175	£575
1679	£125	£450
1680	£80	£275
1682	£125	£450
Sixteenth-dollars, 1677	£65	£225
1678/7	£75	£275
1679/7	£100	£375
1680	£75	£275
1681	£70	£275
Copper twopence, CR crowned	£20	£70
Bawbees, 1677-9	£45	£135
Turners, 1677-9	£30	£100

JAMES VII 1685-9

Silver sixty shillings, 1688, proof only	FDC	£2250
Gold proof only		ext. rare

Struck in 1828, not contemporary.

	F	VF
Silver forty shillings, 1687	£225	£850
1688	£250	£900
Ten shillings, 1687	£135	£475
1688	£175	£650

WILLIAM AND MARY 1689-94

	F	VF
Sixty shillings, 1691	£600	£1750
1692	£600	£1750
Forty shillings, 1689	£250	£850
1690	£250	£695
1691	£200	£595
1692	£175	£550
1693	£175	£550
1694	£250	£695
Twenty shillings, 1693	£375	£1250
1694	£450	£1350
Ten shillings, 1689	*	*
1690	£225	£625
1691	£150	£495
1692	£150	£495
1694	£240	£675
Five shillings, 1691	£175	£425
1694	£175	£425
Copper Bawbees, 1691-4	£50	£140
Bodle, 1691-4	£35	£120

WILLIAM II 1694-1702

	F	VF
Gold Pistole 1701	£4250	£8500
Half-pistole, 1701	£3950	£7500

	F	VF
Silver sixty shillings, 1699	*	*
Forty shillings, 1695	£195	£500
1696	£200	£525
1697	£250	£600
1698	£250	£625
1699	£250	£625
1700	£675	£1750
Twenty shillings, 1695	£225	£625
1696	£195	£525
1697	£325	£875
1698	£175	£500
1698/7	£225	£650
1699	£375	£950

William III 1696 Ten shillings

	F	VF
Ten shillings, 1695	£125	£325
1696	£125	£325
1697	£150	£350
1698	£165	£425
1699	£175	£475
Five shillings, 1695	£85	£250
1696	£80	£225
1697	£80	£225
1699	£80	£225
1700	£80	£225
1701	£110	£400
1702	£125	£400
Copper Bawbees, 1695-7	£85	£375
Bodles, 1695-7	£50	£160

ANNE 1702-14
Pre-Union 1702-7

	F	VF
Ten shillings, 1705	£150	£400
1706	£150	£400
Five shillings, 1705	£60	£165
1706	£60	£165

JAMES VIII 1688-1766 The Old Pretender

Gold Guinea 1716	FDC	£13500
Silver	FDC	£1350
Bronze	FDC	£1350
Crown 1709		unique
Crown 1716, silver	FDC	£2250
Gold		ext. rare
Bronze		ext. rare

The 1716-dated pieces were struck in 1828 from the original dies.

Coincraft

An open letter to Dealers

When a dealer sold us some coins a while ago I asked him why we were not doing more business together, his answer was, that he didn't want to bother us. Hell, we want to be bothered, especially when it comes to business. You will find that Claire, Ian, Barry and myself (Richard) are easy to talk to and we are always interested in buying material. On large lots or collections we are even willing to put up the money for you.

We now have 18 full time and 3 part time staff and we need material to offer our collectors. As the busiest coin firm in the United Kingdom, we now send out 30 different catalogues a year, we need material. Single pieces, hoards, accumulations and of course collections. We buy British and world coins, British and world banknotes, ancient coins and antiquities, medallions, bulk coins and banknotes, in fact almost anything.

Please give us a call and join the many satisfied dealers who do business with Coincraft everyday. We will say yes or no, without messing you around. When we agree a price, we will write you a cheque on the spot. We need you and will treat you right, if you haven't tried us, please do. You will find dealing with Coincraft easy, pleasurable and I hope, profitable.

Richard Lobel
Founder of Coincraft

IRISH COINS

■ HAMMERED ISSUES 995-1661

Most of the Irish coins of this period are in fairly poor condition and it is difficult to find specimens in VF condition upwards.

For more details see *The Guide Book to the Coinage of Ireland AD 995 to the Present Day* by Anthony Dowle or Spink's *Coins of Scotland, Ireland & the Islands* by Patrick Finn (Spink 2002) and *Irish Coin Values* by Patrick Finn (Spink 1979). Prices are for the commonest coins in each case.

HIBERNO-NORSE
OF DUBLIN 995-1150

	F	VF
Silver Pennies, imitative of English coins, many types and varieties from	£400	£800

Hiberno-Norse phase II Penny

Hiberno-Norse phase IV Penny

JOHN AS LORD OF
IRELAND c1185-1199

Silver Halfpennies, profile portrait	£2000	*
Facing head	£125	£300
Farthings	£400	£1100

Different types, varieties, mints and moneyers.

JOHN DE COURCY LORD
OF ULSTER 1177-1205

Silver Halfpenny		unique
Farthings	£1000	£2850

Different types, varieties, mints and moneyers.

JOHN AS KING OF ENGLAND
AND LORD OF IRELAND c1199-1216
Rex/Triangle types

Silver Pennies	from	£55	£150
Halfpennies		£85	£275
Farthings		£800	£1950

Different types, varieties, mints and moneyers.

HENRY III 1216-1272

		F	VF
Silver Pennies, c 1251-1254	from	£55	£150

Dublin only, moneyers DAVI and RICHARD, many varieties.

Edward I Waterford Penny

EDWARD I 1272-1307

	F	VF
Silver Pennies from	£50	£125
Halfpennies	£70	£195

Edward I Farthing Dublin

Farthings	£110	£350

Dublin, Waterford and Cork, many different issues.

EDWARD III 1327-1377

Silver Halfpennies Dublin mint	£6000	*

HENRY VI 1422-1461

Silver Pennies, Dublin mint	ext. rare

Edward IV untitled crown type Groat

EDWARD IV 1461-1483

Silver untitled crown Groats	from	£1000	£2500
Pennies		£1250	£3250
Titled crown Groats		£2250	£5000
Halfgroats		£2500	*
Pennies		£1875	*
Cross on rose/sun Groats		£2500	£6000
Bust/rose-sun Double Groats		£1850	£5500
Groats		£1650	*
Halfgroats		£1500	*
Pennies		£1450	*
'English-style' Groats		£175	£375
Halfgroats		£750	*
Pennies		£75	£185

	F	VF
Halfpennies	£900	*
Bust/rose Groats	£700	£1750
Pennies	£140	£395
Copper crown/cross Farthing	£1000	£3000
Half-farthings	£950	£2500

PATRICIUS/SALVATOR 1463-65

	F	VF
Silver Farthing	£1150	£3250
Three crowns/sun Half-farthings	£1250	£3500

This is an abbreviated listing of the issues of Edward IV which are numerous. There are also many varieties and different mints.

Richard III 'three crowns' Groat

RICHARD III 1483-1485

	F	VF
Silver bust/rose-cross Groats	£1100	£3950
Halfgroats		unique
Pennies		ext. rare
Cross and pellet pennies	£1250	£3250
Three-crown Groats	£675	£1500

Different mints and varieties.

Henry VII early 'three crowns' Groat

HENRY VII 1485-1509
Early issues

	F	VF
Three-crown Groats	£100	£300
Halfgroats	£195	£425
Pennies	£525	£1375
Halfpennies		ext. rare

Henry VII facing bust Groat, Dublin

Later issues

	F	VF
Facing bust Groats	£165	£425
Halfgroats	£825	£2250
Pennies	£825	£2250
Crowned H Pennies	£1250	*

Many varieties. Mints: mainly Dublin, Waterford issues are extremely rare.

LAMBERT SIMNEL, Pretender 1487

	F	VF
Three-crown Groats	£1150	£2950

Different mints and varieties.

HENRY VIII 1509-1547

	F	VF
Silver 'harp' Groats	£85	£200
Halfgroats	£600	£1500

These harped coins carry crowned initials, such as HA (Henry and Anne Boleyn), HI (Henry and Jane Seymour), HK (Henry and Katherine Howard) or HR (Henricus Rex).

Henry VIII posthumous portrait Groat

Posthumous issues

	F	VF
Portrait Groats current for 6 pence	£175	£550
Halfgroats current for 3 pence	£165	£500
Pennies current for 3 halfpence	£475	£1250
Halfpennies current for 3 farthings	£700	£1750

Different busts and mintmarks.

EDWARD VI 1547-1553

	F	VF
Base Shillings 1552 (MDLII)	£825	£2500
Contemporary copy	£50	£225

Mary 1553 Shilling

MARY 1553-1558

	F	VF
Shillings 1553 (MDLIII)	£875	£2500
1554 (MDLIIII)		ext. rare
Groats		ext. rare
Halfgroats		ext. rare
Pennies		ext. rare

Several varieties of the shillings and groats.

PHILIP AND MARY 1554-1558

	F	VF
Base Shillings	£295	£1100
Groats	£100	£475

Several minor varieties.

ELIZABETH I 1558-1603

	F	VF
Base portrait Shillings	£385	£1100
Groats	£110	£475
Fine silver portrait Shillings 1561	£350	£975
Groats	£300	£1000
Base shillings arms-harp	£125	£500
Sixpences	£90	£325
Threepences	£110	£425
Pennies	£30	£100
Halfpennies	£50	£175

JAMES I 1603-1625

	F	VF
Silver shillings	£110	£395
Sixpences	£90	£275

Different issues, busts and mintmarks.

Siege money of the Irish Rebellion 1642-1649

Siege coins are rather irregular in size and shape.

CHARLES I 1625-1649
Kilkenny Money 1642

	F	VF
Copper Halfpennies F	£365	£1100
Copper Farthings F	£550	*

Inchiquin Money 1642-1646

The only gold coins struck in Ireland.

	F	VF
Gold Double Pistole		ext. rare
Gold Pistole F	£45000	*
Silver Crowns	£3000	£7000
Halfcrowns	£2500	£6000
Shillings	£2500	£7000
Ninepences	£5000	*
Sixpences	£4750	*
Groats F	£5000	£13000
Threepences		ext. rare

Three issues and many varieties.

Ormonde Money 1643

	F	VF
Crowns F	£500	£1000
Halfcrowns F	£425	£900
Shillings	£225	£500
Sixpences F	£175	£350
Groats F	£200	£400
Threepences	£135	£300
Halfgroats F	£525	£1250

Many varieties.

Ormonde Money Halfcrown

Ormonde Money Sixpence

	F	VF
Rebel Money 1643		
Crowns	£3850	£9000
Halfcrowns	£4500	£11000

Town Pieces 1645-1647		
Bandon		
Copper Farthings F	*	*
Kinsale		
Copper Farthings F	£500	*
Youghal		
Copper Farthings F	£500	£1750
Brass Twopences		ext. rare
Pewter Threepences		ext. rare
Cork		
Silver Shillings F	£3850	£7250
Sixpences F	£1100	£2750
Copper Halfpennies	£1500	*
Copper Farthings F	£1350	*
Elizabeth I Shillings countermarked CORKE F		ext. rare

Cork 1647 Sixpence

'Blacksmith's' Money 1649

Based on English Tower Halfcrown.

	F	VF
Halfcrown, varieties	£775	£1850

Dublin Money 1649

Crowns	£3500	£9500
Halfcrowns	£2750	£8000

■ CHARLES II TO GEORGE IV

All the issues of this series except Bank of Ireland tokens were struck in base metal.

The series features a large number of varieties, but there is space here for only the main types and best-known variants. A number of rare proofs have also been omitted.

Except for the 'gunmoney' of James II, Irish copper coins are hard to find in the top grades, especially the so-called 'Voce Populi' issues and specimens of Wood's coinage.

We have listed some of the 'gunmoney' of James II in only three grades – Fair, Fine and VF. The majority of these hastily produced coins were not well struck and many pieces with little substantial wear are, arguably, not Extremely Fine.

Dating of gunmoney: in the calendar used up to 1723, the legal or civil year started on March 25 in Great Britain and Ireland, so December 1689 came before, not after January, February and March 1689. Coins dated March 1689 and March 1690 were struck in the same month.

CHARLES II	Fair	F	VF	EF
Armstrong issues 1660-1661				
Copper Farthings	£15	£30	£100	*

St Patrick's coinage				
Halfpennies	£875	£2000	*	*
Star in rev legend	£900	*	*	*
Farthings	£125	£400	*	*
Stars in rev legend	£150	£525	*	*
Cloud around				
St Patrick	£175	£625	*	*
Martlet below king	£150	£525	*	*
Annulet below king	£150	£525	*	*

Charles II St Patrick's Farthing

Regal coinage

Halfpennies, 1680,				
large letters, small cross	£15	£50	£200	*
1680 pellets	£15	£50	£200	*
1681 large letters	£15	£50	£200	*
1681 small letters	£50	£185	*	*
1682 large letters	£15	£50	£200	*

	Fair	F	VF	EF
1682 small letters	£15	£50	£200	£575
1683	£15	£50	£200	£575
1684	£25	£95	£350	*

JAMES II
Regular coinage

Halfpennies, 1685	£20	£65	£225	*
1686	£20	£65	£225	*
1687	£125	£450	*	*
1688	£20	£85	£250	*

Emergency coinage, 'Gunmoney'

Crowns, 1690	£50	£100	£225	£575
1690 horseman, sword				
to E of REX	£125	£225	£550	£1000

James II 1690 'Gunmoney' Crown

Large Halfcrowns,				
1689 July	£15	£60	£185	*
1689 August	£10	£40	£150	*
1689 September	£8	£35	£100	£400
1689 October	£8	£35	£100	*
1689 November	£10	£40	£125	*
1689 December	£10	£40	£125	*
1689 January	£10	£40	£150	*
1689 February	£8	£35	£125	*
1689 March	£8	£35	£125	*
1690 March	£8	£35	£125	*
1690 April	£8	£35	£125	£400
1690 May	£10	£40	£150	*
Small Halfcrowns,				
1690 April	£20	£75	£275	*
1690 May	£10	£30	£150	£350
1690 June	£10	£35	£185	£500
1690 July	£10	£35	£140	£400
1690 August	£12	£40	£165	£475
1690 September	*	*	*	*
1690 October	£35	£110	£450	*
Large Shillings, 1689 July	£8	£25	£90	£225
1689 August	£6	£20	£70	£200
1689 September	£6	£20	£70	£200
1689 October	£8	£25	£90	£225
1689 November	£6	£20	£70	£200
1689 December	£6	£20	£70	£185
1689 January	£6	£20	£70	£185
1689 February	£6	£20	£70	£185

	Fair	F	VF	EF
1689 March	£7	£20	£70	£200
1690 March	£8	£25	£70	£200
1690 April	£8	£25	£90	£225
Small Shillings, 1690 April	£10	£30	£110	£250
1690 May	£7	£20	£80	£225
1690 June	£7	£20	£80	£225
1690 July	*	*	*	*
1690 August	*	*	*	*
1690 September	£20	£135	*	*
Sixpences, 1689 June	£10	£35	£110	£250
1689 July	£8	£30	£100	£200
1689 August	£8	£30	£100	£200
1689 September	£10	£35	£125	£250
1689 October	*	*	*	*
1689 November	£8	£30	£100	£200
1689 December	£8	£30	£100	£200
1689 January	£10	£35	£110	£250
1689 February	£8	£30	£100	£200
1689 March	*	*	*	*
1690 March	*	*	*	*
1690 April	*	*	*	*
1690 May	£15	£45	£140	*
1690 June	*	*	*	*
1690 October	*	*	*	*

Pewter Money

	Fair	F	VF	EF
Crowns	£475	£1750	£4500	*
Groats	£225	£900	£3000	*
Pennies large bust	£300	£700	*	*
Small bust	£325	£750	*	*
Halfpennies large bust	£75	£250	£750	*
Halfpennies small bust	£65	£200	£525	*

Limerick Money Halfpenny

Limerick Money

	Fair	F	VF	EF
Halfpennies	£15	£50	£150	£375
Farthings reversed N	£20	£70	£200	£500
Normal N	£25	£75	£225	*

William and Mary 1693 Halfpenny

WILLIAM AND MARY

	Fair	F	VF	EF
Halfpennies, 1692	£7	£40	£140	*
1693	£7	£40	£140	*
1694	£10	£50	£175	*

WILLIAM III

	Fair	F	VF	EF
Halfpennies, 1696 draped bust	£15	£50	£200	*
Halfpennies 1696 crude undraped bust	£40	£175	£525	*

GEORGE I
Wood's coinage

	Fair	F	VF	EF
Halfpennies, 1722 harp left	£12	£50	£200	*
1722 harp right	£8	£25	£125	£525
1723	£6	£20	£90	£395
1723 obv Rs altered Bs	£7	£20	£90	£395
1723 no stop after date	£7	£20	£90	£395
1723/2	£7	£25	£100	£425
1723 star in rev legend	*	*	*	*
1723 no stop before HIBERNIA	£6	£20	£80	£395
1724 head divided rev legend	£7	£25	£125	£575
1724 legend continuous over head	£10	£30	£150	*
Farthings 1722 harp left	£30	£125	£575	*
1723 D: G:	£10	£40	£195	£725
1723 DEI GRATIA	£6	£20	£80	£325
1724	£8	£30	£95	£400

GEORGE II

	Fair	F	VF	EF
Halfpennies, 1736	*	£10	£50	£300
1737	*	£10	£50	£300
1738	£1	£12	£60	£375
1741	*	£10	£50	£300
1742	*	£10	£50	£300
1743	£2	£15	£60	£395
1744	£1	£12	£60	£325
1744/3	£2	£15	£60	£375
1746	£1	£12	£60	£375
1747	*	£10	£50	£300
1748	£2	£12	£65	£395
1749	*	£10	£50	£300
1750	*	£10	£45	£275
1751	*	£10	£45	£275
1752	*	£10	£45	£275
1753	*	£12	£50	£275
1755	*	*	*	*
1760	*	£10	£40	£275
Farthings, 1737	£1	£12	£65	£300
1738	*	£10	£50	£300
1744	*	£10	£45	£275
1760	*	£8	£40	£250

Voce Populi coinage

	Fair	F	VF	EF
Halfpennies, 1760, Type 1	£35	£150	£425	*
Type 2	£5	£175	£350	*

	Fair	F	VF	EF
Type 3	£75	£175	£400	*
Type 4	£60	£150	£325	*
Type 5	£60	£150	£300	*
Type 6	£60	£150	£300	*
Type 7	£60	£160	£350	£1100
Type 8	£60	£150	£300	*
Type 9	£75	£175	£400	*
Type 9, P before head	£25	£100	£300	£850
Type 9, P under head	£25	£100	£300	£850
Farthings, 1760, Type 1				
loop to truncation	£75	£250	£1250	£3500
Type 2 no loop	*	*	*	*

GEORGE III

London coinage	F	VF	EF	Unc
Halfpennies, 1766	£5	£25	£195	£500
1769	£5	£30	£225	£525
1769 2nd type	£5	£40	£235	£550
1775	£5	£30	£225	£525
1776	£25	£125	£385	*
1781	£5	£20	£160	£450
1782	£5	£20	£160	£400

Soho coinage

Penny 1805	*	£30	£125	£275
Halfpenny 1805	*	£15	£85	£165
Farthing 1806	*	£12	£50	£120

Bank of Ireland token coinage

Silver Six shillings 1804	£85	£250	£525	£875

Bank of Ireland token coinage 1804 Six shillings

Thirty pence 1808	£25	£75	£325	*
Ten pence 1805	£8	£25	£100	£100
Ten pence 1806	£10	£30	£125	£175
Ten pence 1813	£6	£20	£80	£125
Five pence 1805	£6	£20	£80	£125
Five pence 1806	£8	£25	£90	£140

George IV proof penny, 1822

GEORGE IV	Fair	F	VF	EF
Penny 1822	£8	£40	£175	£375
1823	£10	£60	£200	£425
Halfpenny 1822	£5	£15	£110	£225
1823	£5	£15	£125	£250

■ FREE STATE AND REPUBLIC

Proofs exist for nearly all dates of the modern Irish coinage. However, only a few dates have become available to collectors or dealers and apart from the 1928 proofs, are all very rare. They have therefore been omitted from the list.

TEN SHILLINGS	F	VF	EF	Unc
1966	*	£2	£6	£15
1966 proof	*	*	*	£25

HALFCROWNS				
1928	£2	£8	£12	£45
1928 proof	*	*	*	£50
1930	£4	£12	£110	£395
1931	£8	£20	£150	£465
1933	£5	£15	£120	£350
1934	£5	£12	£60	£225
1937	£35	£85	£550	£1450
1938	*	*	*	*
1939	£3	£5	£25	£65
1940	£3	£6	£20	£60
1941	£4	£6	£25	£65
1942	£2	£4	£20	£60
1943	£70	£150	£850	£2600
1951	*	*	£6	£35
1954	*	*	£7	£40
1955	*	*	£5	£20
1959	*	*	£4	£17
1961	*	*	£5	£15
1961 mule normal				
obv/pre-1939 rev	£8	£20	£300	*
1962	*	*	*	£5
1963	*	*	*	£10
1964	*	*	*	£5
1966	*	*	*	£10
1967	*	*	*	£3

FLORINS

	F	VF	EF	Unc
1928	*	£5	£18	£40
1928 proof	*	*	*	£55
1930	£3	£15	£100	£350
1931	£5	£35	£150	£350
1933	£8	£18	£125	£375
1934	£12	£60	£275	£550
1935	£3	£10	£125	£350
1937	£5	£18	£200	£465
1939	£2	£4	£10	£40
1940	£2	£5	£12	£40
1941	£2	£5	£20	£65
1942	£2	£5	£12	£45
1943	£2750	£7000	£12000	*
1951	*	*	£3	£25
1954	*	*	£3	£20
1955	*	*	£3	£20
1959	*	*	£3	£20
1961	*	£3	£6	£40
1962	*	*	£3	£18
1963	*	*	£3	£18
1964	*	*	*	£5
1965	*	*	*	£5
1966	*	*	*	£5
1968	*	*	*	£5

SHILLINGS

	F	VF	EF	Unc
1928	*	£3	£8	£28
1928 proof	*	*	*	£30
1930	£7	£20	£85	£350
1931	£3	£15	£65	£245
1933	£5	£10	£80	£300
1935	£2	£5	£40	£120
1937	£10	£25	£250	£900
1939	*	£3	£8	£35
1940	*	£3	£12	£40
1941	*	£5	£15	£45
1942	*	£5	£8	£28
1951	*	*	£3	£20
1954	*	*	£3	£15
1955	*	*	£3	£18
1959	*	*	£6	£25
1962	*	*	*	£5
1963	*	*	*	£4
1964	*	*	*	£5
1966	*	*	*	£4
1968	*	*	*	£4

SIXPENCES

	F	VF	EF	Unc
1928	*	*	£3	£25
1928 proof	*	*	*	£30
1934	*	*	£12	£65
1935	*	£3	£18	£90
1939	*	*	£5	£35
1940	*	*	£5	£25
1942	*	*	£5	£25
1945	£2	£8	£40	£150
1946	£5	£12	£85	£425
1947	*	£6	£25	£100

	F	VF	EF	Unc
1948	*	£2	£8	£35
1949	*	*	£5	£30
1950	£2	£15	£35	£150
1952	*	*	£4	£20
1953	*	*	£5	£22
1955	*	*	£4	£18
1956	*	*	£3	£12
1958	*	*	£5	£40
1959	*	*	£2	£7
1960	*	*	£2	£7
1961	*	*	£2	£7
1962	*	*	£3	£30
1964	*	*	*	£3
1965	*	*	*	£3
1966	*	*	*	£3
1967	*	*	*	£3
1968	*	*	*	£2
1969	*	*	*	£3

THREEPENCES

	F	VF	EF	Unc
1928	*	*	£3	£18
1928 proof	*	*	£3	£25
1933	£2	£5	£60	£250
1934	*	£3	£15	£65
1935	£2	£5	£25	£150
1939	*	£5	£50	£200
1940	*	*	£10	£40
1942	*	*	£5	£35
1943	*	*	£8	£75
1946	*	*	£5	£30
1948	*	£2	£15	£80
1949	*	*	£5	£30
1950	*	*	£2	£6
1953	*	*	£2	£5
1956	*	*	*	£4
1961	*	*	*	£3
1962	*	*	*	£3
1963	*	*	*	£3
1964	*	*	*	£3
1965	*	*	*	£3
1966	*	*	*	£3
1967	*	*	*	*
1968	*	*	*	*

PENNIES

	F	VF	EF	Unc
1928	*	*	£6	£25
1928 proof	*	*	*	£35
1931	*	£2	£25	£80
1933	*	£3	£40	£150
1935	*	*	£15	£45
1937	*	*	£25	£80
1938				
(possibly unique)	*	*	*	£20000
1940	*	£15	£90	£400
1941	*	*	£6	£30
1942	*	*	£3	£15
1943	*	*	£5	£20
1946	*	*	£3	£15
1948	*	*	£3	£15

	F	VF	EF	Unc
1949	*	*	£3	£15
1950	*	*	£3	£15
1952	*	*	£2	£7
1962	*	*	£2	£3
1963	*	*	*	£2
1964	*	*	*	£2
1965	*	*	*	£1
1966	*	*	*	£1
1967	*	*	*	£1
1968	*	*	*	£1

HALFPENNIES

	F	VF	EF	Unc
1928	*	*	£4	£20
1928 proof	*	*	*	£25
1933	*	£20	£100	£365
1935	*	£10	£80	£225
1937	*	*	£12	£40
1939	*	£10	£30	£140
1940	*	£10	£35	£165
1941	*	*	£5	£25
1942	*	*	£2	£20
1943	*	*	£5	£25
1946	*	*	£15	£65
1949	*	*	£3	£18
1953	*	*	*	£4
1964	*	*	*	£2
1965	*	*	*	£2
1966	*	*	*	£2
1967	*	*	*	£1

FARTHINGS

	F	VF	EF	Unc
1928	*	*	£3	£12
1928 proof	*	*	*	£20
1930	*	*	£5	£18
1931	£1	£3	£8	£30
1932	£1	£3	£10	£35
1933	*	£2	£5	£25
1935	*	£5	£12	£45
1936	*	£6	£15	£50
1937	*	£2	£5	£20
1939	*	*	£3	£12
1940	*	£3	£6	£35
1941	*	*	£3	£7
1943	*	*	£3	£7
1944	*	*	£3	£7
1946	*	*	£3	£7
1949	*	*	£5	£10
1953	*	*	£3	£7
1959	*	*	£1	£4
1966	*	*	£2	£6

DECIMAL COINAGE

50p, 10p, 5p, 2p, 1p, ½p, all face value only.

SETS

1928 in card case	*	*	FDC	£285
1928 in leather case	*	*	FDC	£350
1966 unc set	*	*	*	£10
1971 specimen set in folder	*	*	*	£5
1971 proof set	*	*	*	£9

THE ANGLO-GALLIC SERIES

Anyone interested in studying this series should obtain *The Anglo-Gallic Coins* by E R D Elias, who neatly summarised the series: 'All Kings of England in the period 1154-1453 had interests in France. They were Dukes or Lords of Aquitaine, Counts of Poitou or Ponthieu, Lords of Issoudun or they were even or pretended to be, Kings of France itself, and, in those various capacities, struck coins.

These coins, together with the French coins of their sons, and of their English vassals, are called Anglo-Gallic coins'.

See our table for the English kings' French titles.

KINGS OF ENGLAND AND FRANCE 1154-1453

ENGLAND	FRANCE
Henry II 1154-89 Duke of Normandy and Count of Anjou, Maine and Touraine. By marrying Eleanor of Aquitaine in 1152, he became Duke of Aquitaine and Count of Poitou. He relinquished Aquitaine and Poitou to his son Richard in 1168. In 1185 he forced Richard to surrender Aquitaine and Poitou to Eleanor who governed between 1199-1204.	**Louis VII 1137-80** **Philip II 1180-1223**
Richard I the Lionheart 1189-99 Formally installed as Duke of Aquitaine and Count of Poitou in 1172.	
John 1199-1216 He lost all parts of the Angevin Empire except Aquitaine and part of Poitou.	
Henry III 1216-72 In 1252 he ceded Aquitaine to his son Edward.	**Louis VIII 1223-26** **Louis IX 1226-70** **Philip III 1270-85**
Edward I 1272-1307 He governed Aquitaine from 1252. In 1279 he became Count of Ponthieu. In 1290 the county went to his son Edward.	**Philip IV 1285-1314**
Edward II 1307-27 He was Count of Ponthieu from 1290. In 1325 he relinquished the county of Ponthieu and the Duchy of Aquitaine to his son Edward.	**Louis X 1314-16** **Philip V 1316-22** **Charles IV 1322-28**
Edward III 1327-77 Count of Ponthieu and Duke of Aquitaine from 1325. He lost Ponthieu in 1337 but it was restored in 1360. In 1340 he assumed the title of King of France, which he abandoned again in 1360. He gave Aquitaine to his son, Edward the Black Prince, (b1330-d1376), who was Prince of Aquitaine 1362-1372, although he actually ruled from 1363-1371. In 1369 Edward III reassumed the title King of France.	**Philip VI 1328-50** **John II 1350-64** **Charles V 1364-80**
Richard II 1377-99 The son of the Black Prince succeeded his grandfather, Edward III, as King of England and Lord of Aquitaine.	**Charles VI** **1380-1422**
Henry IV 1399-1413 He adopted the same titles as Richard II.	
Henry V 1413-22 From 1417-1420 he used the title King of the French on his 'Royal' French coins. After the Treaty of Troyes in 1420 he styled himself 'heir of France'.	
Henry VI 1422-61 He inherited the title King of the French from his grandfather Charles VI. He lost actual rule in Northern France in 1450 and in Aquitaine in 1453.	**Charles VII** **1422-61**

HENRY II 1152-68

	F	VF
Denier	£45	£110
Obole	£90	£220

RICHARD THE LIONHEART 1168-99
Aquitaine

	F	VF
Denier	£60	£135
Obole	£60	£135

Poitou

	F	VF
Denier	£45	£100
Obole	£60	£160

Issoudun

	F	VF
Denier	£250	*

ELEANOR 1199-1204

	F	VF
Denier	£65	£145
Obole	£285	*

EDWARD I
During the lifetime of his father 1252-72

	F	VF
Denier au lion	£30	£90
Obole au lion	£45	£120

After succession to the English throne 1272-1307

		F	VF
Denier au lion		£60	£150
Obole au lion		£145	*
Denier á la croix longue		£70	£165
Au léopard, first type		£30	£85
Obole au léopard, first type	£55	£140	
Denier á la couronne		£250	*

EDWARD II

	F	VF
Gros Turonus Regem	ext. rare	
Maille blanche	ext. rare	
Hibernie	£45	£135

EDWARD III
Gold coins

	F	VF
Ecu d'or	£1850	£4000
Florin	£3950	£8000
Léopard d'or, 1st issue	ext. rare	
2nd issue	£2000	£4500
3rd issue	£1850	£4250

	F	VF
4th issue	£2000	£4500
Guyennois d'or, 1st type	£3950	£8250
2nd type	£2250	£5500
3rd type	£1850	£4250

Silver coins

	F	VF
Gros aquitanique au léopard	£190	£565
Tournois à la croix mi-longue	£295	£865
À la croix longue	£140	£300
Sterling	£90	£260
Demi-sterling	£165	£425
Gros au léopard passant	£575	*
À la couronne	£140	£400
Au châtel aquitanique	£185	£575
Tournois au léopard au-dessus	£85	£260
À la porte	£85	£260
Aquitanique au léopard au-dessous	£260	*
Blanc au léopard sous couronne	£75	£165
Gros au léopard sous couronne	£195	£585
À la couronne avec léopard	£165	£465
Sterling à la tête barbue	£300	£825
Petit gros de Bordeaux	ext. rare	
Gros au lion	£140	£400
Demi-gros au lion	£275	*
Guyennois d'argent (sterling)	£95	£250
Gros au buste	£1000	*
Demi-gros au buste	£575	£1450

Black coins

	F	VF
Double à la couronne, 1st type	£110	*
2nd type	£90	£265
3rd type	£185	*
Double au léopard	£70	£175
Sous couronne	£35	£100
Guyennois	ext. rare	
Denier au léopard, 2nd type	£35	£100
Obole au léopard, 2nd type	ext. rare	
Denier au léopard, 3rd type	£40	£120
4th type	£35	£100
Obole au léopard, 4th type	£40	£120
Denier au lion	£45	£145

Some issues of the 2nd and 3rd type deniers au léopard are very rare to extremely rare and therefore much more valuable.

EDWARD THE BLACK PRINCE 1362-72

Edward III 2nd issue léopard d'or

Edward the Black Prince chaise d'or of Bordeaux

ANGLO-GALLIC

Gold coins	F	VF
Léopard d'or	£2250	£5000
Guyennois d'or	£2500	£5500
Chaise d'or	£2250	£5000
Pavillon d'or 1st issue	£2250	£5000
2nd issue	£2250	£5000
Demi-pavillon d'or	*	*
Hardi d'or	£1850	£4500

Silver coins		
Gros	£750	£1875
Demi-gros	£110	£300
Sterling	£75	£165
Hardi d'argent	£50	£135

Black coins		
Double guyennois	£120	£295
Denier au lion	£55	£145
Denier	£60	£150

RICHARD II 1377-99

Gold coins		
Hardi d'or	£2650	£7000
Demi-hardi d'or		ext. rare

Silver coins		
Double hardi d'argent	£750	£2350
Hardi d'argent	£55	£165

Black coins		
Denier	£90	£260

HENRY IV 1399-1413

Silver coins		
Double hardi d'argent	£500	£1450
Hardi d'argent	£40	£125
Hardi aux genêts	£175	£550

Black coins		
Denier	£55	£150
Aux genêts	£150	£385

HENRY V 1413-22

Gold coins		
Agnel d'or	£6000	£15000
Salut d'or	£6750	£18000

Silver coins		
Florette, 1st issue	£90	£225
2nd issue	£150	£385
3rd issue	£65	£175
4th issue	£90	£225
Guénar	£300	£950
Gros au léopard	£395	*

Black coins		
Mansiois		ext. rare
Niquet	£60	£180
Denier tournois	£75	£195

HENRY VI 1422-53

Gold coins	F	VF
Salut d'or	£625	£1250
Angelot	£2000	£5500

Henry VI Salut d'or Paris mint

Silver coins		
Grand blanc aux ècus	£75	£225
Petit blanc	£90	£265
Trésin		ext. rare

Black coins		
Denier Paris, 1st issue	£70	£160
2nd issue	£70	£160
Denier tournois	£75	£175
Maille tournois	£75	£175

The prices of the saluts and grands blancs are for mints of Paris, Rouen and Saint Lô; coins of other mints are rare to very rare.

■ PONTHIEU

EDWARD I

Denier	£95	£250
Obole	£85	£215

EDWARD III

Denier	£150	*
Obole	£225	*

■ BERGERAC

HENRY, EARL OF LANCASTER 1347-51

Gros tournois à la croix longue		£825	£1850
À la couronne		£725	*
Au châtel aquitainique		£825	£1850
Tournois au léopard au-dessus	£550	£1200	
À la couronne			ext. rare
À fleur-de-lis			ext. rare
Au léopard passant			ext. rare
Double		£1150	*
Denier au léopard		£750	*

HENRY, DUKE OF LANCASTER 1351-61

Gros tournois à la couronne avec léopard	£825	*
Au léopard couchant	£825	*
Sterling à la tête barbue	£725	*
Gros au lion		ext. rare

ISLAND COINAGE

Proofs have been struck for a large number of Channel Islands coins, particularly in the case of Jersey. Except for those included in modern proof sets, most are very rare and in the majority of cases have been omitted from the list.

For further information refer to *The Coins of the British Commonwealth of Nations, Part I, European Territories* by F Pridmore (Spink, 1960).

■ GUERNSEY

	F	VF	EF	BU
TEN SHILLINGS				
1966	*	*	*	£2
THREEPENCE				
1956	*	*	*	£2
1959	*	*	*	£2
1966 proof	*	*	*	£2
EIGHT DOUBLES				
1834	*	£12	£65	£385
1858	*	£12	£65	£385
1864	*	£15	£50	*
1868	*	£10	£50	*
1874	*	£10	£50	*
1885 H	*	*	£15	£70
1889 H	*	*	£15	£65
1893 H	*	*	£15	£65
1902 H	*	*	£15	£45
1903 H	*	*	£15	£50
1910 H	*	*	£15	£50
1911 H	*	£15	£40	£100
1914 H	*	*	£12	£45
1918 H	*	*	£12	£45
1920 H	*	*	£5	£25
1934 H	*	*	£5	£25
1934 H 'burnished flan'	*	*	*	£200
1938 H	*	*	*	£12
1945 H	*	*	*	£10
1947 H	*	*	*	£10
1949 H	*	*	*	£10
1956	*	*	*	£7
1956 proof	*	*	*	£10
1959	*	*	*	£3
1966 proof	*	*	*	£3
FOUR DOUBLES				
1830	*	*	£45	£285
1858	*	*	£50	£325
1864	*	£5	£50	*
1868	*	£5	£50	*
1874	*	*	£50	*
1885 H	*	*	£8	£50
1889 H	*	*	£8	£55
1893 H	*	*	£8	£35
1902 H	*	*	£8	£45
1903 H	*	*	£8	£45

	F	VF	EF	BU
1906 H	*	*	£8	£70
1908 H	*	*	£8	£65
1910 H	*	*	£5	£55
1911 H	*	*	£5	£45
1914 H	*	*	£5	£45
1918 H	*	*	£5	£35
1920 H	*	*	*	£30
1945 H	*	*	*	£15
1949 H	*	*	*	£18
1956	*	*	*	£5
1956 proof	*	*	*	£8
1966 proof	*	*	*	£2
TWO DOUBLES				
1858	*	£30	£125	£395
1868	*	£30	£125	£375
1874	*	£30	£125	£325
1885 H	*	*	£20	£40
1889 H	*	*	£20	£45
1899 H	*	*	£20	£45
1902 H	*	*	£20	£45
1903 H	*	*	£25	£45
1906 H	*	*	£25	£50
1908 H	*	*	£25	£50
1911 H	*	*	£45	£90
1914 H	*	*	£45	£90
1917 H	£25	£50	£150	*
1918 H	*	*	£20	£40
1920 H	*	*	£20	£40
1929 H	*	*	£5	£12
ONE DOUBLE				
1830	*	*	£20	£75
1868	*	£40	£100	£350
1868/30	*	£40	£100	£350
1885 H	*	*	£3	£15
1889 H	*	*	£3	£15
1893 H	*	*	£3	£15
1899 H	*	*	£3	£15
1902 H	*	*	£3	£15
1903 H	*	*	£3	£15
1911 H	*	*	£3	£15
1911 H new type	*	*	£3	£15
1914 H	*	*	£3	£15
1929 H	*	*	£3	£15
1933 H	*	*	£3	£15
1938 H	*	*	£3	£12
SETS				
1956 proof				£45
1966 proof				£10
1971 proof				£10

For coins after 1971 refer to the *Standard Catalogue of World Coins* published by Krause Publications annually.

■ JERSEY

CROWN	F	VF	EF	BU
1966	*	*	*	£4
1966 proof	*	*	*	£8

¼ OF A SHILLING

	F	VF	EF	BU
1957	*	*	*	£6
1960 proof only	*	*	*	£75
1964	*	*	*	£4
1966	*	*	*	£4

1/12 OF A SHILLING

	F	VF	EF	BU
1877 H	*	*	£18	£110
1881	*	*	£15	£75
1888	*	*	£15	£65
1894	*	*	£12	£60
1909	*	*	£15	£100
1911	*	*	£10	£50
1913	*	*	£10	£50
1923	*	*	£10	£50
1923 new type	*	*	£12	£60
1926	*	*	£12	£50
1931	*	*	£5	£25
1933	*	*	£5	£25
1935	*	*	£5	£25
1937	*	*	*	£18
'1945' (George VI)	*	*	£5	£12
'1945' (Elizabeth II)	*	*	*	£8
1946	*	*	*	£12
1947	*	*	*	£12
1957	*	*	*	£5
1960	*	*	*	£5
1964	*	*	*	£4
1966	*	*	*	£3
1966 proof	*	*	*	£7

The date 1945 on 1/12 shillings commemorates the year of liberation from German occupation. The coins were struck in 1949, 1950, 1952 and 1954.

1/13 OF A SHILLING

	F	VF	EF	BU
1841	*	*	£70	£265
1844	*	*	£70	£265
1851	*	*	£77	£265
1858	*	*	£70	£265
1861	*	*	£70	£265
1865 proof only	*	*	*	£800
1866	*	*	£40	£135
1870	*	*	£40	£135
1871	*	*	£40	£135

1/24 OF A SHILLING

	F	VF	EF	BU
1877 proof only	*	*	*	£350
1877 H	*	*	£20	£85
1888	*	*	£15	£45
1894	*	*	£15	£45
1909	*	*	£15	£60
1911	*	*	£12	£40
1913	*	*	£12	£35

	F	VF	EF	BU
1923	*	*	£10	£35
1923 new type	*	*	£10	£35
1926	*	*	£12	£45
1931	*	*	£7	£25
1933	*	*	£7	£20
1935	*	*	£7	£15
1937	*	*	£7	£12
1946	*	*	£7	£12
1947	*	*	£7	£12

1/26 OF A SHILLING

	F	VF	EF	BU
1841	*	*	£50	£225
1844	*	*	£50	£250
1851	*	*	£50	£225
1858	*	*	£50	£225
1861	*	*	£45	£195
1866	*	*	£25	£130
1870	*	*	£25	£130
1871	*	*	£25	£130

1/48 OF A SHILLING

	F	VF	EF	BU
1877 proof	*	*	*	£365
1877 H	*	£25	£95	£225

1/52 OF A SHILLING

	F	VF	EF	BU
1841	*	£40	£175	£450
1841 proof	*	*	*	£750
1861 proof	*	*	*	£850

DECIMAL COINAGE

SETS	BU
1957	£30
1960	£15
1964	£12
1966 four coins, proof	£8
1966 two crowns	£10
1972 Silver Wedding five gold, four silver coins	BV
1972 proof	BV
1972 four silver coins	£50

For coins after 1972 refer to the *Standard Catalogue of World Coins* published by Krause Publications annually.

■ ISLE OF MAN

Contemporary forgeries of earlier Isle of Man coins exist.

Copper and Bronze 1709-1839

James Stanley, 10th Earl of Derby, penny, 1709

PENNIES	F	VF	EF	Unc
1709	£60	£250	*	*
1723	£1750	*	*	*
1733	£45	£225	£600	*
1733 proof	*	£500	£850	*

Proof penny in silver, 1733

1733 silver	*	£500	£800	*
1758	£40	£125	£475	*
1758 proof	*	*	£850	*
1758 silver	*	*	£1750	*
1786	£15	£70	£350	£500
1786 plain edge proof	*	*	£750	£1200
1798	£15	£60	£300	£600
1798 bronzed proof	*	*	£425	£700
1798 AE gilt proof	*	*	£1250	£2250
1798 silver proof	*	*	£2000	£3000
1813	£15	£60	£300	£600
1813 bronze proof	*	*	£425	£700
1813 gilt proof	*	*	£1250	£2250
1839	*	£15	£75	£250
1839 proof	*	*	*	£875
1841 proof	*	*	*	£1875
1859 proof	*	*	*	£2850

HALFPENNIES
1709	£75	£185	*	*
1723	£1500	*	*	*
1723 silver	£1500	*	*	*

1733	£65	£250	£500	£750
1733 proof	*	*	£650	£850
1733 silver	*	*	£650	£850
1758	£20	£60	£250	£550
1758 proof	*	*	*	£1250
1786	£10	£50	£200	£395
1786 plain edge proof	*	*	£425	£875
1798	£10	£40	£185	£365

Proof halfpenny, 1798

1798 proof	*	*	£285	£485
1798 silver proof	*	*	£1500	£2500
1798 gilt proof	*	*	*	£1250
1813	£10	£40	£185	£365
1813 proof	*	*	£250	£450
1813 gilt proof	*	*	*	£1250
1839	*	*	£45	£165
1839 proof	*	*	*	*proof
* *		*	£2750	

FARTHINGS
1839	£10	£25	£45	£125
1839 proof	*	*	*	£550
1841 proof only	*	*	*	£1550
1860 proof only	*	*	*	£2850
1864 proof only	*	*	*	£3850

BRITISH PAPER MONEY

Notes signed by the previous Chief Cashier, Andrew Bailey, are generally available at a little above face.

Notes prior to his tenure tend to increase in value, especially the very early notes.

Condition is the most important factor in banknote pricing although it is possible to collect an attractive selection in lower grades; some notes are never seen in better than Very Fine.

We have not listed banknotes prior to 1914 as these are scarce and are generally only available in grades up to Very Fine.

Serial numbers with the prefix 'No' are referred to as 'dot' if 'No' is followed by a full stop and 'dash' if followed by a dash.

Reference numbers are according to Vincent Duggleby's *English Paper Money*. The 8th edition (Pam West, 2011) is a must for the collector.

■ TREASURY NOTES

JOHN BRADBURY

			VF	EF
First issue				
T8	10s	Red on white, six digits	£550	£950
T9	10s	Prefix 'No'	£350	£650
T10	10s	Red on white, five digits	£650	£1200
T1	£1	Black on white, prefix large letters A, B or C	£1400	£2000
T2	£1	No full stop after serial letter	£2100	£3600
T3	£1	Six digits	£500	£850
T4	£1	Large serial number, 'dot' and five digits	£750	£1500
T5	£1	Large serial number, 'dash' and five digits	£800	£1450
T6	£1	Letter, letter, number, number	£800	£1450
T7	£1	Small typeface serial number	*	
Second issue				
T12	10s	Red on white, five digits	£225	£450
T13	10s	Six digits	£280	£500
T11	£1	Black on white	£280	£550
T15	10s	Arabic overprint	£720	£1450
T14	£1	Arabic overprint	£3500	£7000
Third issue				
T16	£1	Green and brown on white	£90	£190
T17	10s	Black serial no with 'dot'	£380	£630
T18	10s	Black serial no with 'dash'	£400	£650
T19	10s	Red serial no with 'dot'	£1700	*
T20	10s	Red serial no with 'dash'	£300	£500

NORMAN FENWICK WARREN FISHER

First issue

T25	10s	Green and brown		

		on white, 'dot'	£160	£340
T26	10s	'Dash'	£160	£340
T24	£1	Green and brown on white	£70	£140

Second issue

T30	10s	Green and brown on white	£100	£240
T31	£1	'Dot'	£65	£140
T32	£1	Square 'dot'	£160	£330

Third issue, Northern Ireland

T33	10s	Green and brown on white	£130	£260
T34	£1	'Dot'	£90	£170
T35	£1	Square 'dot'	£180	£350

Fractionals

727	5s	Violet and green on white from	good	£1000
T28	2s 6d	Olive-green and chocolate from	fine	£3000
T29	1s	Green and brown on white from	fine	£3000

■ BANK OF ENGLAND NOTES

CYRIL PATRICK MAHON 1925-29

			VF	F
B210	10s	Red-brown	£100	£200
B212	£1	Green	£50	£95
B215	£5	Black and white	£320	£540

BASIL GAGE CATTERNS 1929-34

B223	10s	Red-brown	£40	£80
B225	£1	Green, prefix: letters, number, number	£20	£40
B226	£1	Prefix: number, number, letter	£70	£150
B228	£5	Black on white	£220	£450

KENNETH OSWALD PEPPIATT 1934-49

B236	10s	Red-brown, prefix: number, number, letter 1st period	£30	£65
B251	10s	Mauve, 2nd period	£25	£50
B256	10s	Red-brown, prefix: number, number, letter, 3rd period	£60	£120
B262	10s	Metal filament, 4th period	£18	£45
B238	£1	Green, prefix: number, number, letter, 1st issue	£10	£35
B249	£1	Blue (shades), 2nd issue	£6	£16
B258	£1	Green, prefix: letter, number, number, letter, 3rd issue	£10	£35
B260	£1	Metal filament, 4th issue	£8	£16
B241	£5	Black on white, one straight edge, three deckled	£140	£300
B255	£5	Straight edges, metal filament, thick paper	£80	£160
B264	£5	Straight edges, metal filament, thin paper	£80	£140

Fractionals

B253	5s	Olive-green on pale pink background from	£5000	*

			VF	EF
B254	2s 6d	Black on pale blue		
		background from	£5000	*

PERCIVAL SPENCER BEALE 1949-55

			VF	EF
B265	10s	Red-brown, prefix: number,		
		number, letter	£16	£30
B266	10s	Prefix: letter, number,		
		number, letter	£8	£18
B268	f1	Green	£3	£8
B270	£5	Black on white	£65	£100

LESLIE KENNETH O'BRIEN 1955-62

			VF	EF
B271	10s	Red-brown, prefix: letter,		
		number, number, letter	£5	£13
B272	10s	Replacement	£50	£100
B273	£1	Green	£4	£9
B275	£5	Black on white	£80	£145
B277	£5	Blue, pale green and orange,		
		solid blue symbols reverse	£16	£32
B280	£5	Hollow white £5		
		symbols reverse	£16	£80

Queen's portrait			EF	Unc
B281	£1	Prefix: letter number number	£3	£6
B282	£1	Prefix: number number letter	£3	£6
B284	£1	prefix: letter number		
		number letter	£14	£27

JASPER QUINTUS HOLLOM 1962-66

B294	10s	Red-brown, prefix: number,		
		number, letter	£3	£7
B295	10s	Red-brown, prefix: number,		
		number, letter	£3	£7
B288	£1	Green	£3	£7
B292	£1	Green, letter 'G' reverse	£6	£16
B297	£5	Blue	£16	£40
B299	£10	Multicoloured brown	£28	£50

JOHN STANDISH FFORDE 1966-70

B309	10s	Red-brown, prefix:		
		number, number, letter	£3	£7
B310	10s	Prefix: letter, number,		
		number, letter	£3	£7
B311	10s	Prefix: letter, number, number	£7	£13
B301	£1	Green	£4	£10
B303	£1	'G' variety	£6	£12
B312	£5	Blue, prefix: letter,		
		number, number	£16	£40
B314	£5	Prefix: number,		
		number, letter	£18	£45
B316	£10	Multicoloured brown	£24	£50
B318	£20	Multicoloured purple	£160	£30

JOHN BRANGWYN PAGE 1970-80

B322	£1	Green, prefix: letter, letter,		
		number, number	£2	£5
B324	£5	Blue	£24	£50
B332	£5	Multicoloured, prefix: letter,		
		number, number, 1st series	£12	£27

B334	£5	L on reverse, signifies		
		lithographic printing	£12	£27
B326	£10	Multicoloured	£24	£50
B330	£10	Prefix: letter,		
		number, number	£18	£36
B328	£20	Multicoloured purple	£40	£80

DAVID HENRY FITZROY SOMERSET 1980-88

B341	£1	Green	£2	56
B343	£5	Multicoloured, prefix: letter,		
		letter, number, number	£7	£18
B346	£10	Multicoloured, prefix: letter,		
		letter, number, number	£28	£65
B350	£20	Multicoloured purple	£45	£100
B352	£50	Olive green, brown, grey	£65	£110

GEORGE MALCOLM GILL 1988-91

B353	£5	Blue	£8	£20
B357	£5	Multicoloured, Series E	£6	£18
B354	£10	Brown	£16	£32
B355	£20	Multicoloured purple	£50	£105
B358	£20	Multicoloured purple	£35	£75
B356	£50	Olive green, brown, grey	£80	£140

GRAHAM EDWARD ALFRED KENTFIELD 1991-1998

B362	£5	Multicoloured blue	£12	£28
B363	£5	Multicoloured letter, letter,		
		number, number	£10	£22
B364	£5	Multicoloured blue	£6	£13
B360	£10	Multicoloured brown	£25	£60
B361	£50	Olive green, brown, grey	£80	£150
B366	£10	Multicoloured brown	£12	£28
B369	£10	Multicoloured brown	£12	£26
B371	£20	Multicoloured purple	£35	£75
B374	£20	Multicoloured purple	£35	£65
B377	£50	Red	£60	£100

MERLYN VIVIENNE LOWTHER 1999-2004

B380	£5	Multicoloured blue	£6	£14
B393	£5	Multicoloured blue	£5	£9
B395	£5	Multicoloured blue	£5	£8
B382	£10	Multicoloured brown	£18	£30
B388	£10	Multicoloured And 'Co'	£10	£20
B390	£10	Multicoloured The 'Co'	£12	£20
B384	£20	Multicoloured purple	£45	£80
B386	£20	Multicoloured purple	£22	£34
B385	£50	Red	£55	£95

ANDREW JOHN BAILEY 2004-

B398	£5	Multicoloured blue	face	£8
B400	£10	Multicoloured brown	face	£15
B402	£20	Multicoloured purple	£25	£28
B405	£20	Adam Smith reverse	face	£25
B404	£50	Red	face	£60

A new £50 will be issued at the end of 2011 featuring James Watt and Mathew Boulton, signed by the new chief cashier, Chris Salmon. According to press releases, this was originally due to be issued at the end of 2010. Other denominations with Salmon signature will follow.

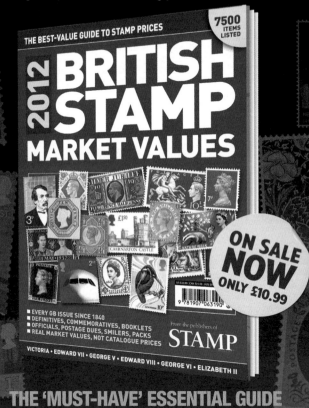

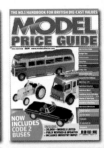

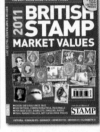

LINDNER
Das Original

Solid Wood Case Premium

Pure wood case containing 3 wooden trays with recess to enable easy removal from case. Several different combinations of red inserts, which are compatible with the standard Lindner coin boxes, are available.

Item 2493-1 Wood Case 3 trays, 1 each 48, 25 20 compartments

Price £53.40

REBECK L Coin Holders

Self adhesive coin holders with extra space for writing on. Can be used in landscape or portrait format. Overall size of each coin holder 50mm 70mm. Packet of 25, available in the following sizes
17.5 mm, 20.0 mm
22.5 mm, 25.0 mm
27.5 mm, 30.0 mm
32.5 mm, 35.0 mm
37.5 mm, 39.5 mm

Price £3.20

Item 2493-1

Südafrika
Krugerrand
1oz Fine Gold
1974

REBECK L Coin Holder Storage Cases

Specially made for the Rebeck L coin holders these solid wood boxes, fitted with brass latches, have a detachable lid making scrolling through.

Small box to hold 80-100 coin holders, overall size 295mm x 60mm x 80mm Single compartment with 1 fixed and 1 movable wooden wedge.**Ref RCB1**   **£8.30**

Large box to hold 400-500 coin holders, overall size 235mm x 300mm x 80mm Five compartments supplied with 1 fixed and 5 movable wooden wedges.
Ref RCB2   **£18.80**

CALL 01736 751910   WWW.PRINZ.CO.UK

PRINZ PUBLICATIONS UK LTD, UNIT 3A HAYLE INDUSTRIAL PARK, HAYLE, CORNWALL, TR27 5JR
UK POSTAGE: ORDERS UP TO £60 POSTAGE £3.00. ORDERS OVER £60 POST FREE. OVERSEAS POSTAGE CHARGED AT COST

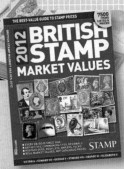